IMAGES
*of America*

# SUMMIT

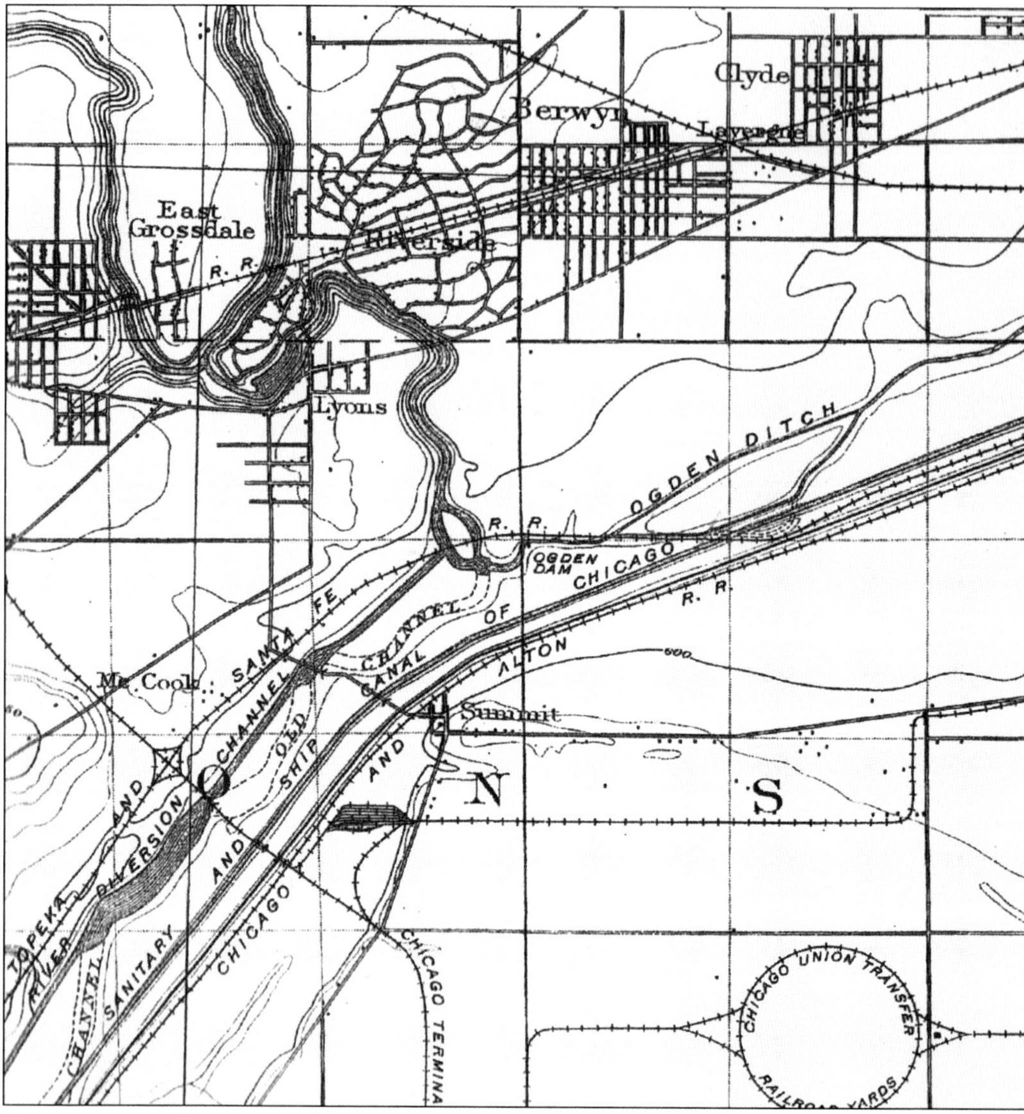


**Topography, Riverside Quadrangle, Illinois, 1901 Edition.** This map shows the landforms in and around Summit as surveyed between 1890 and 1899. Note the high ground on which the old settlements of Riverside and Summit sit and the glacial sluiceway between them through which old Lake Chicago once flowed. (Courtesy of the U.S. Geological Survey Photographic Library.)

*On the cover*: **Parlin Family.** This *c.* 1910 photograph shows the Cyrus E. and Jane Parlin family in front of the 1868 "Long John" Wentworth farmhouse at Summit, which was annexed to Chicago in 1923. Recorded as part of the Works Progress Administration Historic American Buildings Survey in 1936, this building and the 4,700-acre Wentworth estate have undeniable historic ties to early Summit. (Courtesy of the Summit Area Historical Society.)

IMAGES
*of America*

# SUMMIT

Robert Kott

ARCADIA
PUBLISHING

ISBN 978-0-7385-5248-4

Published by Arcadia Publishing
Charleston, South Carolina

Printed in the United States of America

Library of Congress Catalog Card Number: 2008923929

For all general information contact Arcadia Publishing at:
Telephone 843-853-2070
Fax 843-853-0044
E-mail sales@arcadiapublishing.com
For customer service and orders:
Toll-Free 1-888-313-2665

Visit us on the Internet at www.arcadiapublishing.com

*To everyone—pioneers, present citizens,*
*and posterity of the Summit area*

# CONTENTS

# ACKNOWLEDGMENTS

Very special thanks are due to my collaborator Bruce Beveridge, Summit Public Library District senior historical archivist, without whose abilities, support, and valuable counsel this book would not have been feasible. Bruce also provided access to the growing Summit Public Library collections, which have great potential under his guidance. Thanks are also due to Jeff Ruetsche, my editor at Arcadia Publishing, and publisher John Pearson, whose skillful work produced a worthy final product and whose understanding was immeasurable.

Special thanks are offered to geologist Don Mikulic of the Illinois State Geological Survey and archaeologist Kenneth Farnsworth of the University of Illinois; Summit village president Joseph Strzelczyk, who provided access to documents; Ellen Finelli and Colleen Allen of the United States Geological Survey Photographic Library in Denver, Colorado; the Illinois State Museum; Jesse White, State of Illinois archivist, and the Illinois Regional Archives Depositories; Vitaly Muzyka of the Bedford Park Public Library; the Chicago Historical Society; the officially dormant but still supportive collections of the Summit Area Historical Society; committeeman Steve Landek of the Lyons Township Democratic Organization; Pastor Wheeler Parker Jr., Helen Maletich, Patricia Kirk, Paul Rush, and Joseph Bestwina Jr. of Summit; Ted Ronczkowski of Bridgeview; Dorothy Ridder, Paul Garklavs, and Paul Welko of Chicago; Bill and Colleen Walen of Homer Glen; Fred and Deb Kott of Countryside, who went to great lengths to aid the production of this book; and Nicole Lucia Bauza for providing encouragement when it was most needed. My sincere thanks to all who contributed to this effort in any way great or small. Issues of the *Des Plaines Valley News* from 1915 to 1928 were also valuable sources.

Every attempt has been made to properly credit the photographs contained in this book to their respective sources. If there are errors in photograph credits, I ask that the mistake be forgiven. All images, unless otherwise noted, are from the Summit Area Historical Society.

# INTRODUCTION

Summit occupies land of great antiquity and strategic and transportational importance. It was considered home by residents from about present-day Narragansett Avenue west along Archer Avenue to the area of the western terminus of the Chicago Portage and Summit Ford, and into present-day McCook and south to a point near present-day Justice. Traditionally it once included the Point of Oaks, the area of the Chicago Portage National Historic Site, and the banks of the Des Plaines River. An examination of historic newspaper articles from the 1833 to 1925 period attests to this.

After Summit's incorporation in June 1890, and with the formation of the Clearing Industrial District and later Metropolitan Sanitary District of Greater Chicago, it became a nearly landlocked community of lesser size. Today it comprises a 2.3-square-mile village, including the Argo neighborhood, the Summit-Argo Post Office service area, and the larger Argo-Summit/ Bedford Park Elementary School District No. 104.

Waterways comprise 0.2 square miles or 6.58 percent of the village. Summit is 13 miles southwest of Chicago's downtown and had a racially diverse population of 10,637 inhabitants in the 2000 census. It is primarily Mexican (44 percent), Polish (12 percent), and African American (12 percent), with lesser Irish (4 percent), Italian (3 percent), Latino (2 percent), and Arab (2 percent) populations.

Known for its extremely diverse ethnic mix, it was first peopled by Native Americans, seasonal fur traders, French, English, native mixed-blood pioneers, Scots, and eastern Yankees in the 1830s; Irish "canallers" by the late 1830s; and Germans in the 1840s. There was a second flood of immigration here in the 1880–1910 period with Poles, Croatians, Slovaks, Russians, Italians, and Dutch with some African Americans, Mexicans, and Greeks arriving by 1910. Since then there have been several spikes in immigration, adding Yugoslavians, Arabs, East Indians, and most recently a large influx of Mexicans and other Latin Americans.

Historically Summit was known for the quality of its produce, especially vegetables grown on local farms for sale in Chicago, with urbanization taking hold by 1907 with the establishment of the Corn Products Refining Company corn-milling and processing plant (one of the largest in the world). After 1918, manufacturing and services diversified, but the natural advantages of Summit as a transport and distribution center have always flourished with food-processing companies with attendant rail yards, waterways, and highways playing a major role in its progress and economics.

Summit, Lyons, Riverside, and the city of Chicago have an intertwined and inseparable geological and historical relationship; all are parts of the much larger entity called the Chicago metropolitan area. The further we go back in time, the more regional our heritages become. Political fragmentation into "legally determined" municipal units is often misleading and unnecessarily divisive. Political boundaries change, but history does not. We share in the common roots of this region—its advantages, problems, and prospects—and we face a common future.

The Lake Chicago Outlet northern channel, now containing the Lower Des Plaines River, was left when ponding meltwaters behind the last Wisconsin glacier carved through the encircling Wedron Formation glacial deposits at Summit and conducted the overflow of Lake Chicago down a nearly two-mile-wide passage to the Illinois River 14,000 years ago. The younger trickling Des Plaines River claimed southwesterly flow through it when falling water levels in the Lake Michigan Basin became separated by the surficial continental divide, with flow from the Chicago River to the east. By 2,000 years ago, the Chicago Portage water and/or land route between the eastern and western watersheds became a natural portal to the North American interior. This primarily water route depended on seasonal variations in water levels between the Chicago River and Lower Des Plaines River. It has been estimated that at the time of the spring freshets and during times of high water of both watersheds, there was a continuous waterway between Lake Michigan, the Chicago River, and Lower Des Plaines for about 48 days a year, resulting in no real portage or land carry between waterways. Falling water levels required boat carries or portages of between one to more than seven miles between the navigable waterways of this route for 173 days per year. The remaining 144 days of the year required land carries on the nearby North or South Portage Roads between frozen or parched waterways of the route in excess of 7 miles up to even as far as 100 miles.

Still, the stage was set 2,000 years ago for the Des Plaines Valley to contribute to the growth and progress of the Chicago region by providing the most convenient land and water routes from Lake Michigan to the Illinois River and hinterlands.

The human prehistory of the Summit Beach began around 12,000 years ago with generations of Native Americans beginning with those of the Paleo-Indian period. As these first humans to enter our area carried on hunting activity here, they left behind distinctive stone tools indicating Eskimo-type subsistence heavily dependent on hunting larger animals for meat and gathering plant foods to a lesser extent. Next came the Archaic period (with early, middle, and late components), between 10,000 and 2,600 years ago, that saw an increasingly concentrated riverine hunting and gathering culture grow here as our environment became more hospitable to smaller game animals and food plants. The earliest presently known artifact find from the Summit Beach region include stone tools of this period of cultural history.

Between 2,600 and 1,000 years ago, the Woodland period (divided into early, middle, and late components) came into vogue, and the use of pottery in addition to diagnostic stone tools is noted, especially with the adoption of the more sedentary and well-established, far-ranging influence of the middle-Woodland-period culture with its dense deposits of flamboyant artifact assemblages, earthworks, and richly outfitted burial mounds. These people still focused on hunting, gathering, and fishing and utilized corn to a limited extent by about 1,300 years ago. The late-Woodland-period hallmarks include the addition of effigy and geometric mounds, which were sometimes used for burials and which thoroughly perplexed the early white settlers of the general Chicago area that found them long after their construction.

The final prehistoric period found in our area is the Mississippian period, which saw committed corn agriculture, use of shell tempering in clay pottery, and a diet more focused on floodplains and backwaters.

Our local Mississippian-period people lived in hamlets and frequently in a more conservative Woodland manner, living in smaller residential sites near waterways, utilizing corn to a lesser extent than other Illinois Mississippian people, making either shell-tempered clay for pottery (Fisher ware) or grit-tempered pottery (Langford ware) between 900 to about 1640, and developing the use of the bow and arrow over the earlier atlatl. The historic period began in 1673 when Fr. Jacques Marquette and Louis Jolliet, returning from their exploration of the Mississippi River, documented Illini-speaking Kaskaskia-band American Indian near Starved Rock that undoubtedly used canoes, hunted almost exclusively along the Illinois River, and knew of the Chicago Portage Route. It was with their guidance that Father Marquette and

Jolliet became the first documented Europeans to travel up the Illinois River–Des Plaines River, Mud Lake–Chicago River route and became the first of many documented Europeans to visit the future site of Chicago passing over Summit Ford and through what would eventually become the village of Summit. It is believed by many that on his second visit to the Kaskaskia village, determined to minister to the American Indians as he had promised, sickly Father Marquette actually camped in the Summit locale in the winter of 1674–1675. Later there was a small settlement of French families along the Des Plaines River south of the Chicago Portage west terminus near the head of the Point of Oaks at the very least in the 1740s.

During historic times, the records show that many American Indian tribes either resided along or passed through the Chicago Portage Route at different times; these included primarily the Illini, Miami, Sac, Fox, and Chippewa-Ottawa-Potawatomi Indians, among others. Some passed through during American Indian wars like the Iroquois; however, the only American Indians to ever cede the entire portage route land to the U.S. government were the united Chippewa-Ottawa-Potawatomi at the Treaty of St. Louis 1816. Historic-period occupation sites are characterized by the presence of trade goods of European or American manufacture dating roughly from 1670 to 1850.

Although the native American Indians appreciated the natural advantages of the Summit locale and used dugout canoes for at least 3,000 years, their way of life seemed to limit their conception of the strategic importance of this area—its true territorial, military, and transportation potential, something the Europeans and Americans seized on after 1673. Louis Jolliet, René-Robert Cavelier, sieur de La Salle, the later British, and the even later U.S. government did, however. In the Treaties of 1795, 1816, and 1833, the federal government began extinguishing the American Indians' claim to the entire region by entering into "mutually beneficial" treaties with them that gradually displaced the American Indians by the 1830s, when they were technically moved west of the Mississippi River and the sale of government land to speculators and pioneer settlers began. Prior to 1831, Summit had been substrate to two ancient American Indian trails that followed the high ground Calumet Beach and lower Toleston Beaches, the first partially becoming the later Archer Road (1831), one of the first improved roads of Cook County, and the second following much of present Douglas Avenue used as the South Portage Road, which extended from about what is now Twenty-ninth Street and California Avenue, joining with the North Portage Road just past Summit Ford in present-day McCook. The originally much wider Portage Creek extended into Summit, as did the deeper southern channel and portion of Mud Lake. Overlooking these strategic trails and the Des Plaines Valley, the early glacial lake beach nearby, because of its high and dry location on the old continental divide, became the central point of an extensive but sparsely populated settlement site, called the Summit or Summit.

The origin of the name *Summit* goes back to at least 1836, although the future town area itself may have been platted and subdivided as early as 1822. More research must be done along these lines; however, Summit was referred to as a growing settlement area by 1836 when William Gooding laid out plans for constructing the Illinois and Michigan Canal in three divisions, the Summit Division (from Chicago to Lockport), the Middle Division (from Lockport to Seneca), and the Western Division (from Seneca to LaSalle). The Summit Division was the first excavated by 1837 with the Middle Division being completed in 1848, years later because of building, financial, and bedrock-removal difficulties. A man named Van Austen is said to have had a tavern at Summit Ford prior to 1834 and is suspected of tending to the Laughton Tavern at Riverside, just as did Stephen White after 1834 when the brothers both died. However, documentary proof of this is lacking. Alfred Andreas (author of *History of Cook County*, published in 1884) considered Russell Heacock the first real resident of Summit.

With purposeful exploitation and improvement by influxes of settlers over time, local trails became roads, fords became bridge sites, and along the portage route canals were dug to improve the commercial transport and sanitation capabilities of Chicago and its satellite cities. Railroads and rail yards were built, swamps were drained, and prairies were claimed for habitation and industry. An efflorescence of agriculture, stone quarries, commercial and industrial growth, and prosperity was not far away. Summit grew and expanded by acquiring the Corn Products Subdivision by annexation in 1911, and a twin city complex was born that attracted further transport facilities and industry and urban expansion. The city of Chicago also grew spectacularly and expanded to its present municipal boundaries. Although progress has required the alteration or improvement of many old transportational landmarks through Summit, they are still with us today in the current highways, waterways, railroads, roads, and bridges that reflect upon the geological legacy Summit fell heir to.

# One

# Nature's Legacy

The Summit region has been under six successive seas in the past 500 million years and has been scoured by glacial ice and water at times—this is clear from drill cores. Most of Summit's high-elevation beach emerged when the levels of glacial Lake Chicago fell, exposing beaches about 12,000 years ago and continuing to expose more contiguous land areas on the Lake Chicago basin and Lake Chicago Outlet river channel until 2,000 years ago. The entire region was repeatedly bulldozed earlier by continental glaciers from the north beginning about 1.5 million years ago, which left a unique topography after their latest erosive and depositional action.

This topography included glacial moraines, the Lake Chicago Plain, and the glacial Lake Chicago Outlet, with its deepest Summit branch establishing water flow to the Illinois and Mississippi Rivers, the Riverside Spit and Summit Beach deposits, the Des Plaines River, and the surficial continental divide, which was to play a role in this area's desirability for human travels.

The land Summit sits upon was known for beautiful wet and dry prairies, some forested land (including the Point Aux Chenes), very fertile riverside floodplains, and an abundance of natural springs, animals, and plants.

Quoting historians Robert Knight and Lucius Zeuch of the Chicago Historical Society,

> The Des Plaines River between the present sites [1928] of Riverside and Summit with the immediately adjacent territory was one of the most important locations—if not the most important—in early North America. The best route connecting the St. Lawrence and Mississippi waterways passed through here. Here was the gateway to the Illinois Valley and here was the focal point where the most traveled Indian trails converged before passing down the valley, these trails followed along ridges or the beaches formed by the various stages of ancient glacial Lake Chicago which had its outlet here.

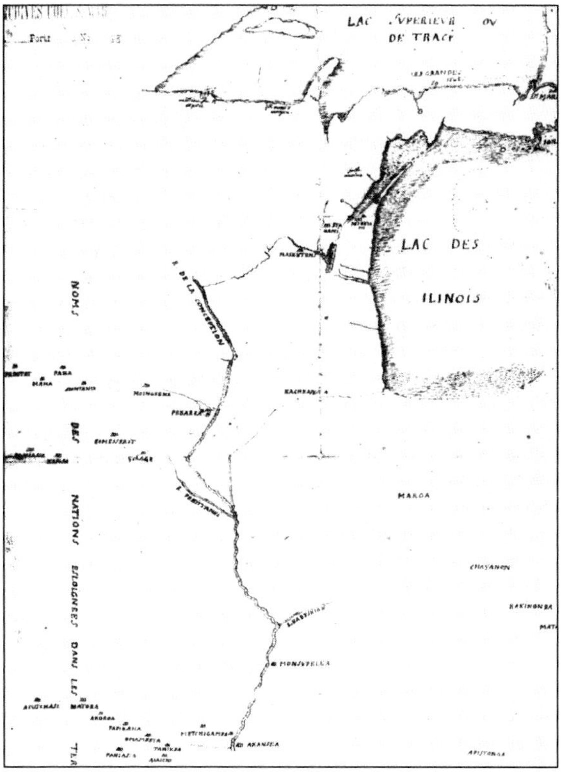


**THE MARQUETTE MAP, 1673–1674.** Drawn by Fr. Jacques Marquette in Green Bay, Wisconsin, this represents the only known holographic map of the waterways encountered on the 1673 voyage to find the destination of the "Great River" (Mississippi). (Courtesy of the Illinois State Museum.)

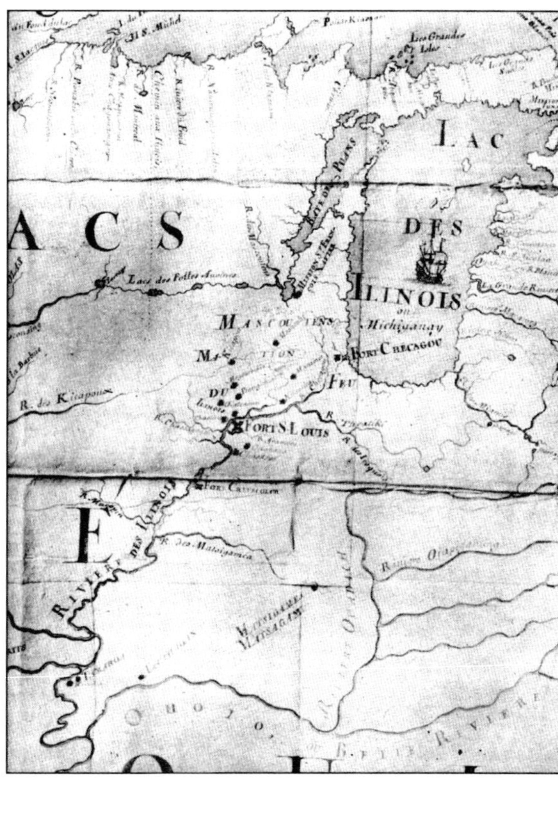


**JEAN BAPTISTE LOUIS FRANQUELIN MAP, 1688.** Jean Baptiste Louis Franquelin was the royal hydrographer of Canada for a time and the France-based draughtsman of René-Robert Cavelier, sieur de La Salle, from 1684 to 1687. This map variation close-up shows the Great Lakes and Mississippi Valley more accurately. Note the string of French forts and missions between Chicago and Peoria, which were the focus of local French and American Indian activities. (Courtesy of the Illinois State Museum.)

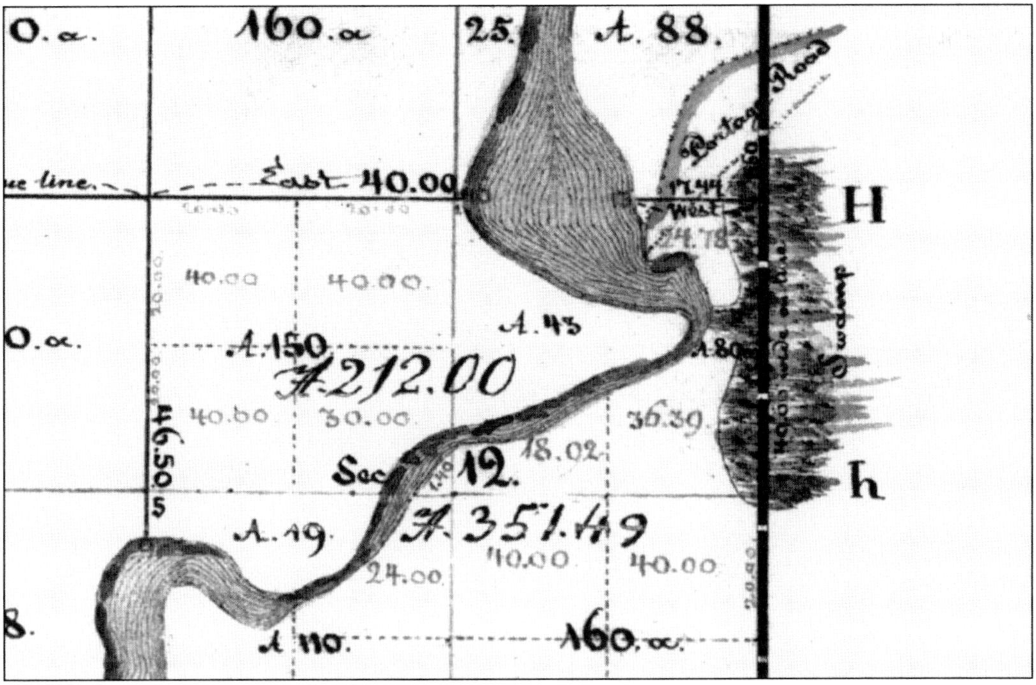


**SECTION 12, 1834.** The configuration of the Lower Des Plaines River is seen here with the wide Portage Creek and Mud Lake extending into Summit. This was drawn by E. T. Langham, surveyor general, on November 29, 1834. (Courtesy of the Illinois State Archives.)

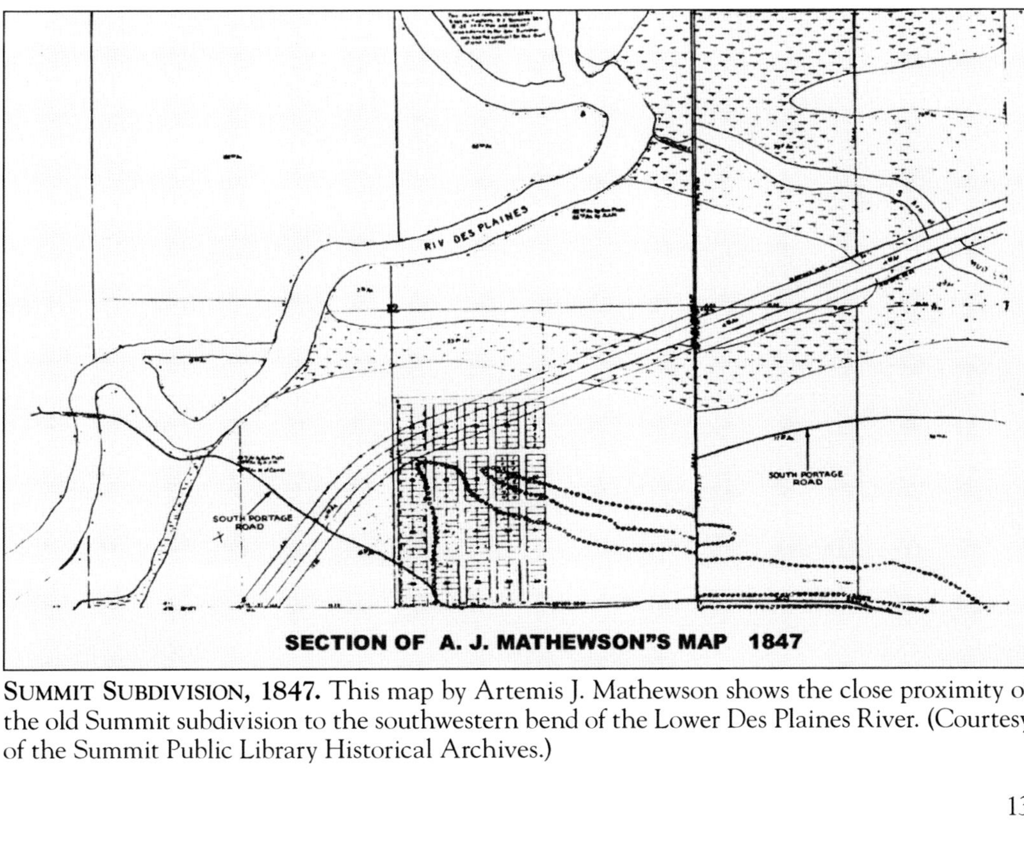


**SUMMIT SUBDIVISION, 1847.** This map by Artemis J. Mathewson shows the close proximity of the old Summit subdivision to the southwestern bend of the Lower Des Plaines River. (Courtesy of the Summit Public Library Historical Archives.)

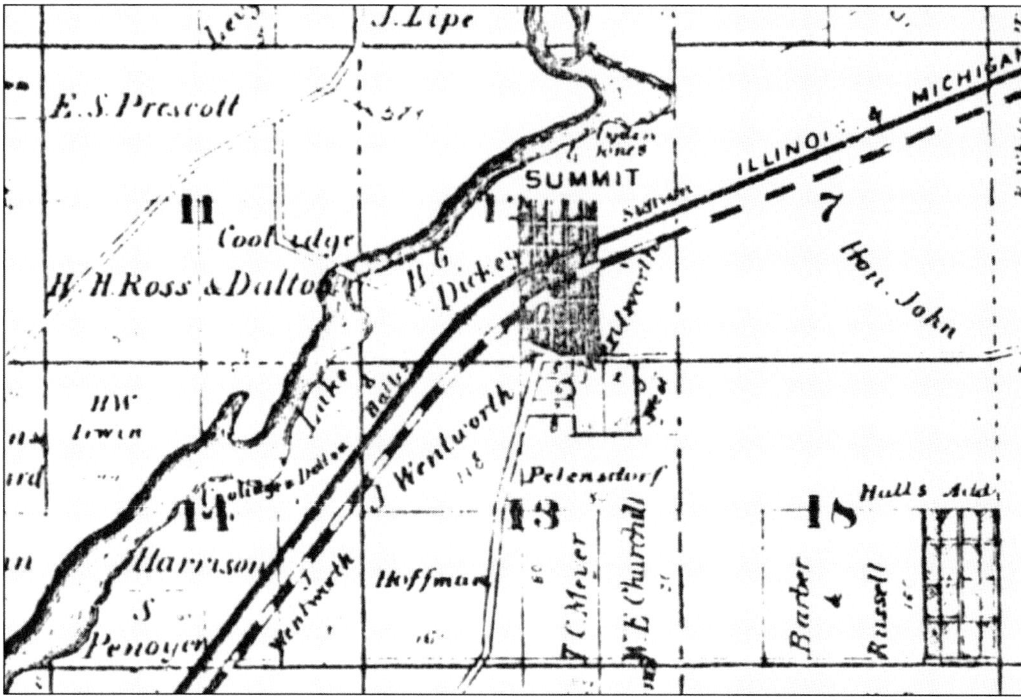


**JAMES VAN VECHTEN PLAT, 1870.** This map shows the Summit subdivision as it appeared at the foot and crest of the Summit Beach. Note its bisection by the Illinois and Michigan Canal; the Chicago, Alton and St. Louis Railroad; and both Archer Avenue and southwesterly proceeding Archer Road. Adjacent is "Long John" Wentworth's Summit farm—2,440 acres that at one time supported 10 dwellings and numerous barns and stables by itself. (Courtesy of the Illinois State Geological Survey and University of Illinois at Urbana-Champaign Library.)

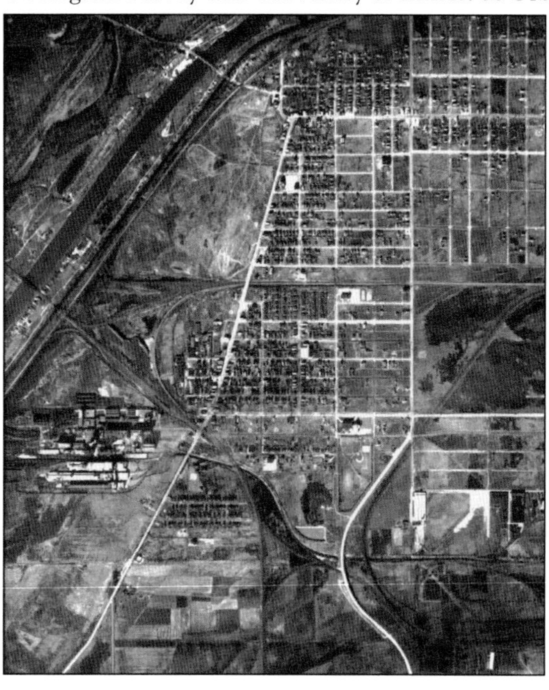

**SUMMIT/ARGO REGION AERIAL VIEW, NOVEMBER 1938.** Considerable urban sprawl in this region has been fed by urbanization, commerce, and industry and improvement in modes of travel and traditional transportation routes. By this time, much of the growth in the Argo and south Summit area is apparent. (Courtesy of the Illinois State Geological Survey.)

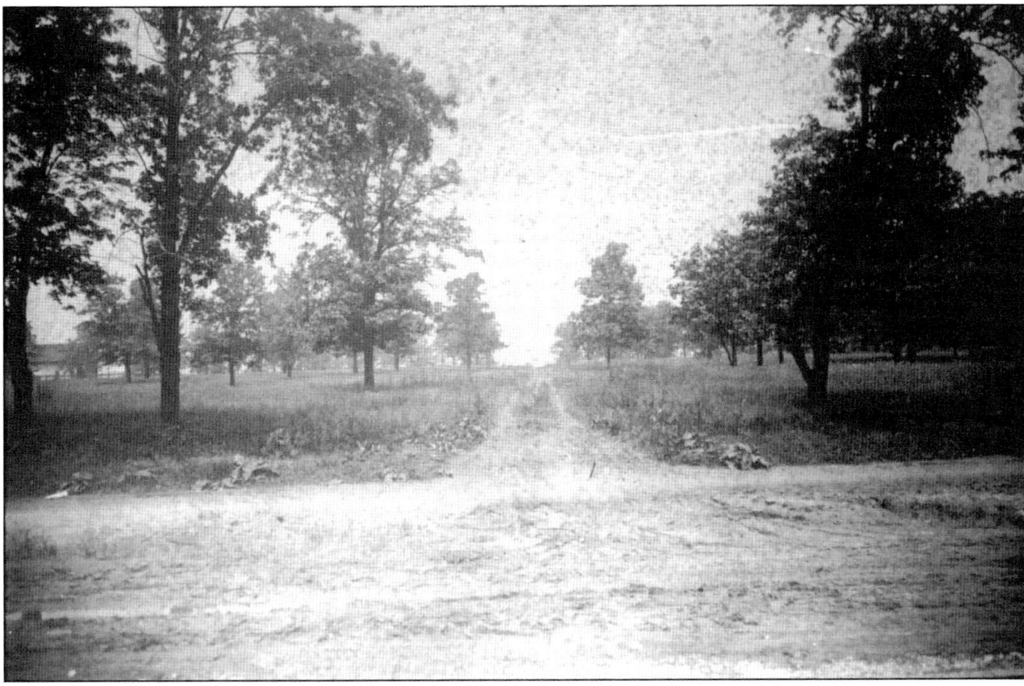

**ARCHER AVENUE AND SEVENTY-THIRD COURT, 1915.** Little more than a mud road on the Summit Beach, the area in this photograph features a few houses interspersed on the high-ground forest overlooking the Lake Chicago Plain. This area is now densely urbanized.

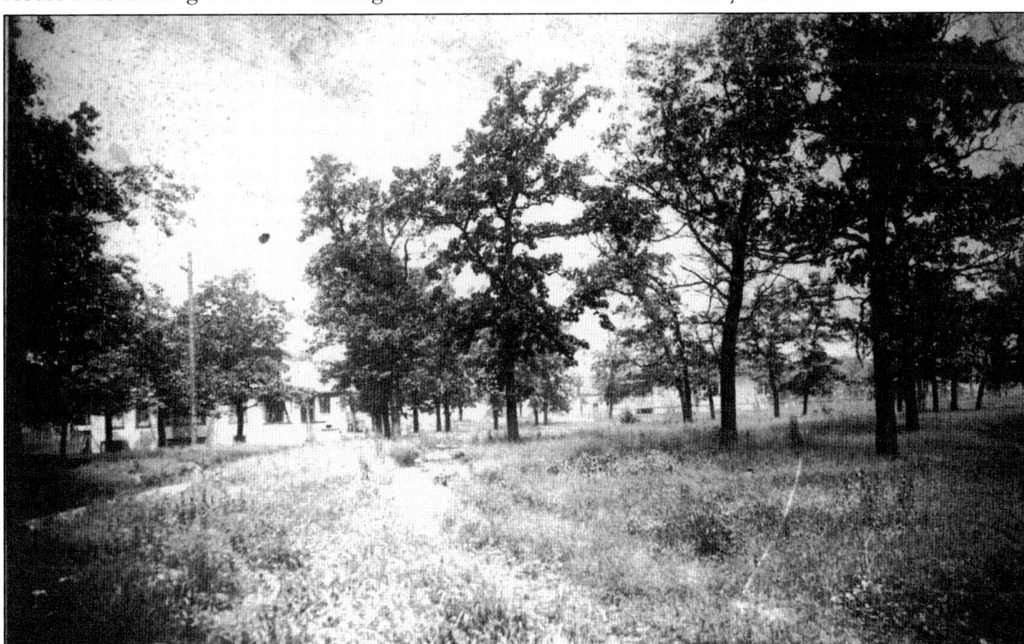

**ARCHER AVENUE AND SEVENTY-THIRD AVENUE LOOKING NORTH, 1915.** Here the mixed oak forest that existed on the sandy Summit Beach crest overlooking the Lake Chicago basin can still be discerned at the foot of this beach. To the north lies the parallel South Portage Road, just out of sight.

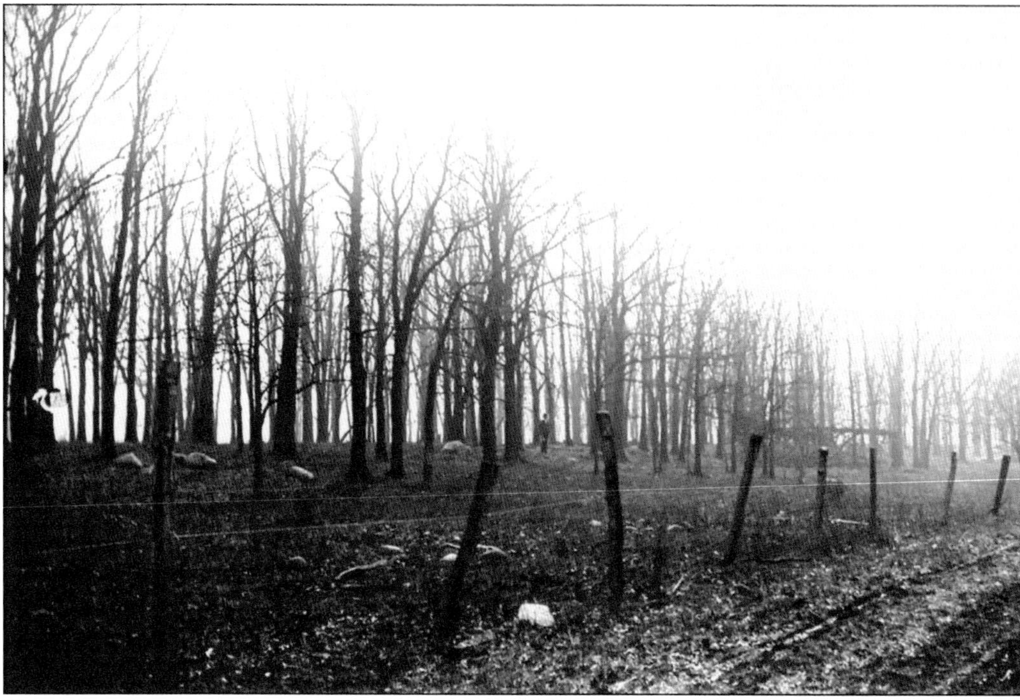

**TREES ON SUMMIT BEACH OVER THE LAKE CHICAGO OUTLET, 1903.** Today this land once visited by prehistoric man is covered with homes, businesses, and transportation routes. (Courtesy of the Summit Public Library Historical Archives.)

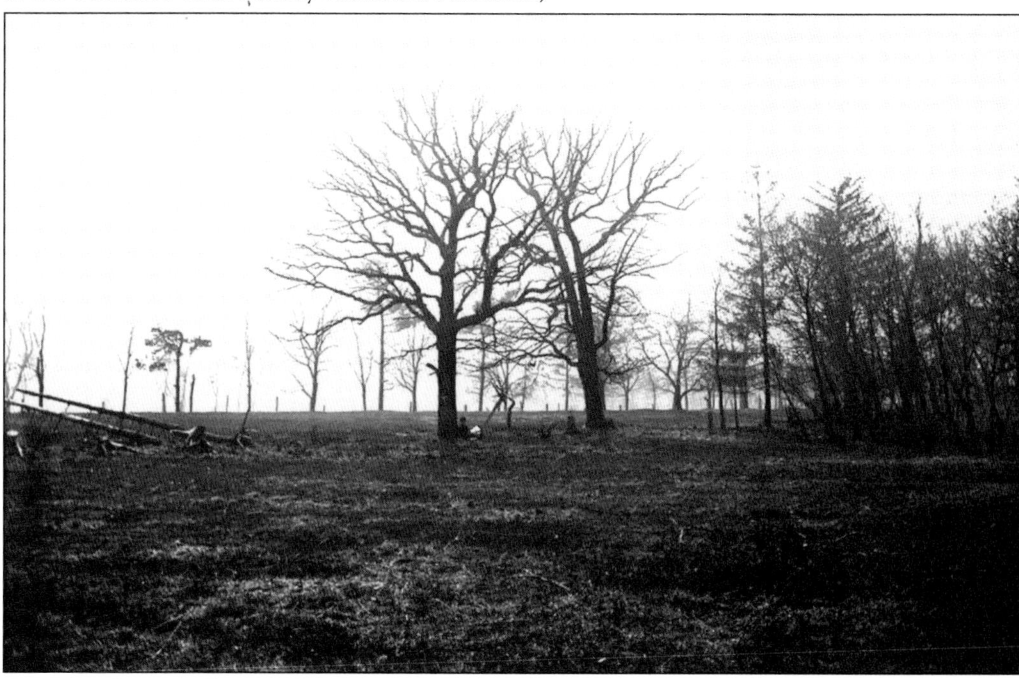

**OAKS ON SUMMIT BEACH CREST OVER THE LAKE CHICAGO OUTLET, 1903.** Local topography featured mixed oak forests and disturbed prairie before urban sprawl. (Courtesy of the Summit Public Library Historical Archives.)

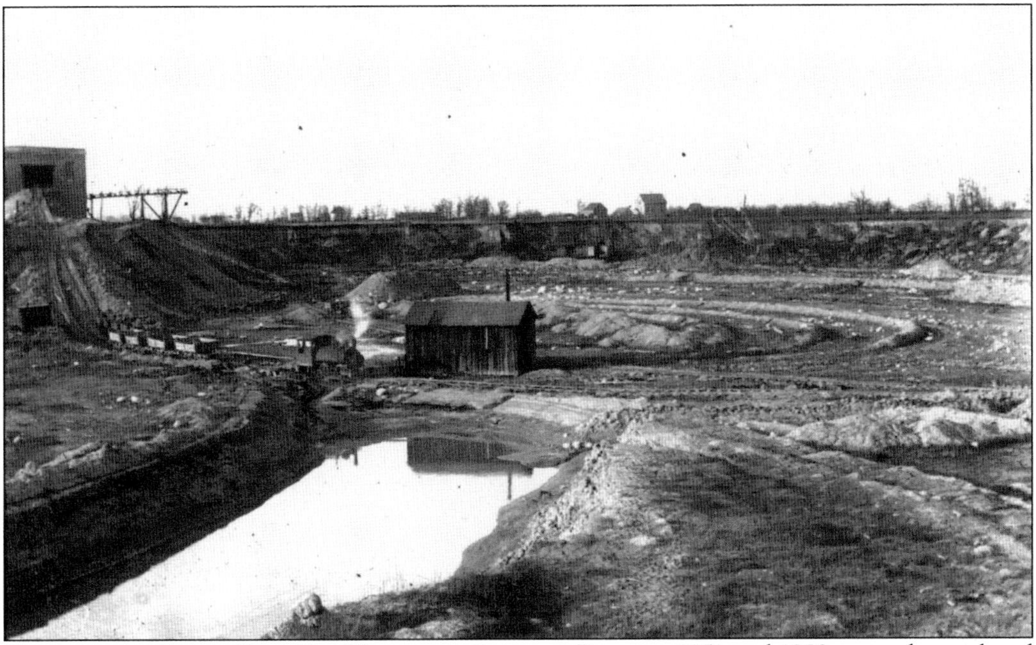

**Gravel and Brick Clay Pit North of Summit.** Between 1851 and 1882, several gravel and clay pits were opened in Summit. Here abundant deposits of gravel for road improvement and brick clay were exploited. Peter Kern operated one near Center Avenue, now the site of Hanover Park. (Courtesy of the Summit Public Library Historical Archives.)

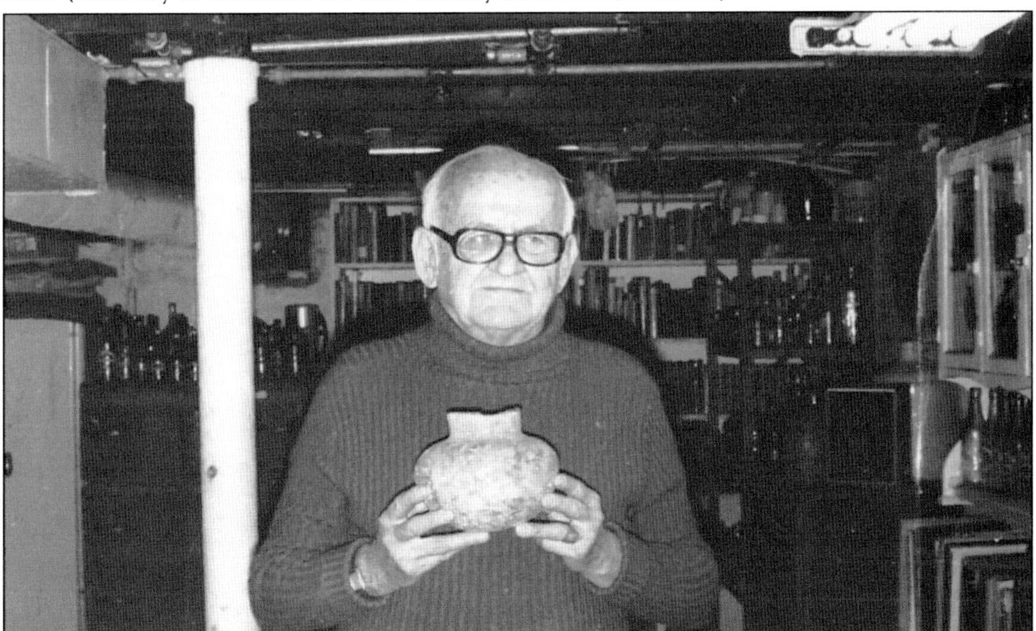

**Joseph Panzer and Mississippian-Period Clay Pot, 1975.** A lifelong resident of Summit, Joseph Panzer collected this artifact from the Illinois and Michigan Canal excavation near the 1895 Marquette monument. Although hunted since at least 12,000 years ago, there was no appreciable settlement of Summit until about 5,000 years ago. This site has been continuously occupied since about AD 900.

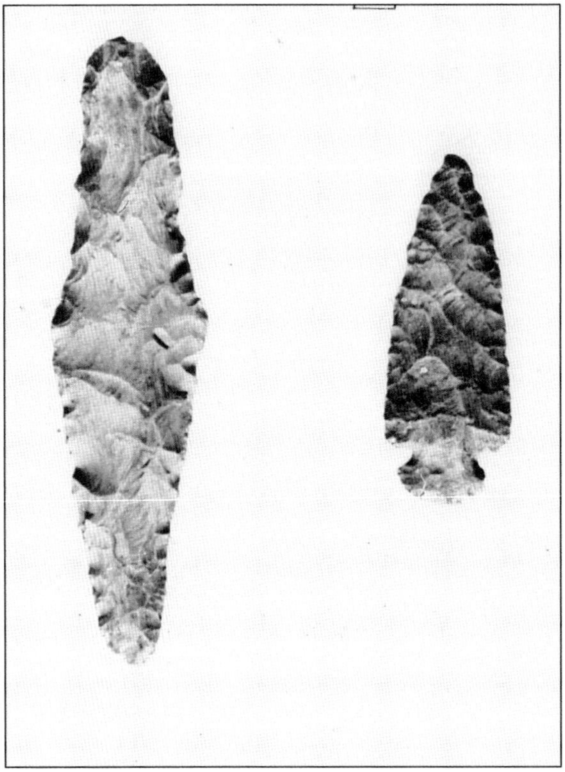

**PREHISTORIC STONE IMPLEMENTS FROM SUMMIT.** Collected in 1914 by a Mrs. Raguse, while planting lilac bushes near her home along the old Toleston Beach level, are a 9,000-year-old St. Charles point (right) and a 3,000-year-old Morse knife. They were identified by Kenneth Farnsworth of the University of Illinois.

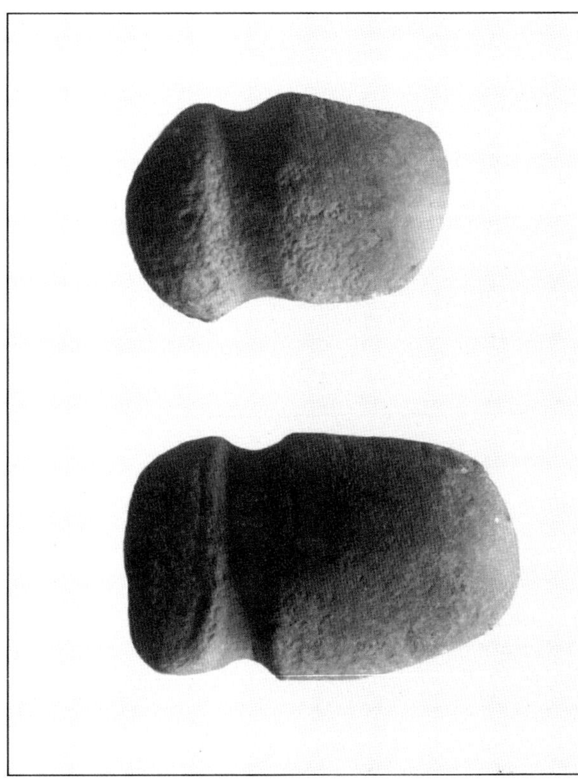

**PREHISTORIC STONE AXES FROM SUMMIT.** Five known fully grooved Archaic-period ax heads found in Summit date between 6,000 and 7,000 years old. They were found in local gravel pits along with other artifacts of the late Woodland/ Mississippian periods. Kenneth Farnsworth of the University of Illinois identified them.

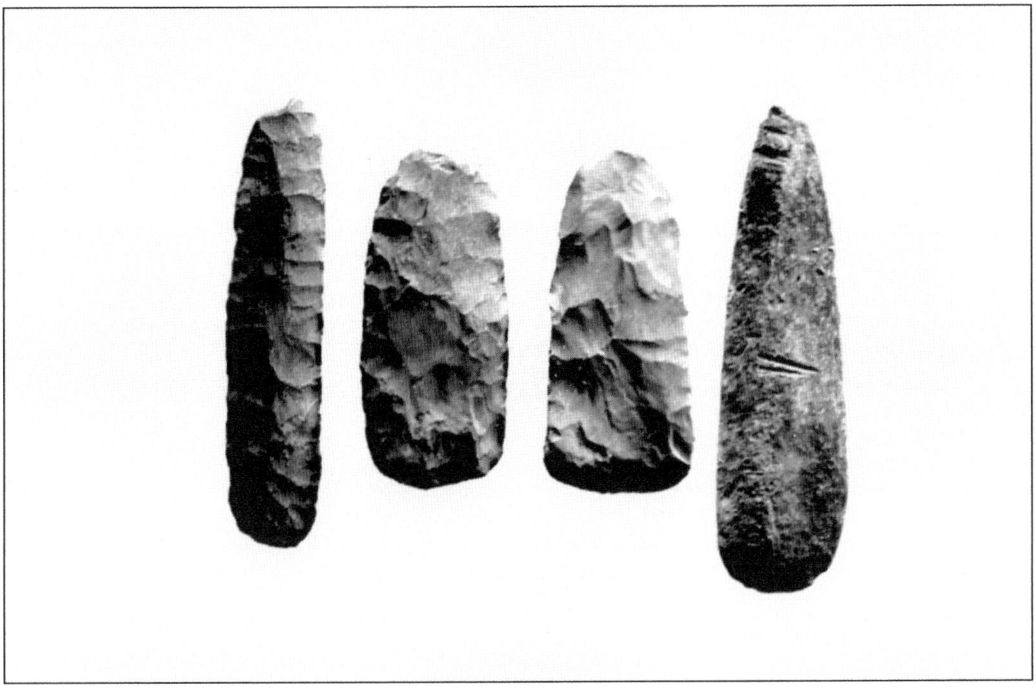

**Stone Implements from the Summit Beach.** A chert pick, two chert adzes or gouges, and a sandstone tool sharpener, probably a Mississippian woodworking tool kit, were found by Joseph Panzer of Summit in the local gravel pits, now modern-day subdivisions. These artifacts probably date about AD 900 to 1200. They were identified by Kenneth Farnsworth of the University of Illinois.

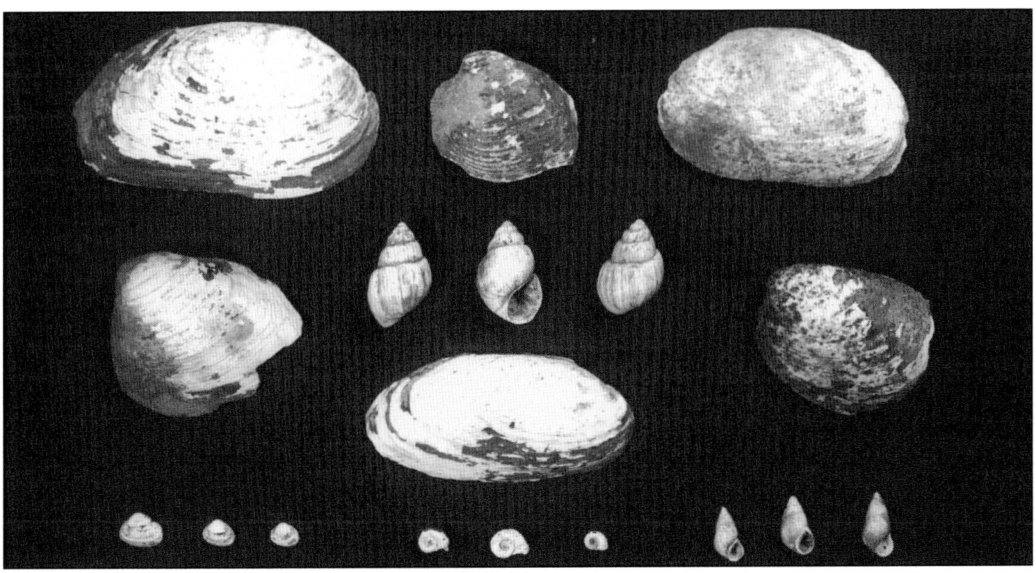

**Fossil Mollusks from Summit.** These fossil mollusks from the Lake Chicago Outlet indicate active water flow from the confluent Nipissing Great Lakes between 7,000 and 4,000 years ago. From left to right are the following genera: (top row) *Lampsilis*, *Fusconaia*, and *Lasmigona*; (second row) *Pleurobema*, three *Campeloma* snails, and *Pleurobema*; (third row) *Elliptio*; (bottom row) three *Sphaerium*, three *Helisoma* snails, and three *Goniobasis* snails.

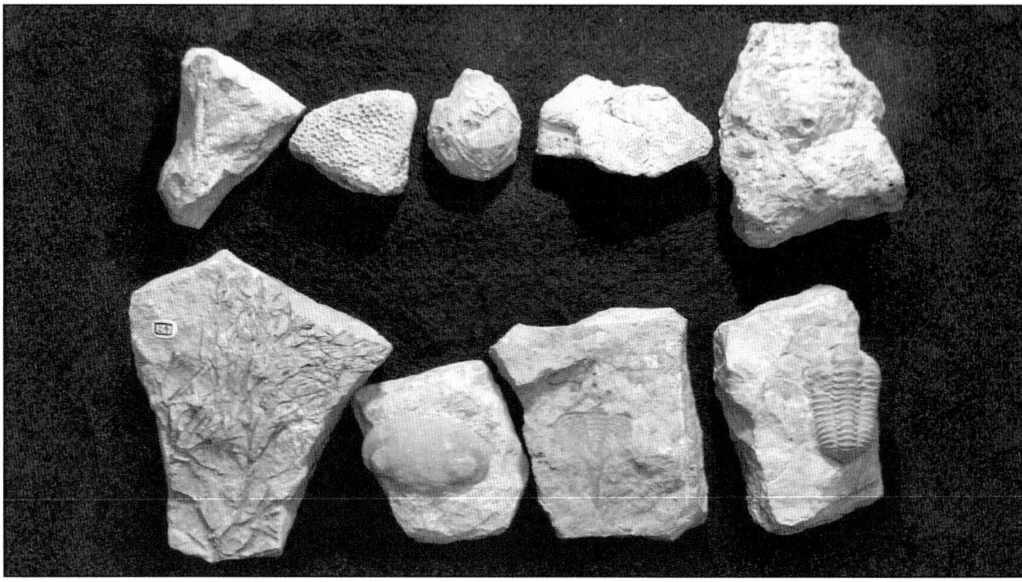

**BEDROCK FOSSILS.** Under a mantle of soil, sand, and clay are bedrock strata from sea deposits with embedded fossils. Here are more common types found in local quarries. The top row is from the Racine Formation, about 395 million years old; from left to right are crinoid stem, *Favosites* coral, *Caryocrinites* cystoid, *Fenestella* bryozoan, and *Eucalyptocrinus* crinoid. The bottom row is from the Sugar Run Formation, about 400 million years old; from left to right are crinoid rootlets, *Bumastus* trilobite, *Dalmanites* trilobite, and *Sthenarocalymene* trilobite.

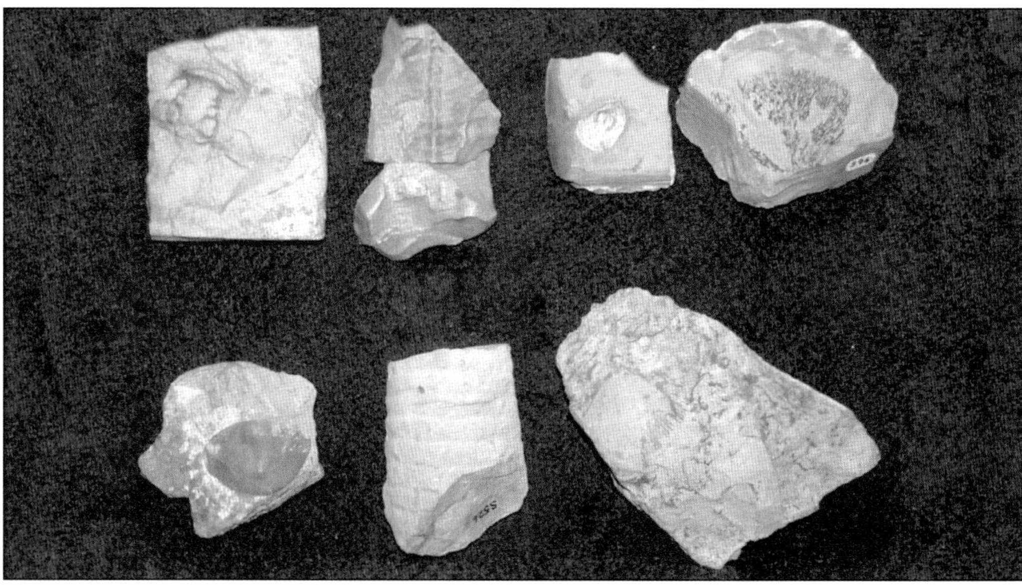

**MORE BEDROCK FOSSILS.** The top row is from the Wilhelmi Formation, about 425 million years old; from left to right are *Flexicalymene* trilobite, *Conularia* conularid, *Lingula* brachiopod, and *Dictyonema* graptolite. The bottom row is from the Fort Atkinson Limestone Formation, about 435 million years old; from left to right are *Stenoparia* trilobite, *Dawsonoceras* cephalopod, and *Strophomena* brachiopod. The fossils in this particular illustration are from the Chicago Metropolitan Water Reclamation District Deep Tunnel Project and are rarely seen in the township.

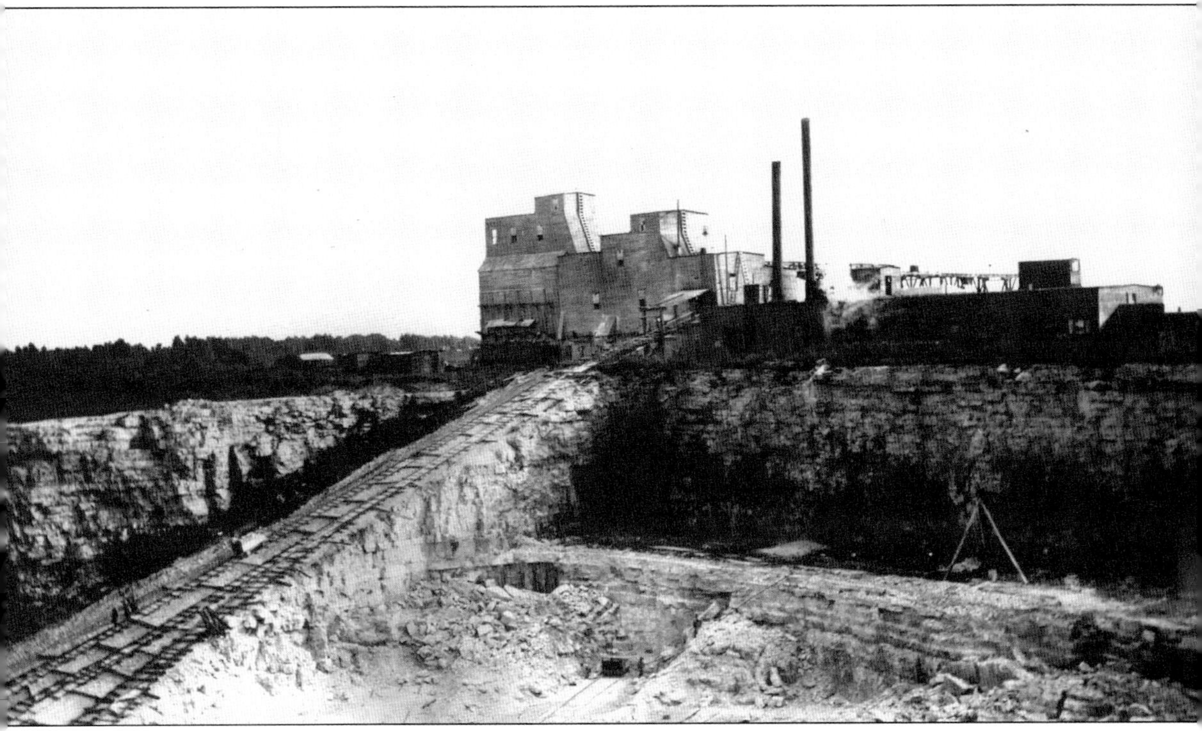

**DOLESE AND SHEPARD SUMMIT QUARRY, 1907.** This photograph shows the quarry and crushing plant looking southeast. This is one of several quarries in Niagaran dolomite located in Summit between 1865 and 1926 that provided the basis of a profitable industry here during the village's early years. They were centered along Summit-Lyons Road (later referred to as Lawndale Avenue) west of town in the northeast quarter of the southeast quarter of section 11, township 38 north, range 12 east. Although gravel and brick clay pits in Summit provided some road-building and construction materials starting in the 1850s, the later spread of the quarrying industry played a more major role in the local economy as the need for quality agricultural lime and later crushed stone for paving material revved up to full gear. Abandoned by the 1920s, these quarries became recreational "swimming holes" for a time before they were filled with local and Chicago garbage, landscaped, and built over. This information was provided by Don Mikulic of the Illinois State Geological Survey. (Courtesy of the U.S. Geological Survey Photographic Library, photograph by E. F. Burchard.)

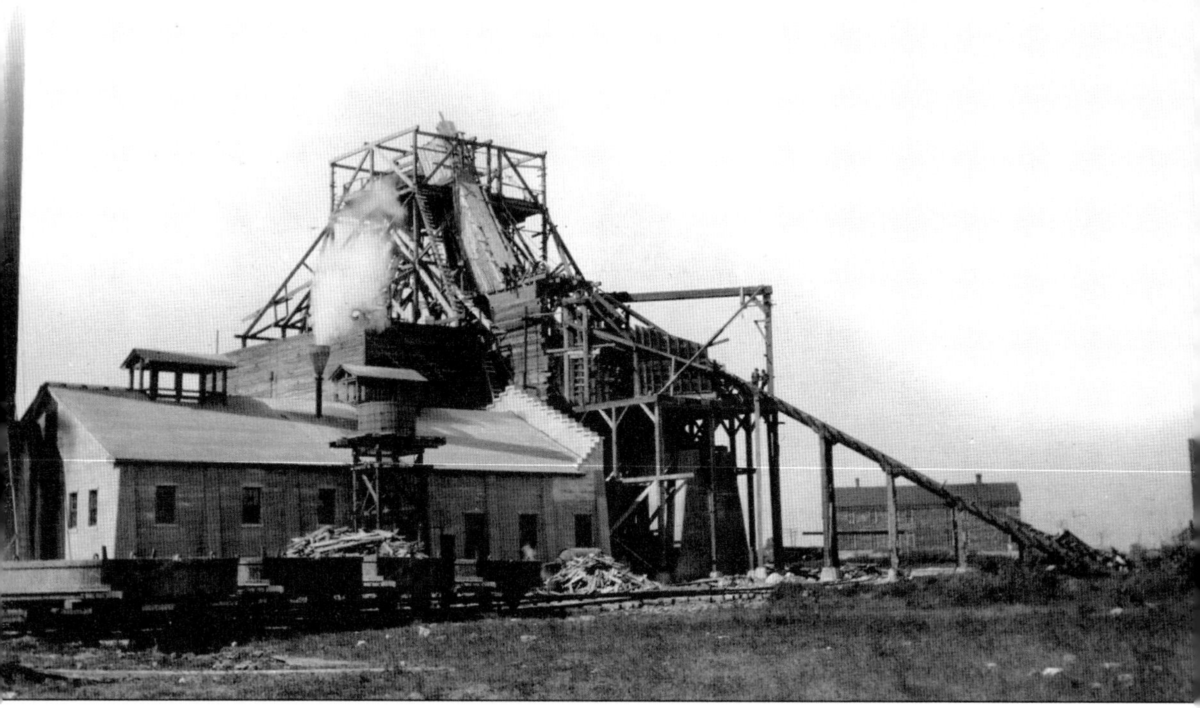

**Artesian Stone and Lime Company, 1907.** Pictured is an operating stone crusher in the old Summit quarrying district. The stone quarried here was deposited as calcareous ooze in the extensive Silurian Sea about 400 million years ago that through time and compaction became rock strata planed by glaciers and partially exposed by Chicago Outlet River flowage. (Courtesy of the U.S. Geological Survey Photographic Library, photograph by E. F. Burchard.)

# *Two*

# PORTAGE AT THE SUMMIT

In 1673, Frenchmen Louis Jolliet and Fr. Jacques Marquette journeyed from Green Bay with others to the western "Great River" (Mississippi) to confirm its destination. They proceeded to the mouth of the Arkansas River, where they turned back, realizing they were headed to the Gulf of Mexico and hostile hands. On their return trip north, they entered the Illinois River where they found an Illini-speaking American Indian village and were led to the Chicago Portage Route that they afterward documented.

Their eastward turn from the south-flowing Lower Des Plaines River took place just north of Summit at the Point aux Chenes (Point of the Oaks) where they encountered the seasonal Mud Lake swamp ground to the east. Their portage took place across the continental divide here on one of the portage trails because of unavoidably low water levels. They portaged to the Chicago River and canoed into Lake Michigan. Early travelers utilized the portage roads primarily before the Illinois and Michigan Canal was dug, fording the Des Plaines River at points that were shallow and solid enough to accommodate. Summit's ford was located where old Lincoln Avenue (now Lawndale Avenue) crossed the river and the north and south portage roads joined before proceeding to southwestern destinations.

The site of Marquette and Jolliet's portage between the Des Plaines and Chicago Rivers (at approximately 4800 South Harlem Avenue) was commemorated by the Cook County Forest Preserve District in 1930 with a picnic grove and monument. Now an important nexus in the federal Illinois and Michigan Canal National Heritage Corridor of 1984, it was upgraded to include the Guido Rebechini monument of Marquette, Jolliet, and an American Indian brave in 1989 and a footbridge placed over the meager altered remnant of what is left of Portage Creek in 2007. Early historians and surveyors routinely made references to the portage at the Summit. The close proximity of the physical elevation rise at Summit is undoubtedly the reason why.

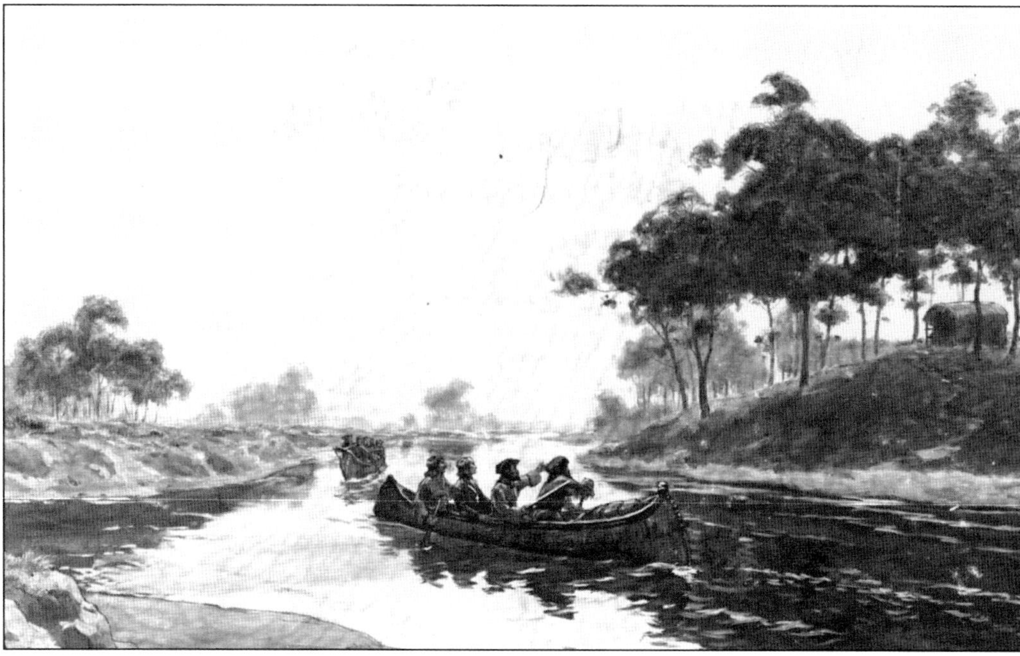

**THE SUMMIT AND MARQUETTE.** The eastward 1673 portage starting point was just north of the foot of what the French termed the Point aux Chenes, or the Point of Oaks, a wooded high point above the generally treeless prairies along the southwestern bank of the Des Plaines River valley and Mud Lake. (Courtesy of the Summit Public Library Historical Archives.)

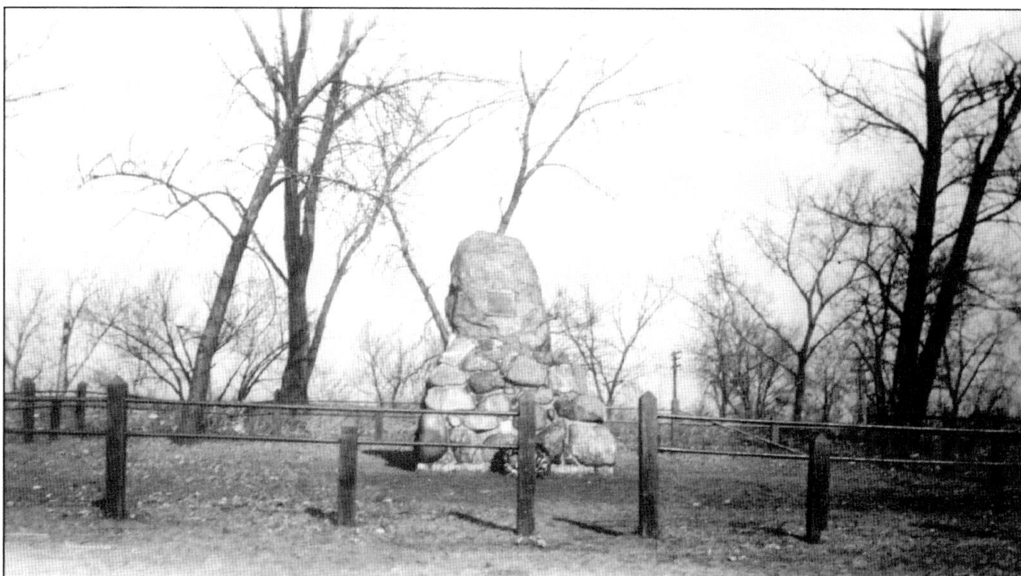

**SUMMIT MARQUETTE MONUMENT, 1895.** The Summit Marquette monument was erected on a sandy ridge just northwest of the Point of Oaks at the urging of Ossian Guthrie (1826–1908), chief engineer of the old Illinois and Michigan Canal Bridgeport Pumping Works and "the father of Chicago's drainage system," and Edward G. Mason, then president of the Chicago Historical Society. Built by the Chicago and Alton Railroad, it celebrates the site where Fr. Jacques Marquette camped temporarily during the freshet of 1674–1675.

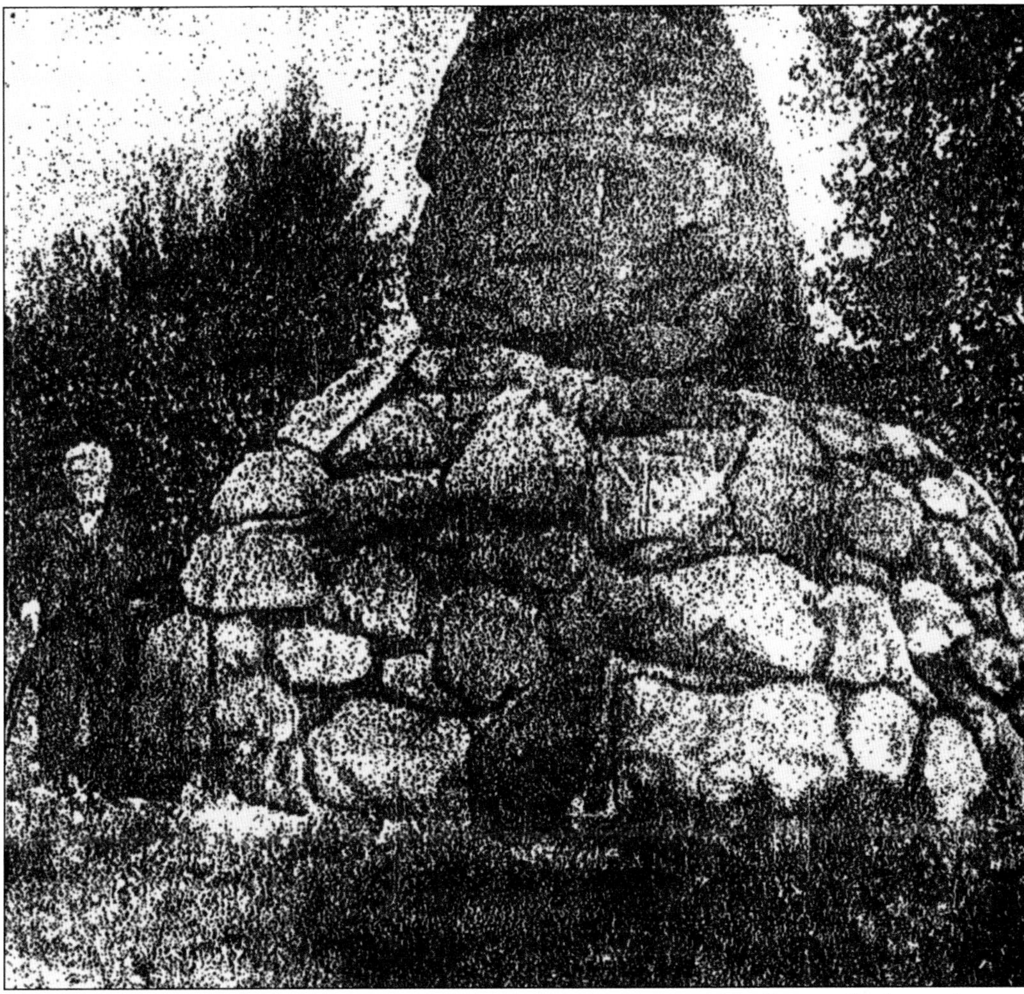

**OSSIAN GUTHRIE AND MARQUETTE MONUMENT, SUMMIT, 1895.** Originally located across from the old Chicago and Alton Railroad station, this monument commemorates one of three spots researched over a lifetime by Guthrie: the 1673 portage route, the 1674 Damen Avenue (Robey Street) Marquette cabin site, and the 1674–1675 temporary Marquette encampment. Guthrie arrived at the three sites by interviews since 1847 on the original topography of the area, the Marquette journal, and the fieldwork and surveys of the Chicago Drainage Canal commissioners. On May 23, 1906, Guthrie took executive committeeman Samuel H. Kerfoot Jr. and members of the Chicago Historical Society on an expedition to these sites. Guthrie was an inventor at age 18, dabbling in steam engines, and was design engineer of the pumps used to conduct water into the Illinois and Michigan Canal, later becoming master mechanic and chief engineer of the Bridgeport works. In 1885, he devised the plan to purify the Chicago River by digging a new drainage canal. He was an early proponent of the glacial theory of the origin of the Chicago Outlet, an honorary member of the Western Society of Engineers, and a noted pioneer, historian, and geologist. Guthrie was the grandson of the doctor who discovered chloroform in 1831. (Courtesy of the Summit Public Library Historical Archives.)

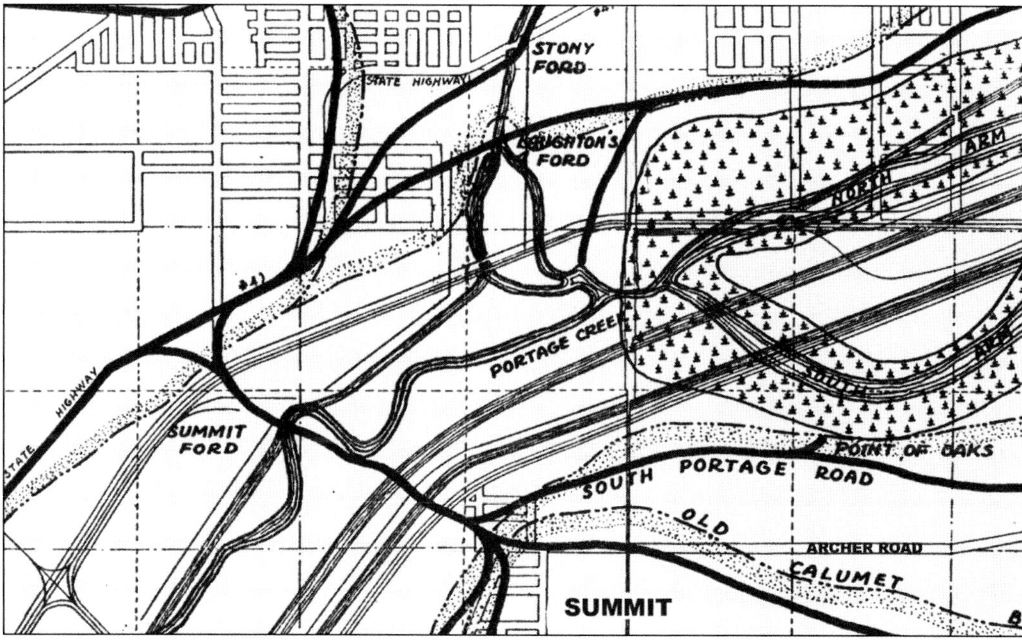


**THE CHICAGO PORTAGE ROUTE, 1673–1836.** The Chicago Portage Route was used as the most direct water-to-land route between the future site of Chicago and the Lower Des Plaines River and points west. This seasonally varying route included the north and south portage trails and Mud Lake channels. Its period of greatest economic importance proceeded the 1831 improvements of Archer Road and later transport roads, railroads, and canals through the same corridor. (Courtesy of the Chicago Historical Society.)

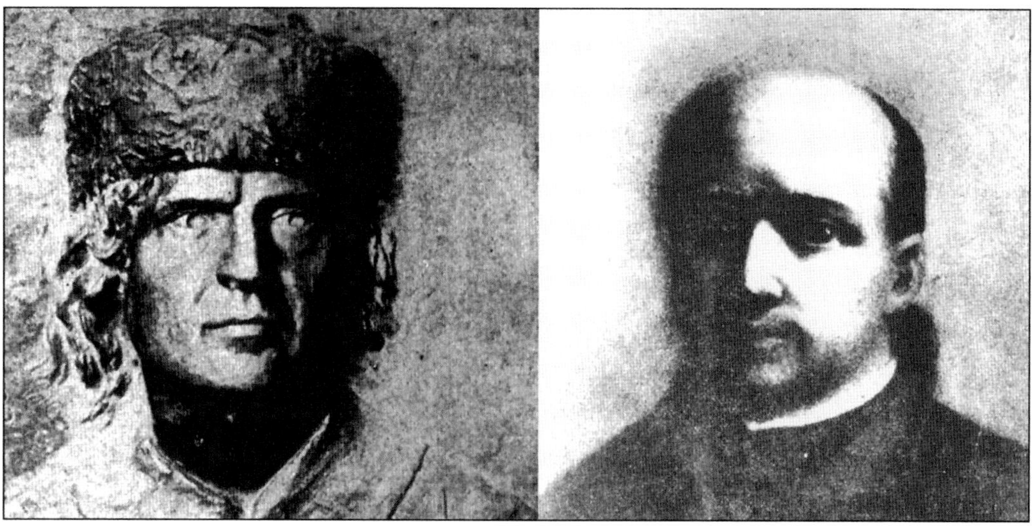

**JOLLIET AND MARQUETTE.** The first documented Europeans to use the Chicago Portage Route, led by American Indians in 1673, were Louis Jolliet and Fr. Jacques Marquette. Jolliet was a Canadian explorer (born in 1645 in Trois Rivieres, Canada, and died in 1700) and proposed the digging of a canal through the portage at Chicago in 1674. Marquette, who was born in Laon, France, in 1637, established three noted missions in New France and died at Ludington, Michigan, on the return from the Illini Kaskaskia village in 1675. (Courtesy of the Summit Public Library Historical Archives.)

**WEST TERMINUS CHICAGO PORTAGE ROUTE MONUMENT, 1930.** The West Terminus Chicago Portage Route monument was erected by the Chicago Historical Society to showcase the remains of the altered Portage Creek and the North Portage Road access to the Lower Des Plaines River. This location has been accepted by Ossian Guthrie as the place that Jolliet and Marquette began their September 1673 eastern portage, making them the first documented Europeans to traverse this seasonal obstruction to the Chicago River.

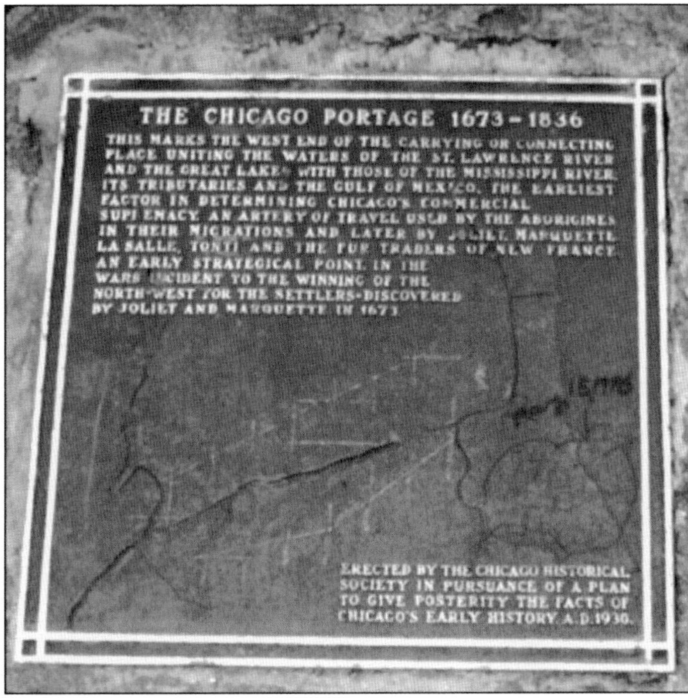


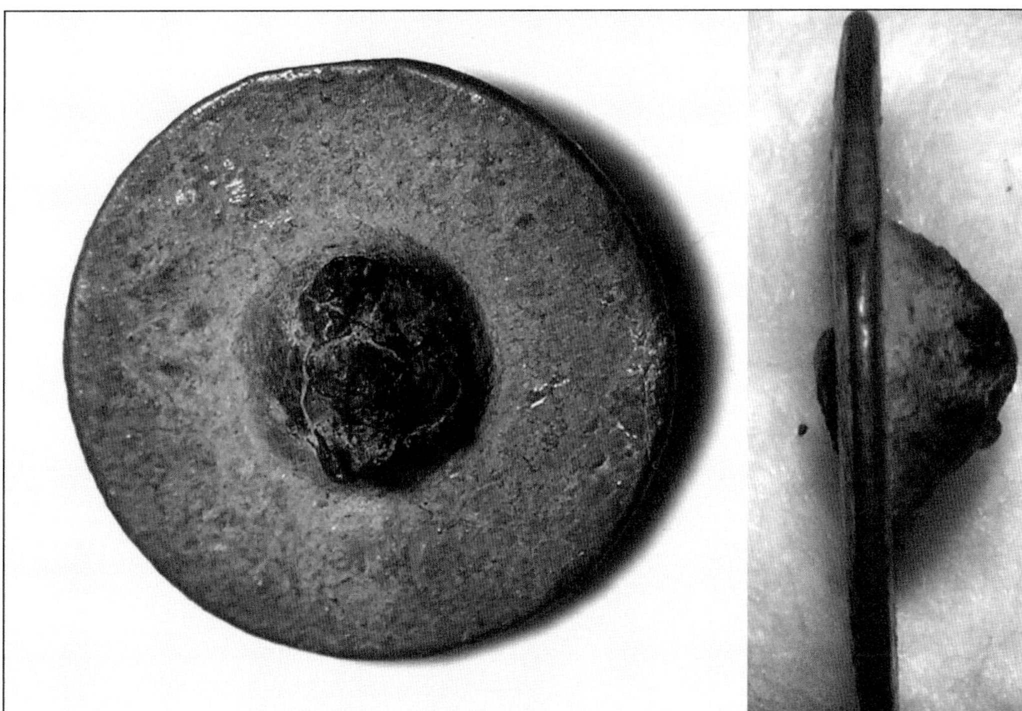

**HISTORIC WHITE METAL AND IRON SHANK TUNIC BUTTON, 1780–1820.** Possibly lost by some French or British traveler in the marshland—perhaps during an arduous summer portage—such buttons were reused as late as 1830. This was identified by Kenneth Farnsworth of the University of Illinois.

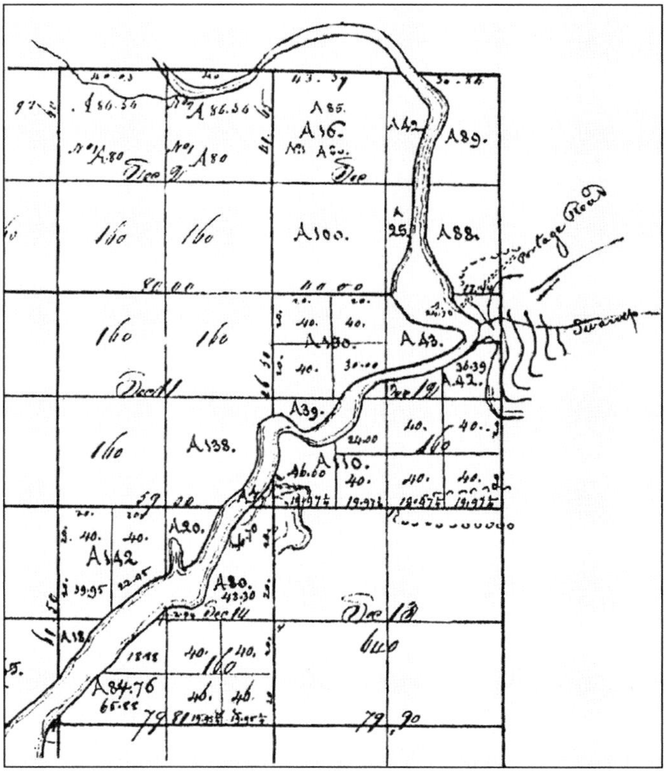


**FEDERAL PLAT OF SUMMIT AREA, 1821.** This survey plat shows the Summit area with the North Portage Road, the original Portage Creek basin, and the western and southern side of Mud Lake. The original Summit section was divided into 40-acre tracts in 1821. (Courtesy of the Summit Public Library Historical Archives.)

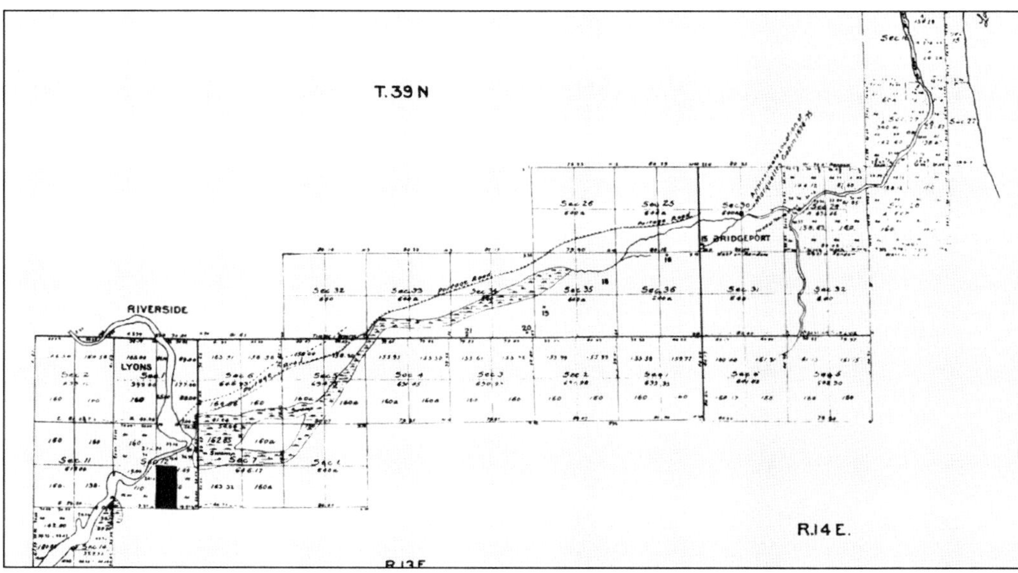


**FEDERAL SURVEY BY JOHN WALLS, 1821.** After the Treaties of Greenville in 1795 and St. Louis in 1816, the American Indians ceded the full tract containing the site of Chicago, the portage, and the section reserved for the Illinois and Michigan Canal connected to the separate military tract set aside in 1812 by Congress and surveyed in 1816. With the formation of the State of Illinois in 1818 and serious efforts in the building of the Illinois and Michigan Canal, portions of the federal lands were surveyed for possible sale by 1821. This included the old Summit village area. (Courtesy of the Summit Public Library Historical Archives.)

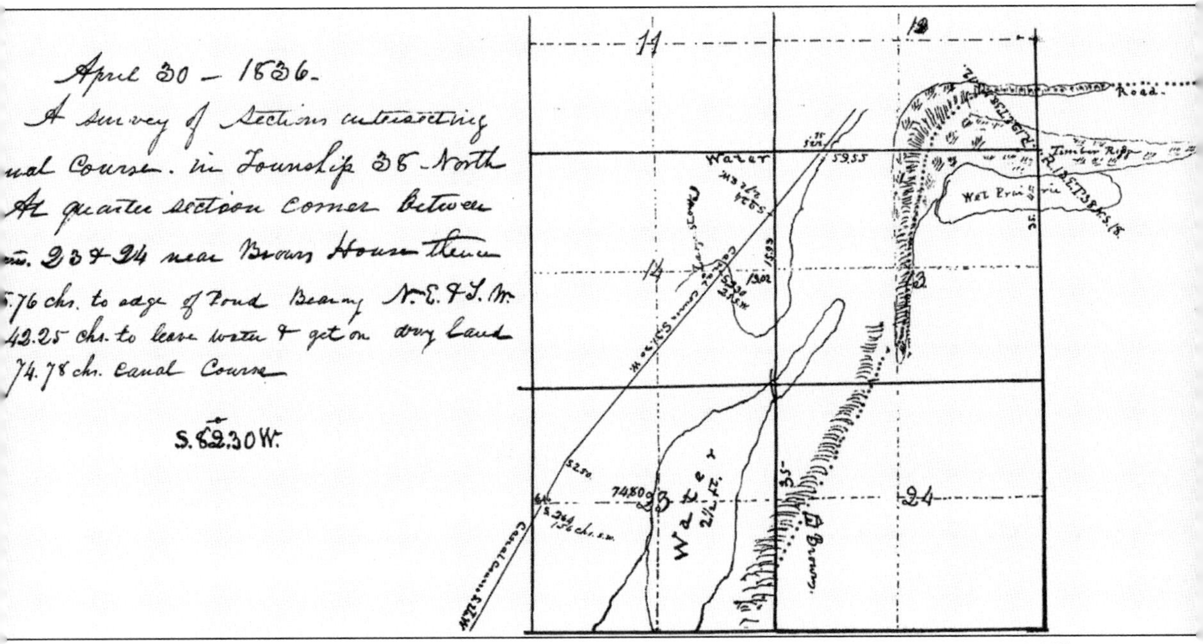


**ILLINOIS AND MICHIGAN CANAL COMMISSIONER'S SURVEY OF ARCHER AVENUE, 1836.** The State of Illinois, with land granted by the federal government, made arrangements to join the Illinois River with Lake Michigan—the Illinois and Michigan Canal. The government gave to the state all the odd-numbered sections of the unnamed congressional townships along the intended canal route, with the government taking all the even-numbered sections. The present village of Summit is within parts of sections 11, 12, and 14, and all of section 13 in township 38 north, range 12 east of the third principal meridian. In 1836, Col. William B. Archer laid out the current Archer Avenue from Chicago to Joliet to facilitate canal construction. Once an American Indian trail, Archer also became known as "the Road to Widow Brown's" in 1831—a link between Chicago and Joliet. The route was impassable most of the time until it was properly graded. The Point of Oaks can be seen here as indicated by a grove of trees. (Courtesy of the Summit Public Library Historical Archives.)

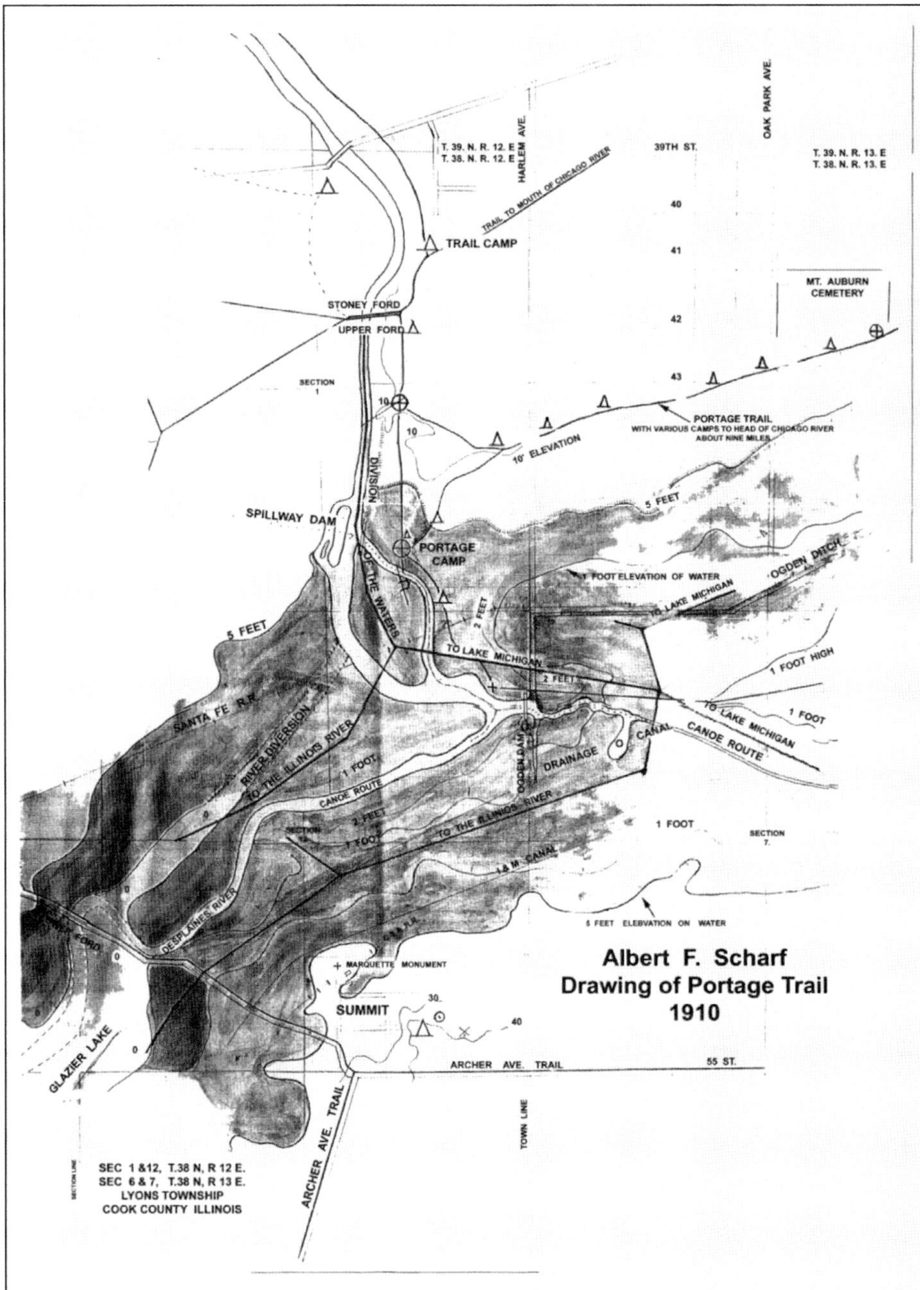


**SCHARF MAP, 1910.** This 1910 map by Albert F. Scharf, an early Chicago archaeologist, shows the location of an American Indian village site in Summit accompanied by burial mounds near the old Summit depot. His analysis of seasonal flood crests on the local topography substantiates the work of Ossian Guthrie indicating the 1674 landing site of Fr. Jacques Marquette during the flood that forced him from his Damen Avenue cabin site to higher ground. This map also indicates that the assumed Laughton trading post site to the north with the north portage trail, most often accessed by canoe, would both have been inundated at high water levels. (Courtesy of the Chicago Historical Society.)

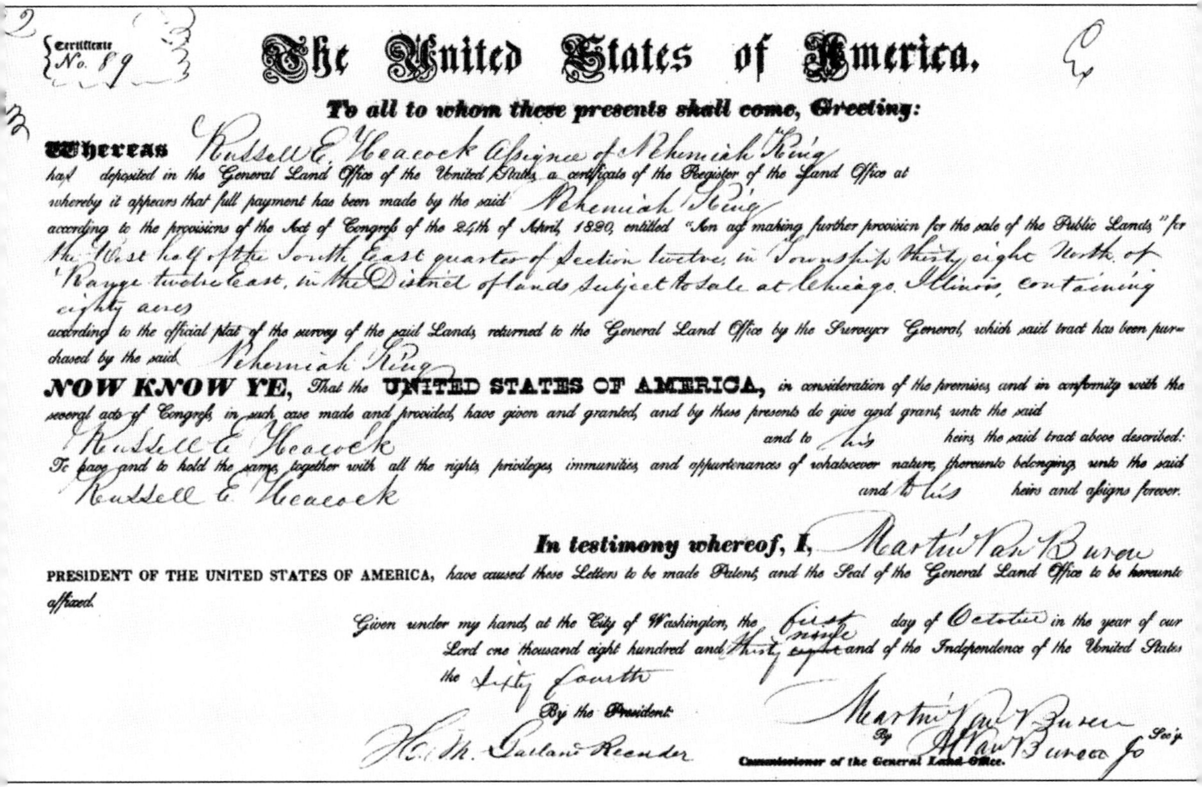
Certificate No. 89

The United States of America,

To all to whom these presents shall come, Greeting:

Whereas Russell E. Heacock Assignee of Nehemiah King has deposited in the General Land Office of the United States, a certificate of the Register of the Land Office at whereby it appears that full payment has been made by the said Nehemiah King according to the provisions of the Act of Congress of the 24th of April, 1820, entitled "An act making further provision for the sale of the Public Lands," for the West half of the South East quarter of Section twelve, in Township thirty eight North of Range twelve East, in the District of lands subject to sale at Chicago, Illinois, containing eighty acres according to the official plat of the survey of the said Lands, returned to the General Land Office by the Surveyor General, which said tract has been purchased by the said Nehemiah King

NOW KNOW YE, That the UNITED STATES OF AMERICA, in consideration of the premises, and in conformity with the several acts of Congress, in such case made and provided, have given and granted, and by these presents do give and grant, unto the said Russell E. Heacock and to his heirs, the said tract above described: To have and to hold the same, together with all the rights, privileges, immunities, and appurtenances of whatsoever nature, thereunto belonging, unto the said Russell E. Heacock and to his heirs and assigns forever.

In testimony whereof, I, Martin Van Buren PRESIDENT OF THE UNITED STATES OF AMERICA, have caused these Letters to be made Patent, and the Seal of the General Land Office to be hereunto affixed.

Given under my hand, at the City of Washington, the first day of October in the year of our Lord one thousand eight hundred and thirty nine and of the Independence of the United States the sixty fourth

By the President: Martin Van Buren

By M. Van Buren Jr Sec'y

H. M. Garland Recorder

Commissioner of the General Land Office.

**FEDERAL LAND PATENT, 1839.** The original subdivision of Summit was in the southeast quarter of section 12, township 38, range 12 east. The Summit subdivision is indicated on very early federal plats and was subdivided by their surveyors by 1821. It is not yet known if any of the property was actually purchased then, but it came into the possession of Nehemiah King, a federal surveyor, by 1835. This patent shows that pioneer Russell E. Heacock was an assignee for King and that Heacock purchased the 80 acres in 1839. Historical records show that this section was settled by 1834 with an inn and stagecoach stop, but others settled here earlier, including American Indians from ancient times. It has been continuously occupied since about AD 900. (Courtesy of the Bureau of Land Management.)

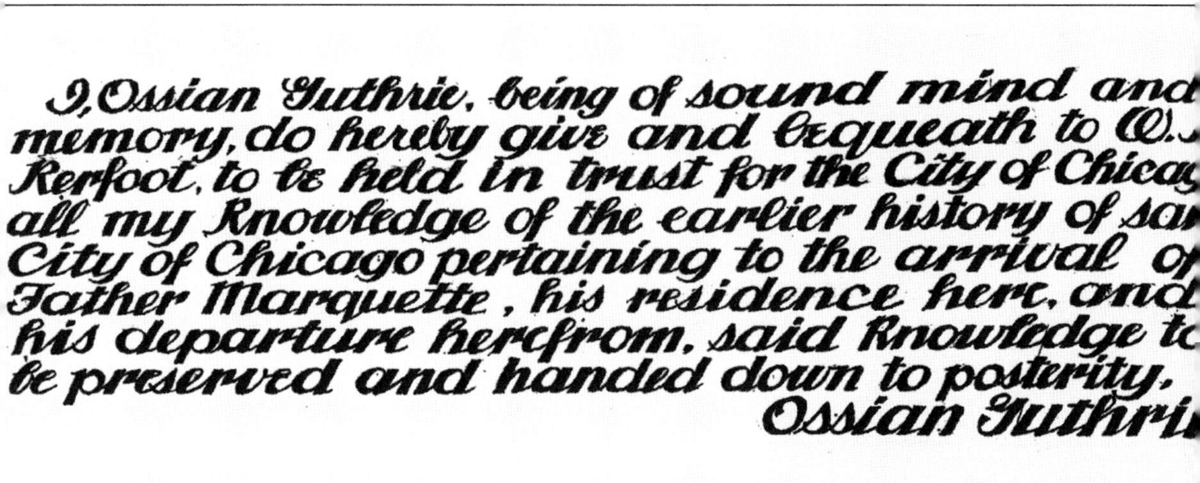

I, Ossian Guthrie, being of sound mind and
memory, do hereby give and bequeath to W. J
Kerfoot, to be held in trust for the City of Chicag
all my knowledge of the earlier history of sai
City of Chicago pertaining to the arrival of
Father Marquette, his residence here, and
his departure herefrom, said knowledge to
be preserved and handed down to posterity.
Ossian Guthri

**OSSIAN GUTHRIE'S BEQUEST, 1906.** Sensing his mortality in 1906, Ossian Guthrie, well-known and beloved resident of Chicago since 1844, willed to the inhabitants of Chicagoland and the world all his accumulated knowledge regarding the history and topography of the portage routes taken by Fr. Jacques Marquette and Louis Jolliet in 1673, and later by Marquette in 1674–1675. Guthrie spent almost 60 years of life studying the geology, oral accounts, documentaries, and survey history of the region and was determined that his knowledge would not go to waste. Childless, although married five times, this honorary member of the Western Society of Engineers and the Chicago Historical Society transmitted his knowledge to posterity. He was a geologist, writer, historian, civil engineer, and inventor and was called "the father of Chicago's drainage system" for his foresighted 1885 design plan for the Chicago Sanitary and Ship Canal, built in 1900. He died on October 25, 1908, leaving as his personal legacy to Summit, the Marquette monument, which was moved and altered in 1968. (Courtesy of the Summit Public Library Historical Archives.)

# *Three*

# Early Settlers and the Birth of Summit

The federal government and the State of Illinois sold off land tracts to early speculators even before the commencement of Illinois and Michigan Canal construction. Public land records show that Nehemiah King bought the full west half of the southeast quarter of section 12 in June 1835, with Alexander Dale taking the entire east half of the same quarter in February 1835. Hyram Pearsons acquired most of the northwest quarter of section 14 in December 1835, while much of sections 11 and 13 were bought after the canal was completed.

By 1835, Summit had a stagecoach house with a blacksmith, hotel, and tavern located at Archer and Lawndale Avenues, called the Summit Corner by residents. The property was leased by Dr. John T. Temple of Chicago and later by Frink and Walker and other coach concerns. The tavern was run by a list of men such as Levi Osterhoudt, a Mr. Skinner, Stephen White (later of Lyons), and most notably Denis O'Brien from 1845 to 1893.

The early farmers in Summit and contiguous lands sold produce in Chicago and were well known for the quality of their products, but the Illinois and Michigan Canal brought most of the village pioneers. Many Irish immigrants traveled out to Illinois to work on the canal, including some who had previously dug the Erie Canal. As some of these canal workers traded in their canal script in lieu of land, the Summit settlement grew, consisting mostly of Irish laborers who intermingled with the original pioneers from the eastern states.

With the Illinois and Michigan Canal came the dolomite quarries. Quarries were dug for the use of the canal but later prospered with agriculture and the building, and rebuilding, of Chicago. Many early settlers in Summit worked at the local quarries, often rooming in leftover canal boardinghouses, while others took up farming or the mercantile business. Property development remained at a standstill, however, while under the watchful eye of Summit Farm owner "Long John" Wentworth. The next boom for the area came with the construction of a second canal dug by the Chicago Sanitary District in the 1890s.

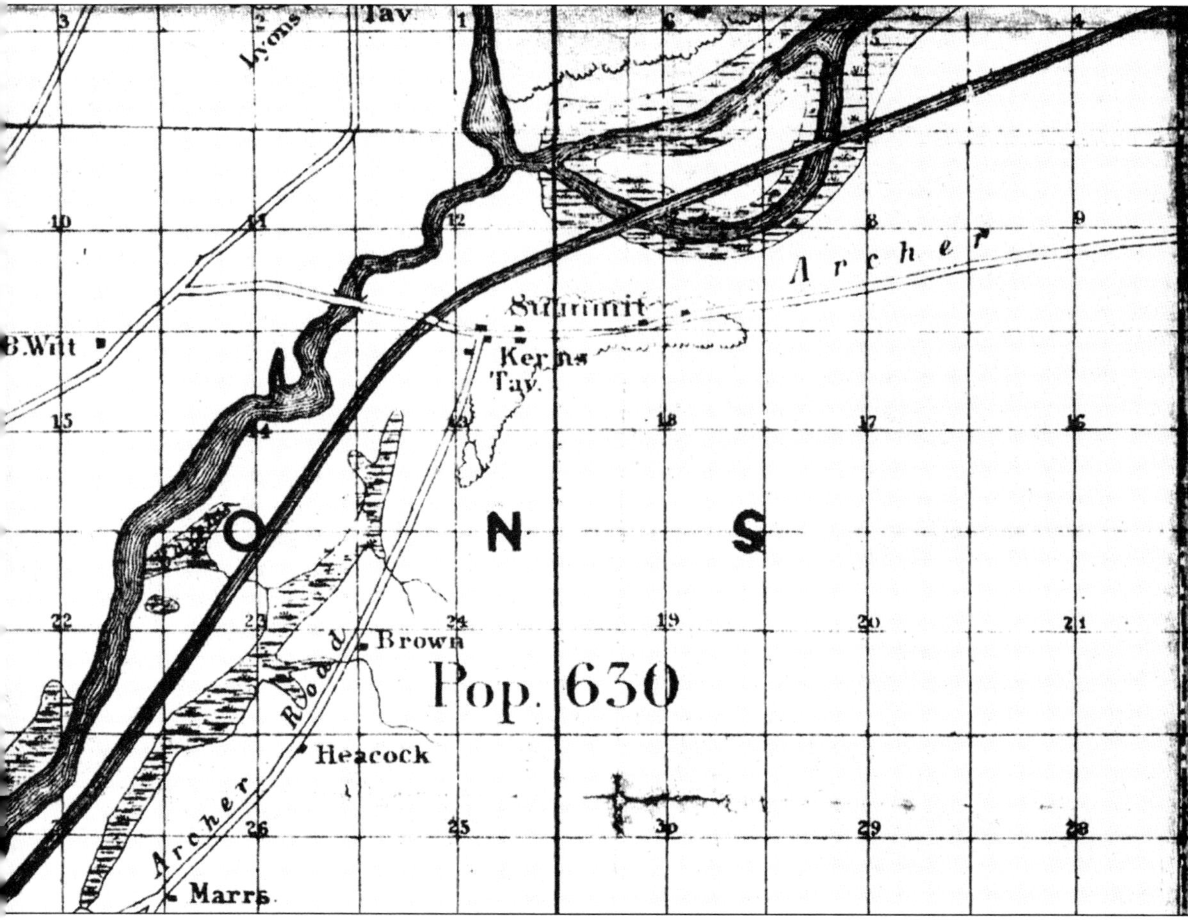


**MAP OF SUMMIT AND SURROUNDING LAND, 1851.** This map dating from 1851 shows Summit, the location of the stage house on the north side of Archer Avenue where it turns from east and west to north and south, and the location of the Kern Brothers' Tavern. Special note should be taken at the location of esquire William "Scotch" Brown's house in modern-day Bedford Park and Russell Heacock's residence located at what is now the entrance to Resurrection Cemetery at about 7200 South Archer Avenue. These farms were located on the east side of Archer, as before the Illinois and Michigan Canal was completed, the west side was a marsh most of the year. Peter Kern owned most of present-day Summit and operated a general store and a quarry on his property. William Brown and Russell Heacock were residing in their country homes when they fell victim to the cholera epidemic of 1849 that killed them and many of their family members. Heacock was buried on Brown's farm. Evidence of these farmhouses and Kern's holdings has long since disappeared from the landscape.

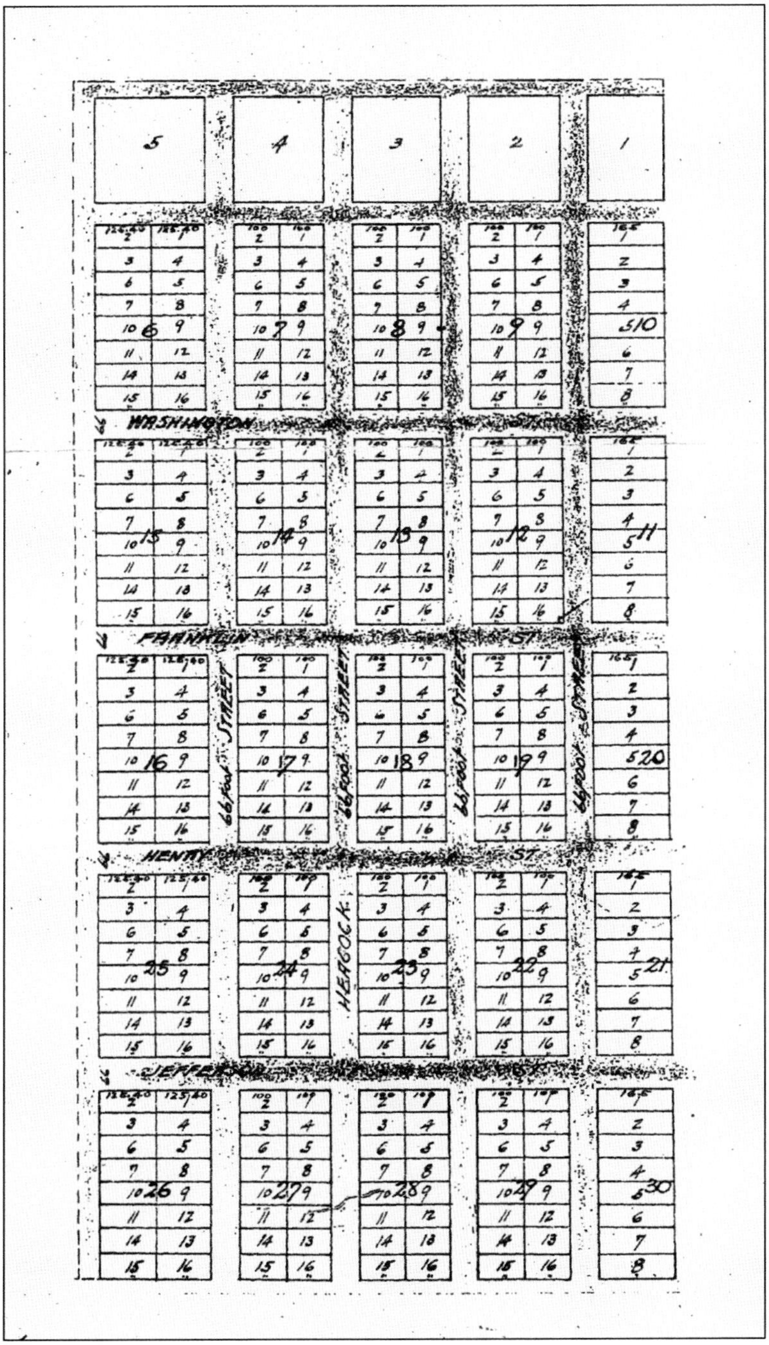


**SUMMIT SUBDIVISION.** This 1830s-era county plat shows the original Summit subdivision of the southwestern half of the southeast quarter of section 12, township 38. Subdivided before the Illinois and Michigan Canal or railroad were constructed, the lots are shown extending north nearly to the Des Plaines River. Archer Avenue is the southern boundary of the tracts. A Heacock Street is shown, as are Jefferson, Henry, Franklin, and Washington Streets. Block 27 is the property at the corner of Center and Archer Avenues, where the stagecoach stop was located. (Courtesy of the Summit Public Library Historical Archives.)

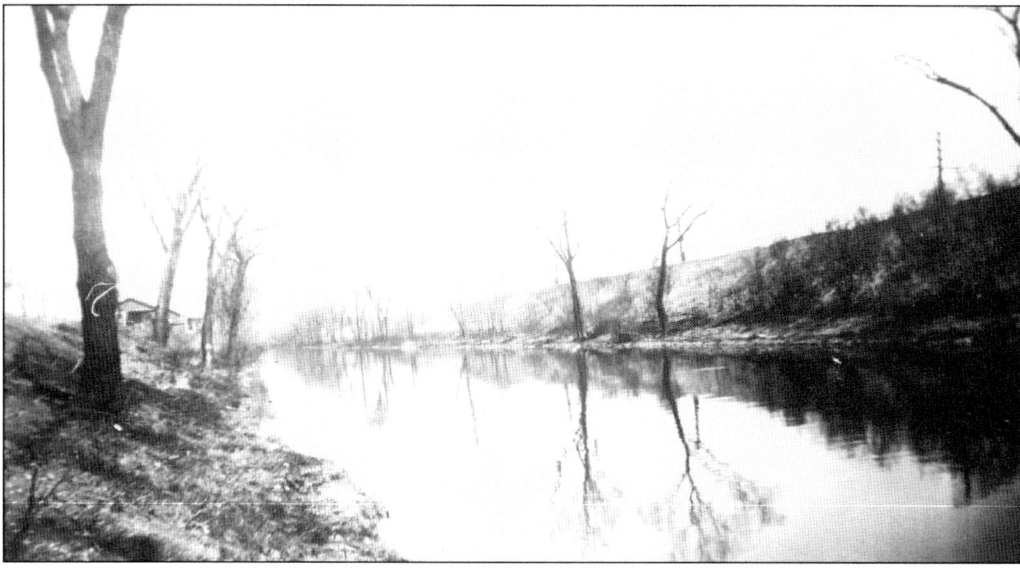

**THE TADPOLE DITCH.** The Illinois and Michigan Canal was the lifeblood of Chicago. It connected Lake Michigan with the Illinois River and was the draw for many of Summit's early settlers. Built between 1836 and 1848, the canal accommodated the shipment of commerce to and from the city via mule-drawn barges, and later by steam vessels. It was replaced by the Chicago Drainage Canal from Lockport to Chicago in 1900 and fell into disuse.

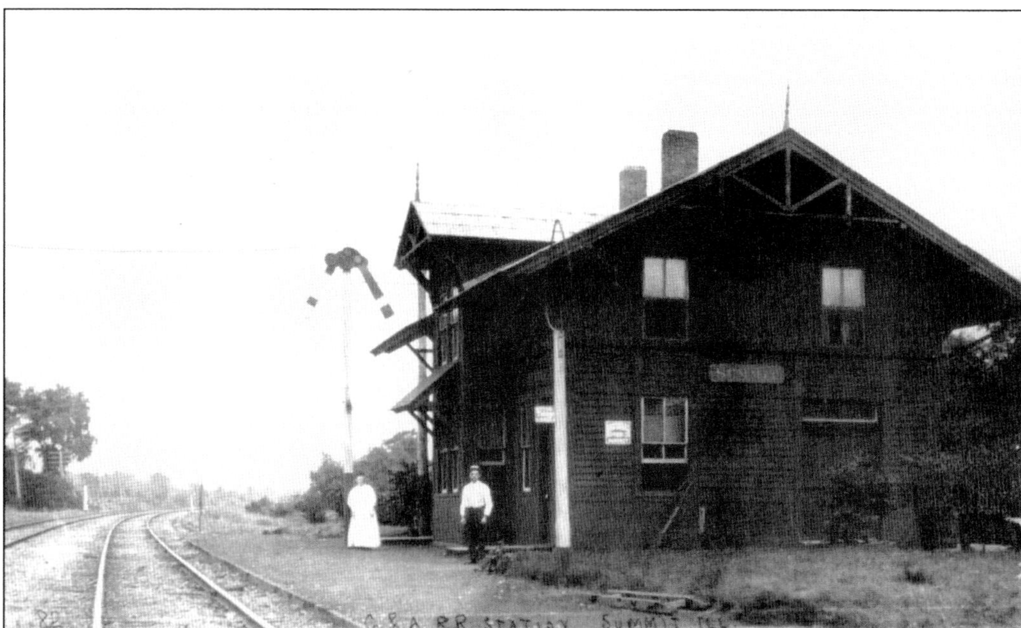


**CHICAGO AND ALTON RAILROAD.** The Joliet and Chicago Railroad was opened in 1856, traveling between Joliet and Chicago. In 1857, the railway was reorganized as the St. Louis, Alton and Chicago Railroad. In 1862, it became the Chicago and Alton Railroad. Summit's station, seen here, dates to before 1890. It was also used as a telegraph office and post office distribution point.

# Garden City Cemetery Notice.

The First Annual Election of the Garden City Cemetery Association is to be held in the school house at the Summit, on the last Tuesday in March, for the election of Trustees and a Superintendent, for the ensuing year, or until others are chosen by a majority of lot holders. Every lot holder taking five hundred feet will be entitled to one vote, or two persons may together purchase a lot, and between them control one vote. Persons desiring to become members of this Association can do so by subscribing as above, and advancing $1 to the agent, J. BLANCHARD, and his signature to this card will secure a free ticket on Tuesday, March 31st, 1868, on the regular morning train.

R. B. BARNES,
WM. SALTENSTOLL,
And others.

March 23, 1868.

P. S.—Free Tickets can be had at this office, No. 11

GARDEN CITY REST. A portion of Peter Kern's property was bought by Leonard Kent, who opened a private graveyard called the Garden City Rest in 1867, after the original Chicago Cemetery was closed. The graveyard was located at Seventy-fourth Avenue and Archer Avenue.

SHEEP FOR SALE.—Six

**SOUTH DOWN BUCK LAMBS,**

For sale from Ewes had from imported stock by the Bucks, presented to the Mayor of Chicago by the Prince of Wales, and which are fit for service this season, for sale at the

**Summit Farm, Cook County, Ill.**

Apply on the premises, or address the subscriber, care of Hon. John Wentworth, Chicago, Ill.

no26-x513 1td&w CHAS. L. REED.

SUMMIT FARM, 1862. "Long John" Wentworth owned the Summit Farm and visited there almost daily. After retirement, Wentworth lived at the estate house located off the corner of Archer and Harlem Avenues. The farm offered fine cattle, milk, turkeys, sheep bred from English stock, honeybees, and racehorses. Wentworth had racing interests and also raised fine Thoroughbred horses.

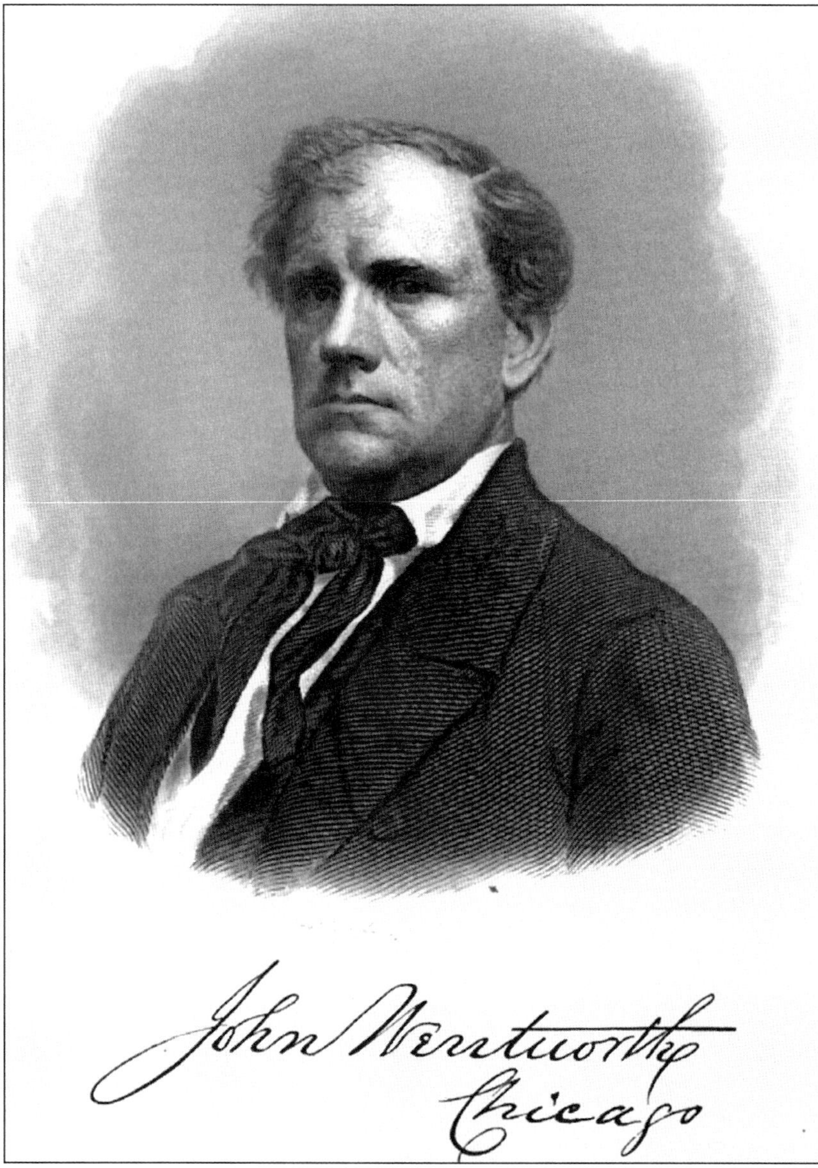


**"LONG JOHN" WENTWORTH.** "Long John" Wentworth—born on March 5, 1815, and died on October 16, 1888—was a Republican mayor of Chicago from 1857 to 1858 and 1860 to 1861 and served 12 years in the U.S. House of Representatives. He was a towering man at six feet six inches tall. He came to Chicago in 1836, later becoming managing editor of Chicago's first newspaper, the *Chicago Democrat*, eventually becoming its owner and publisher. Having lived at the Sherman House in Chicago, he moved to his farm on the Summit in 1868. Long John died at the estate and was buried in Rosehill Cemetery. After his death, the estate was managed by nephew Moses Wentworth. Summit was like Long John's private domain just out of reach of Chicago, under the charge of Denis O'Brien, nicknamed "Mayor O'Brien," one of Long John's fellow horse breeders and proprietor of the stage house. Many of Summit's pioneers worked on Long John's farm or bought their property from him. After his death, Summit quickly incorporated, as Long John was no longer there to protect his—or their—interests from the slowly encroaching city.

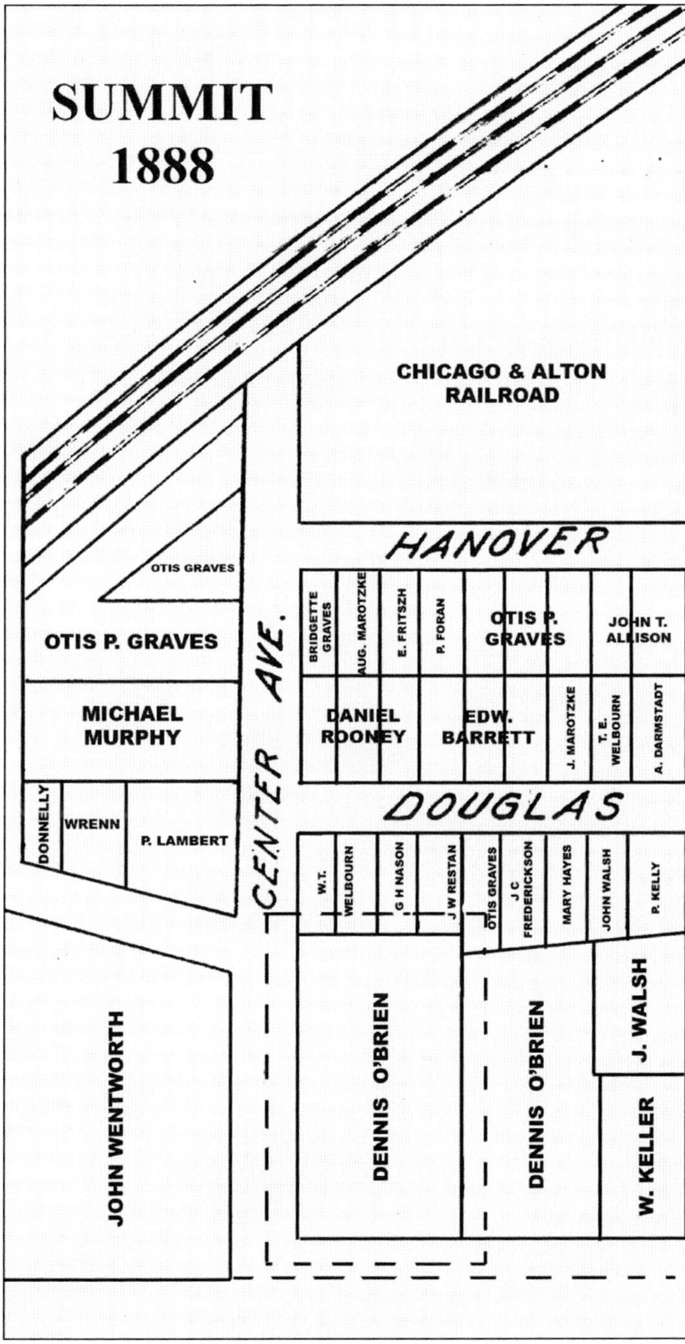


**SUMMIT SUBDIVISION, C. 1888.** The west half of the southeast quarter of section 12 took on a different appearance after John Wentworth's death. A resubdivision took place, and the lots were laid out as they are seen today. The dashed lines seen here indicate the original pre–Illinois and Michigan Canal block 27. Wentworth bought up thousands of acres at every convenience. His landholdings consisted of some 4,700 acres including present-day Summit, Garfield Ridge, Clearing, Bridgeview, and Willow Springs. He was joined in this endeavor by William B. Ogden, who also owned land in the area. Ogden, Chicago's first mayor from 1837 to 1838, died in 1877.

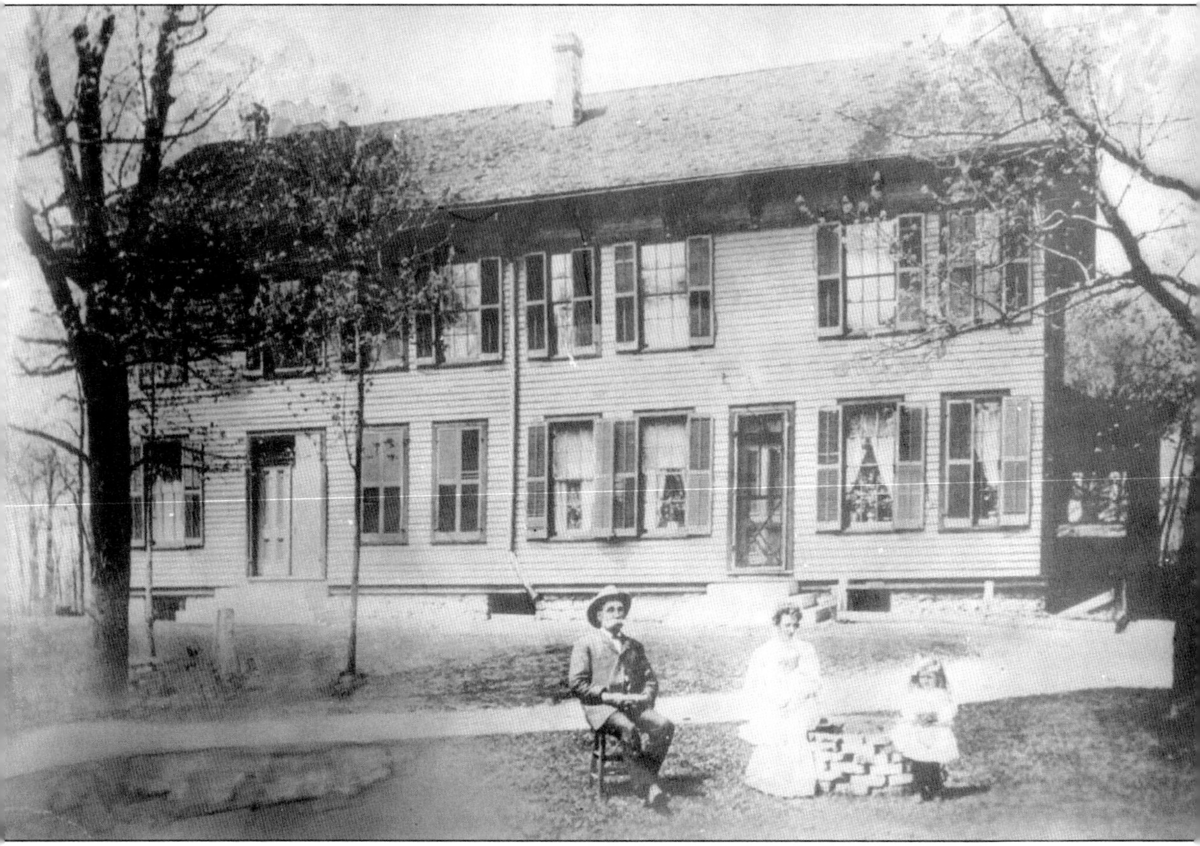

**CYRUS E. PARLIN.** Farm foreman and horse breeder Cyrus E. Parlin bought the Summit Farm from the Wentworth estate, including "Long John" Wentworth's 18-room farmhouse and back buildings located at 7200 Archer Avenue. Parlin was originally a lumberjack from Maine brought in to take charge of Wentworth's cattle and horses. Parlin would become quite successful with the farm and was one of the founders of Summit State Bank, organized on October 11, 1910. He was also on the first highway commission of Stickney Township for six years after its inception. The house stayed in the Parlin family for many years and then passed to the Ridder family. Even though this residence was the home of a past Chicago mayor and statesman, having seen the likes of great men like the Prince of Whales, it was never given the historical landmark status it deserved. It was torn down in 1968.

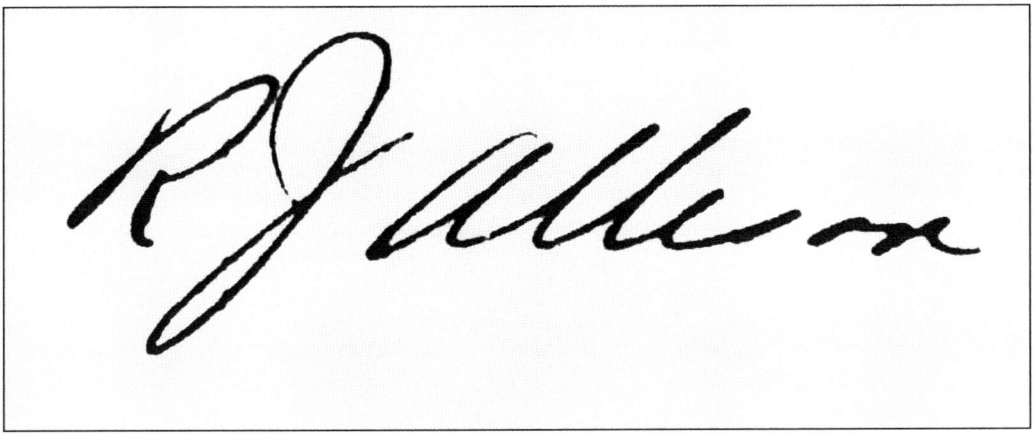

**ROBERT J. ALLISON.** Robert J. Allison was originally an Illinois and Michigan Canal boatman. He was well respected and nicknamed "Honest Jack" by his friends. He was a merchant, postmaster, and landowner in Summit. Allison died on September 25, 1891, shortly after becoming Summit's first mayor. He was the father of John T., Robert D., Nancy, Sarah, Agnes, Frank, and Kate.

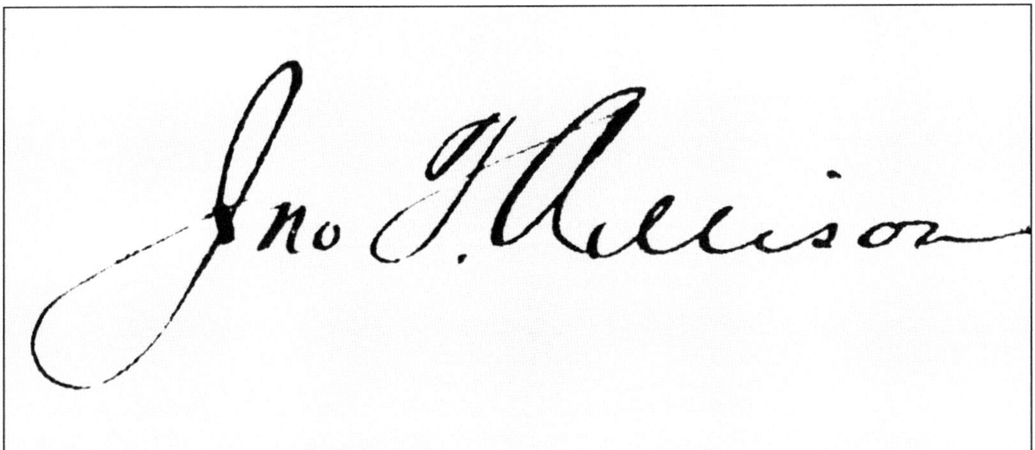

**JOHN T. ALLISON.** A son of Robert J. Allison was John T., a stone contractor and quarry foreman, as well as an early Summit mayor. He dealt heavily in real estate and was active in township politics. John T. Allison would erect an estate at Wildwood in modern-day Willow Springs, and it was here that he died in April 1926.

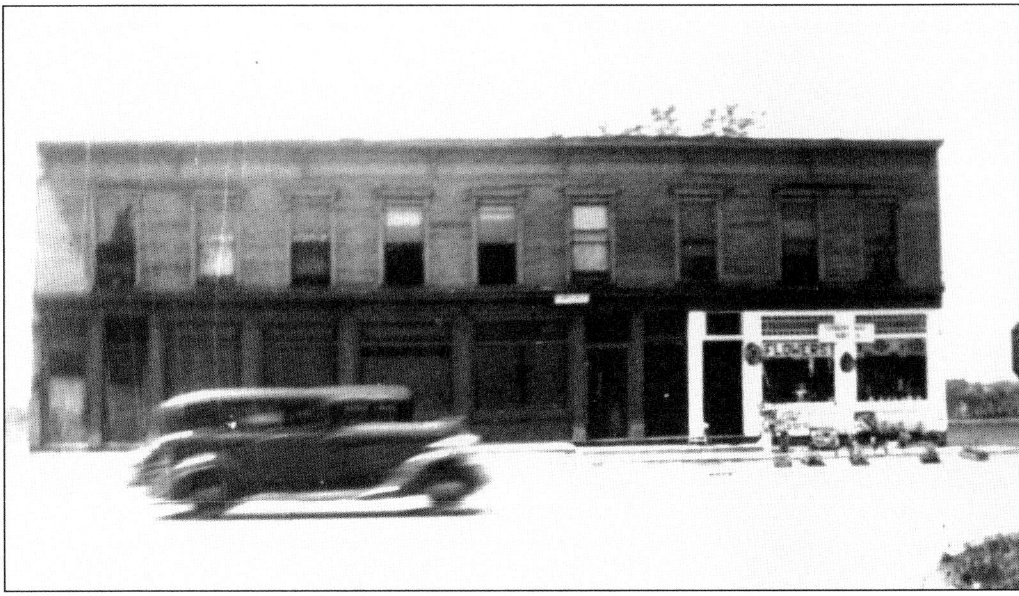


**FLAT BUILDING, MID-1930S.** This building housed business fronts encompassing 5552, 5554, and 5556 South Archer Avenue. It was owned by Robert J. Allison, Summit's first board president, who was postmaster intermittently from the 1860s until his death in 1891. The rightmost storefront was possibly the site of the village's first board meetings.

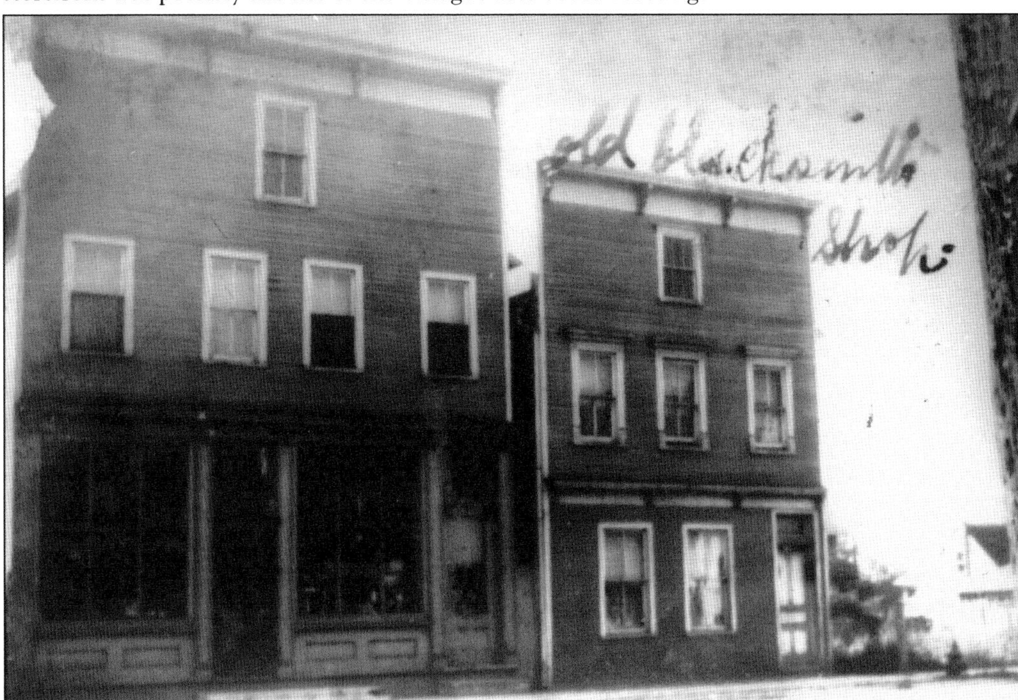

**SCHROEDER BLACKSMITH.** Pioneer resident Gottlieb Schroeder came to Summit from Prussia in 1875 and later built this blacksmith shop at 7429 West Archer Avenue (right) and a store and flat building (left) at 7427 Archer. The stables sheds were in the back. Son-in-law Carl Greb obtained these two buildings after Gottlieb's death in 1915.

**WELBOURN ESTATE.** William T. Welbourn purchased this land from Moses Wentworth in 1894 and later built this house. In 1896, the Michigan Central Railroad put in tracks along the south end of the property. The house was later owned by Judge Sam Herzog, who probably installed the jail cell in the basement that has become legendary in the village.

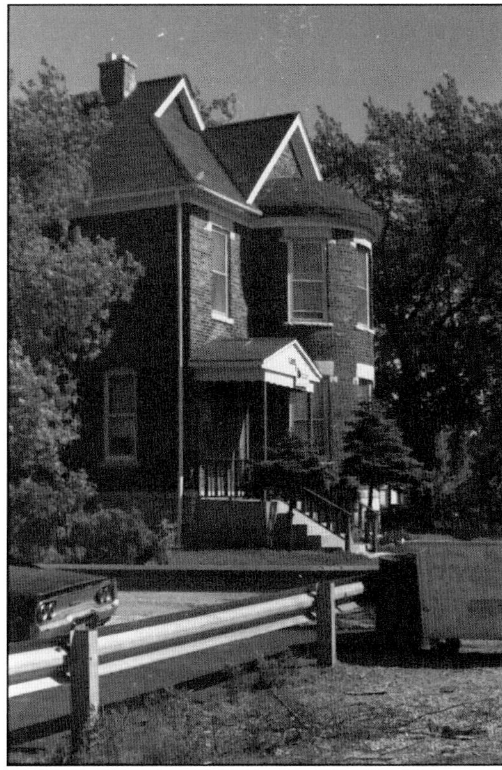

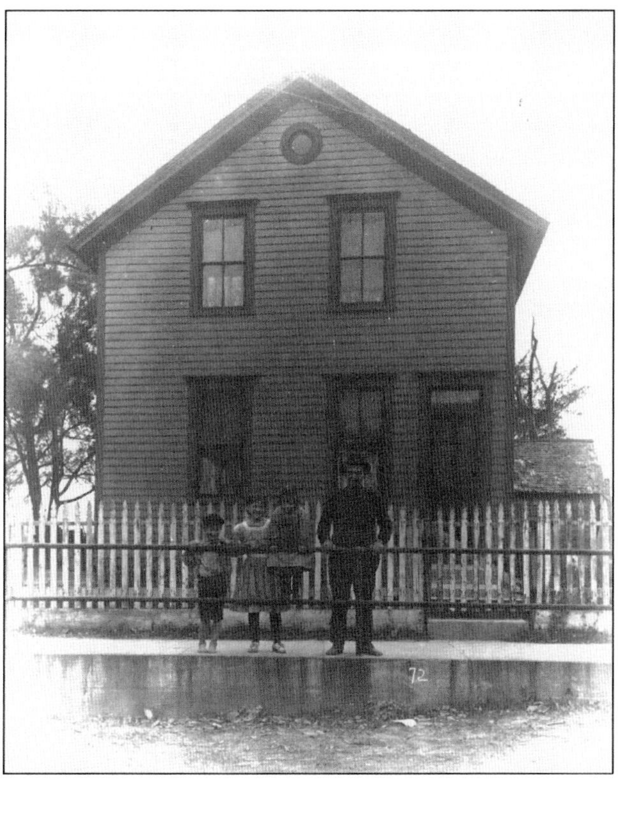

**JOHN KIRK RESIDENCE.** Seen here is the residence of John Kirk at 7665 Lincoln Avenue. John Kirk and brother William came to Summit as Illinois and Michigan Canal supervisors. They purchased canal land where William stayed and raised his family. William's son John built the house pictured here. John started a long line of public servants with son Edward J. and grandson John J. becoming long-standing Summit village clerks. Edward was a beer vendor but built a paint store in 1924 at 7336 Archer Avenue. The man in this picture was a friendly transient who lived along the canal. (Courtesy of Patricia Kirk.)

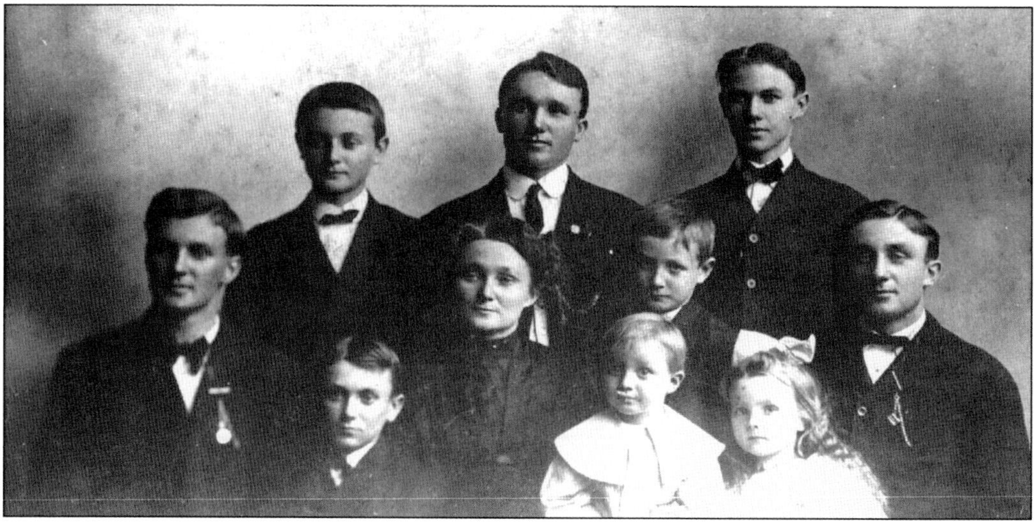

**LAMBERT FAMILY.** The children of pioneer Patrick Lambert and wife Maime are shown here. Patrick came to Summit to work on the Illinois and Michigan Canal and stayed. His offspring include past mayors of Summit and community leaders. Patrick died at age 96 in 1935.

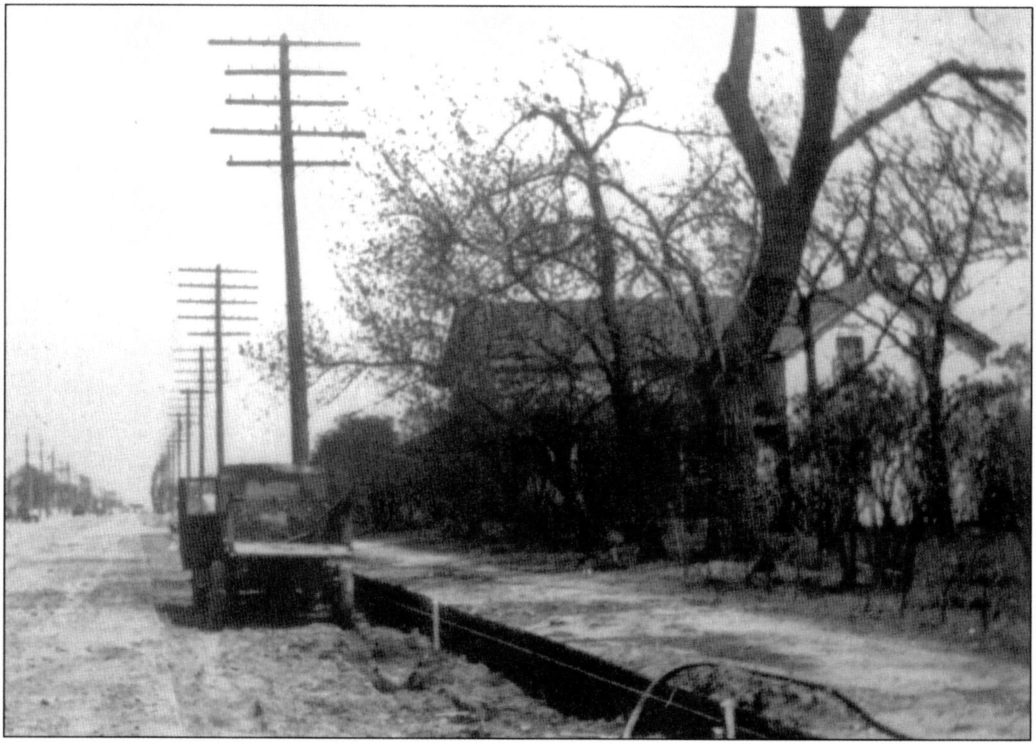

**OTIS P. GRAVES HOME, 1935.** Otis P. Graves came from New York State and eventually bought land at Seventy-fourth Avenue and Archer Avenue in 1869 where he built his home. He was an early village trustee and served on the school board for many years. Graves owned numerous land tracts in town. He ran the old Kern stone quarry on the site of Summit Park. He passed away at age 84 in 1920.

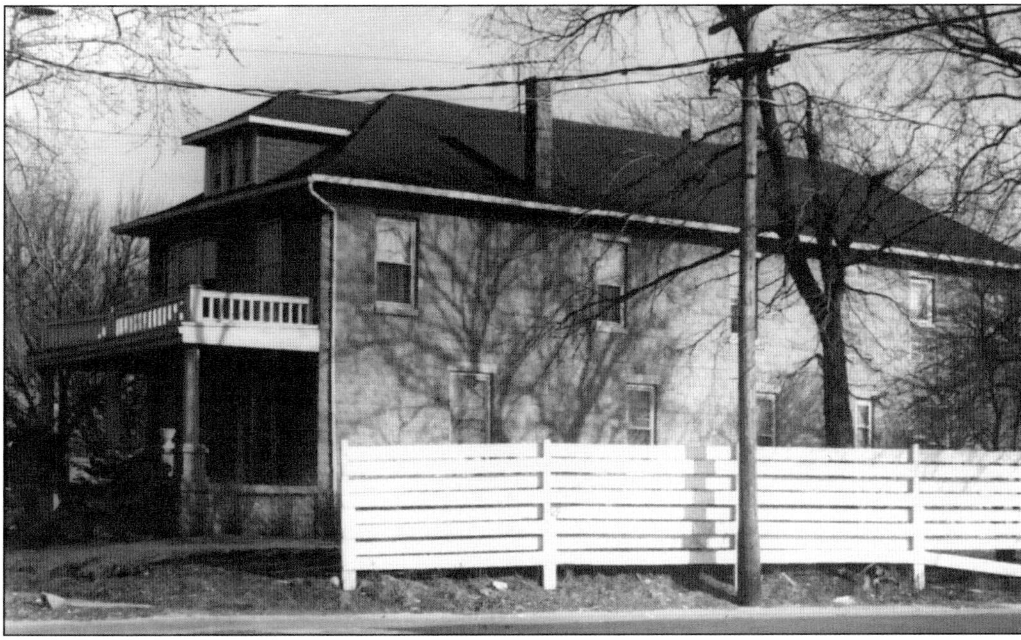

**JOSEPH J. MARSHALL.** Joseph J. Marshall arrived in the 1890s with the construction of the Chicago Drainage Canal and opened a general store at 7454 Archer Avenue. A successful quarry engineer, village trustee, and building contractor, he erected this house at 7503 West Fifty-sixth Street in 1912. He always stated that the home was located on the site of an old American Indian signal station.

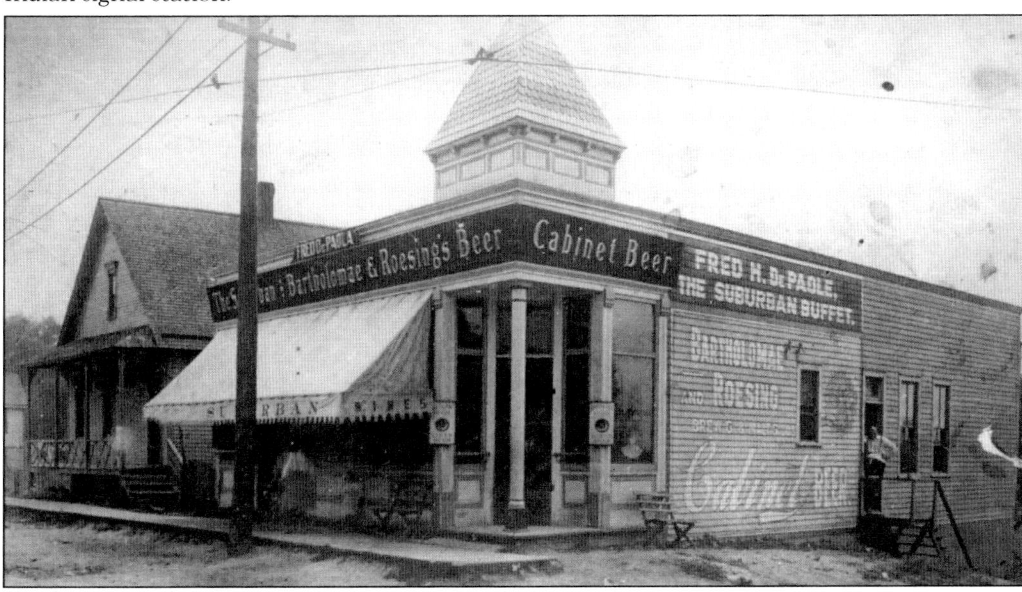


**FRED DEPAOLE.** Fred DePaole's Bartholomae and Roesing tavern is seen here around 1903. This view is looking southwest from the Summit Corner at Archer Avenue and Lawndale Avenue. DePaole ran a tavern in Summit as early as 1899 but leased this property from Angela Swalls in 1902 (Swalls's house is seen in the background) and erected this building, which he occupied until 1917. In 1926, the property was owned by Frank Starai, who removed this wooden structure for a brick building.

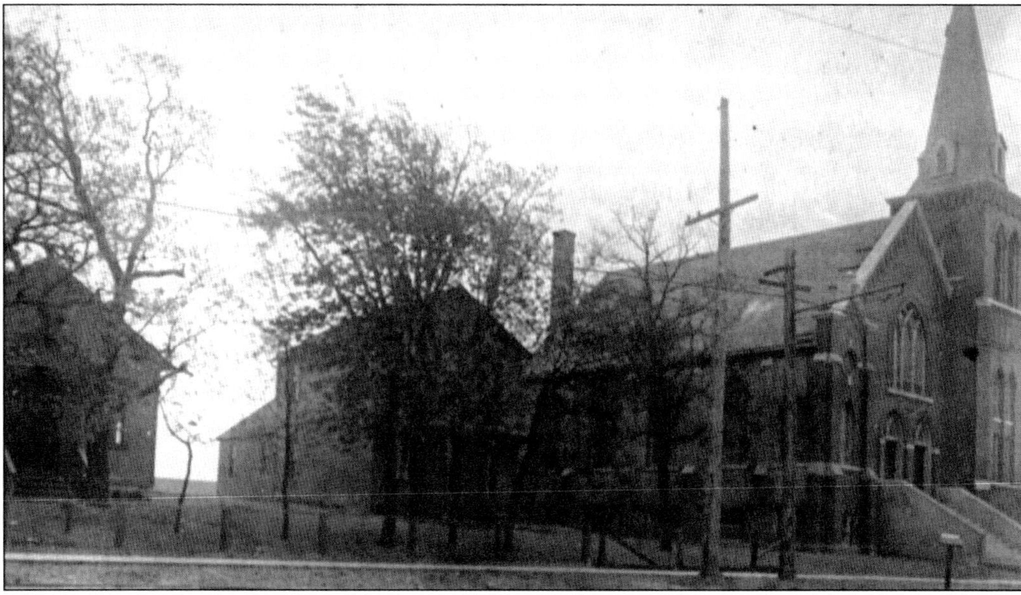

**ZION LUTHERAN CHURCH.** The oldest church congregation of Summit is Zion Lutheran Church, started by German farmers in 1871. By 1872, a church (left) and parsonage (middle) were built on land donated by member Frederich Petersdorf. A regular day school with a teacher was formed in 1913 when the brick church building (right) was built, with the old church being used as a schoolhouse. A brick grade school building beside the old church was erected in 1949. (Courtesy of the Summit Public Library Historical Archives.)

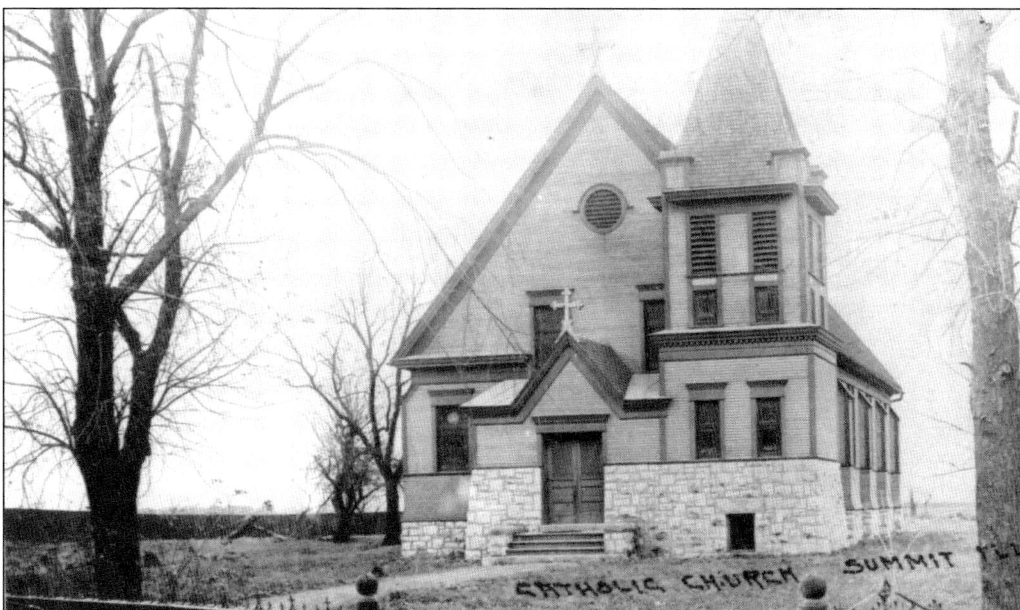


**FIRST ST. JOSEPH CHURCH.** Early Catholics in the community attended either St. Mary's in Lyons or St. James at Sag Bridge. By 1900, the Summit members of St. Mary's Parish separated and a mission church was started utilizing the village hall. St. Joseph Parish was founded in 1902, and this church was built at Sixtieth Street and Archer Avenue. In 1916, a grade school was built at Sixty-first Place and Seventy-fifth Avenue. The church building burned in 1918.

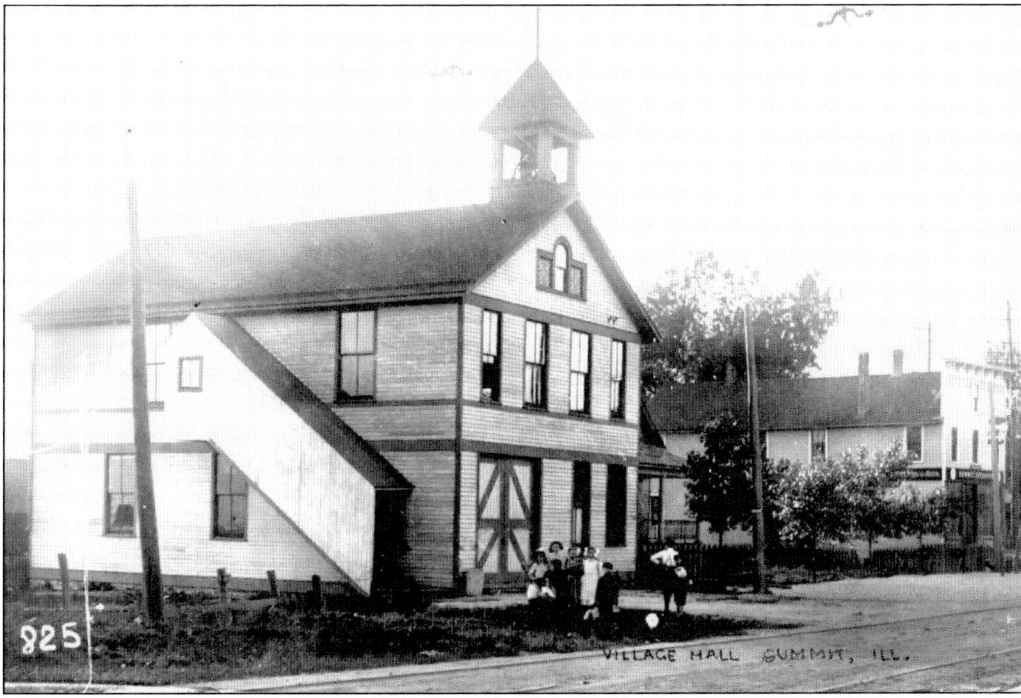


**ORIGINAL VILLAGE HALL.** The newly formed village of Summit acquired land from Moses Wentworth and built this hall in 1898. The first board meeting held in the building was on January 3, 1899. Built by the S. L. Derby Company of Lemont, the dimensions were 30 by 50 feet, with two stories. The second floor was rented as a hall, and the first event was a boxing match. (Courtesy of the Paul Rush collection.)

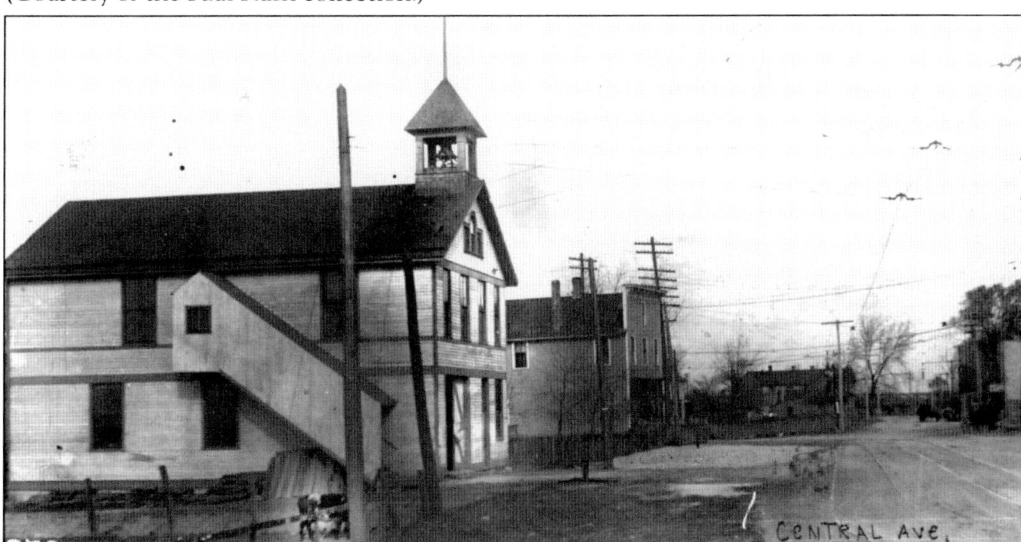


**VILLAGE POUND.** The village hall accommodated the police department, fire apparatus, board meetings, and, alongside the property, the village pound. Responding to problems with stray cattle and livestock, the board voted that a pound be built. William Keller was appointed the first pound marshal in 1895. In this image, a goat is waiting to be claimed by its owner. Stray livestock would plague the village for years to come. (Courtesy of the Paul Rush collection.)

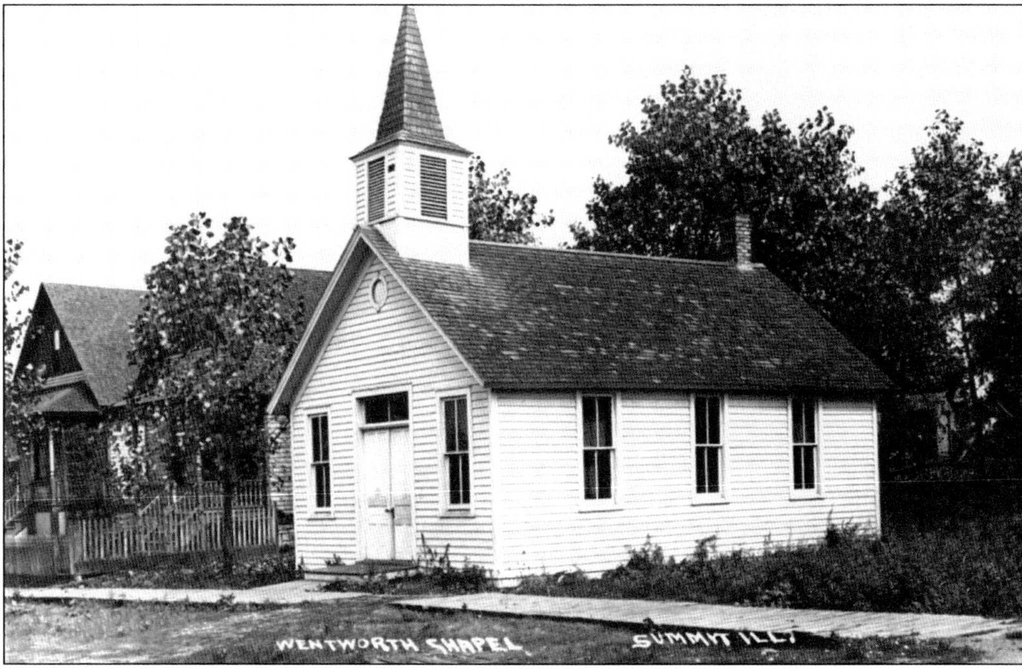


**WENTWORTH CHAPEL.** Located at the northeast corner of Douglas and Hunt Avenues was the first home of the Summit Congregational Church. The church had a Sunday school in Summit in 1890 but no permanent meeting place. Moses Wentworth donated property to the congregation, and it built this structure in 1895. The building was upgraded through the years but eventually sold to the Holy Cross Greek Orthodox Church in the early 1960s, when the Congregationalists moved to a new site. The building burned in 1976. (Courtesy of the Paul Rush collection.)

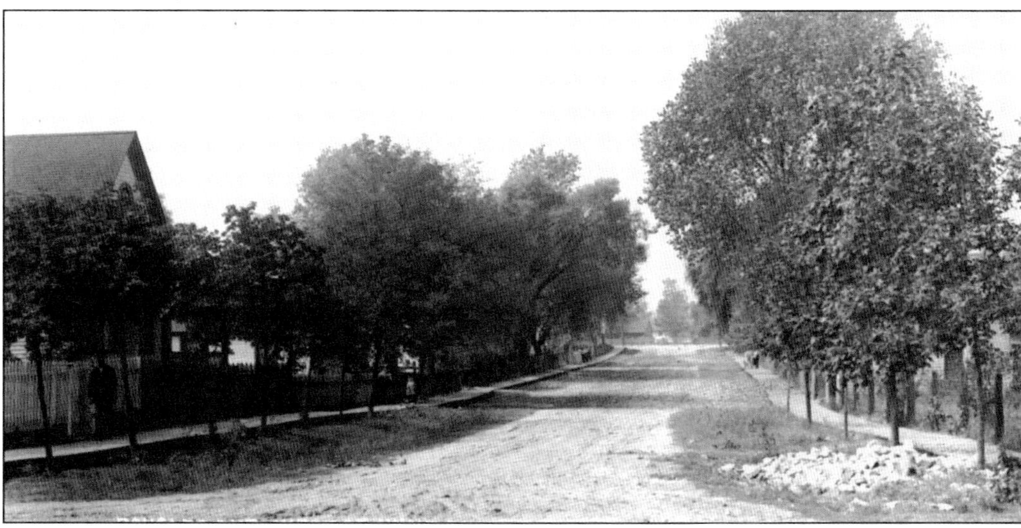

**DOUGLAS WEST OF HUNT.** Taken from the center of Douglas Avenue west of the intersection with Hunt Avenue, and near the Wentworth Chapel, this image depicts an early Summit street scene around 1906. The house to the left is the original Walsh residence, sold in 1920 to Patrick Murphy. The Murphys ran a boardinghouse out of the building at one time. The wooden sidewalk was constructed in 1900. (Courtesy of the Paul Rush collection.)

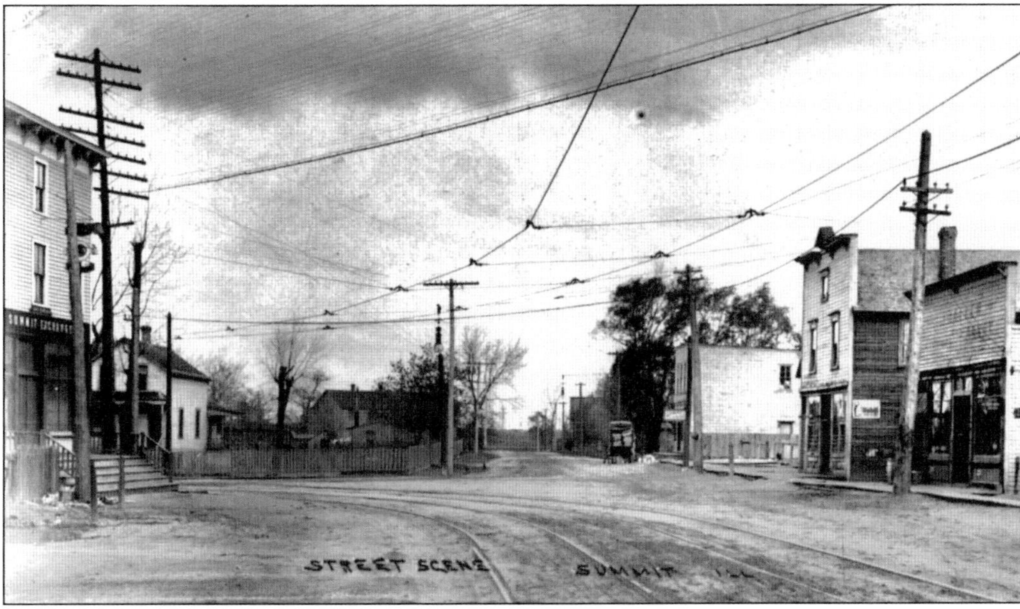


**CENTER AND LINCOLN AVENUES.** Lawndale Avenue was initially called Lincoln Avenue from Center Avenue to the west embankment of the Des Plaines River bridge. This view from about 1906 shows the corner of Lincoln and Center looking north. To the left is the original Summit telephone exchange in the Mesich brothers' building. Behind it is the home of Patrick Lambert. The buildings on the east side of Center are, from left to right, Berletich's Saloon, a vacant Kabaker's General Store, and O. W. Keller's Grocery. (Courtesy of the Paul Rush collection.)

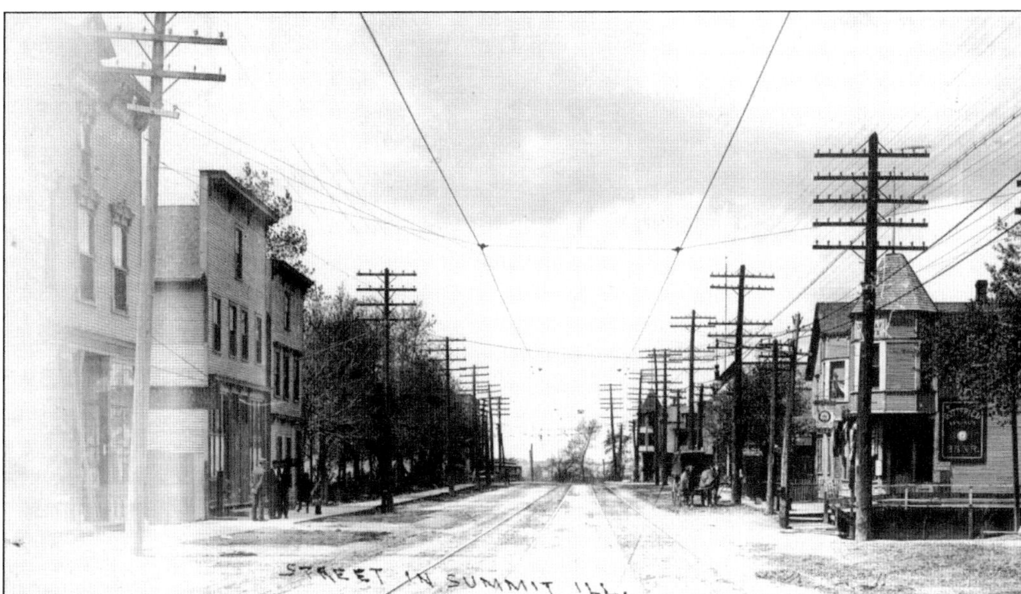


**WESTBOUND ARCHER AVENUE FROM HUNT AVENUE, C. 1910.** John Maloy's post office and grocery building is seen to the far right, as the camera points west on Archer Avenue. To the left are the three buildings of Gottlieb Schroeder. Carl Greb occupied the farthest structure on the left, where he had a general store. (Courtesy of the Summit Public Library Historical Archives.)

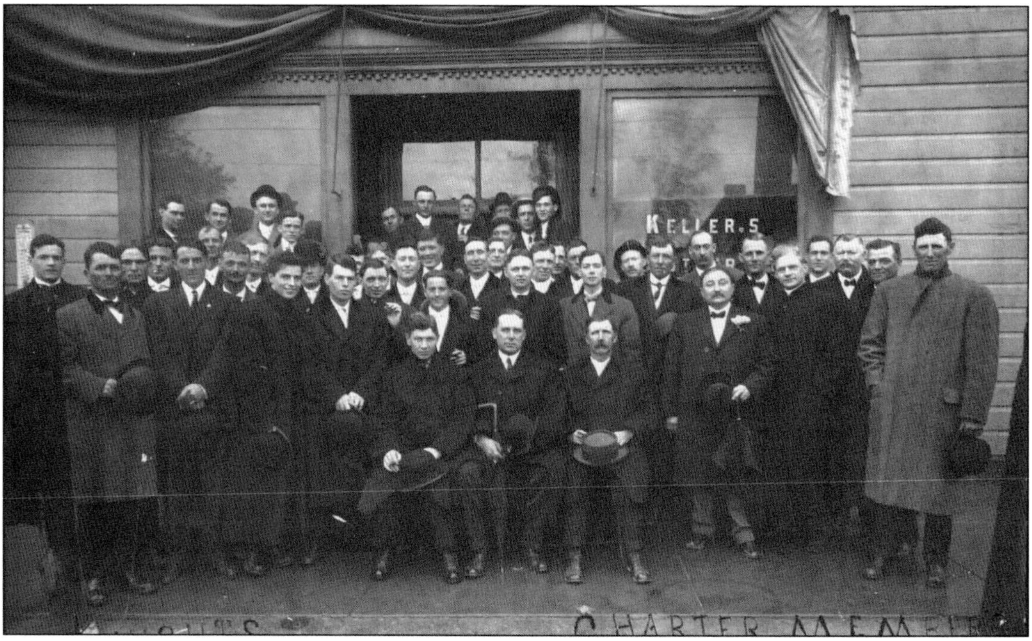


**KELLER'S RESTAURANT.** The charter members of St. Joseph's Council Knight's of Columbus No. 1642 pose in front of Fred Keller's restaurant on May 12, 1912. Located at 7444 Archer Avenue, this building later became the Frederick and Hayes Funeral Home until 1938. A dance hall was upstairs and catered to village board meetings for a time. The building is no longer standing. (Courtesy of Patricia Kirk.)

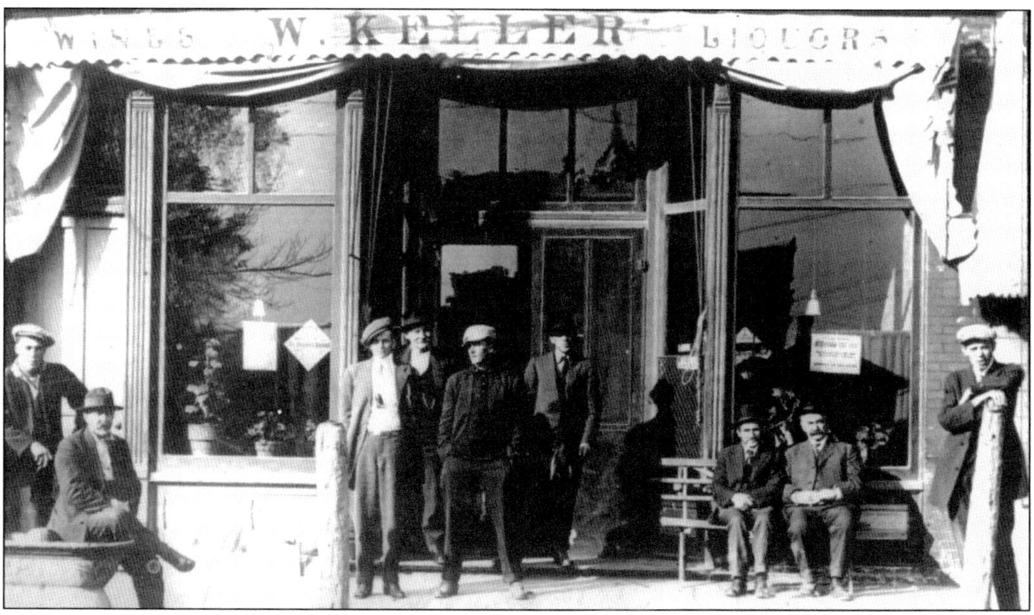


**KELLER'S LIQUORS.** This image from about 1913 shows men outside William Keller's liquor store. On the second floor was a hotel. Built in mid-1880s, 7446 Archer Avenue was home to many tenants after Fred Keller's death in 1909. Wife Caroline kept the business going for a while, but from 1925 to 1937 it was an A&P grocery, then an early home of Foran Funeral Home. This is the oldest commercial building standing in Summit to this day.

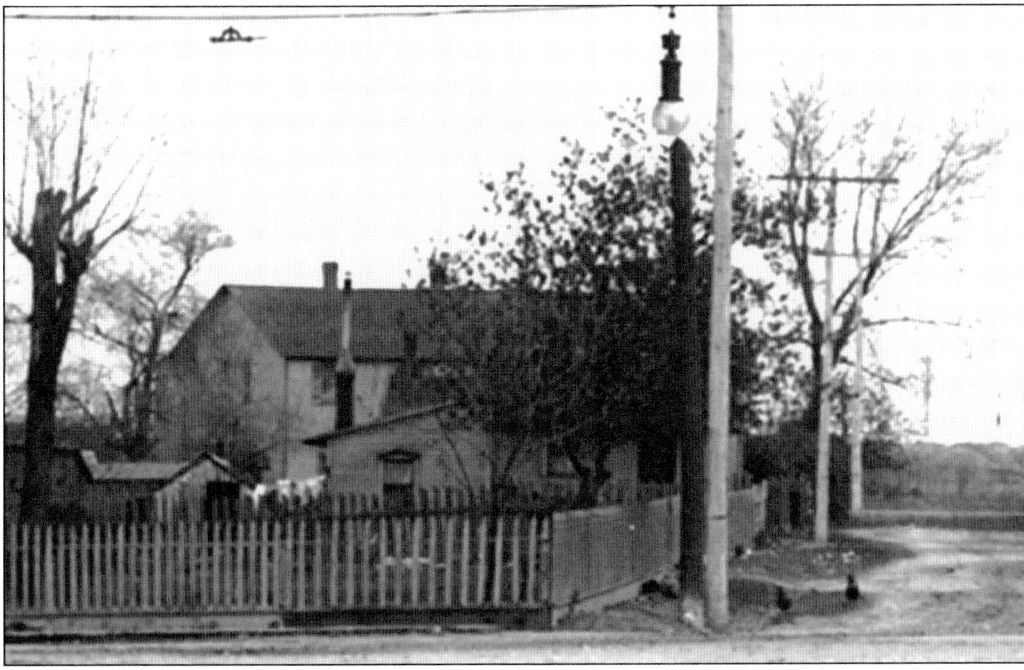

**First Summit School.** As early as 1846, this old canal boardinghouse was used as a school. Seen here in 1906, the two-story frame building was on the property of Otis P. Graves, school board president. The building was later operated by Tony Pechnik as a boardinghouse, tavern, and small bowling alley for local Croatians working at the quarries. The building was gone by 1911.

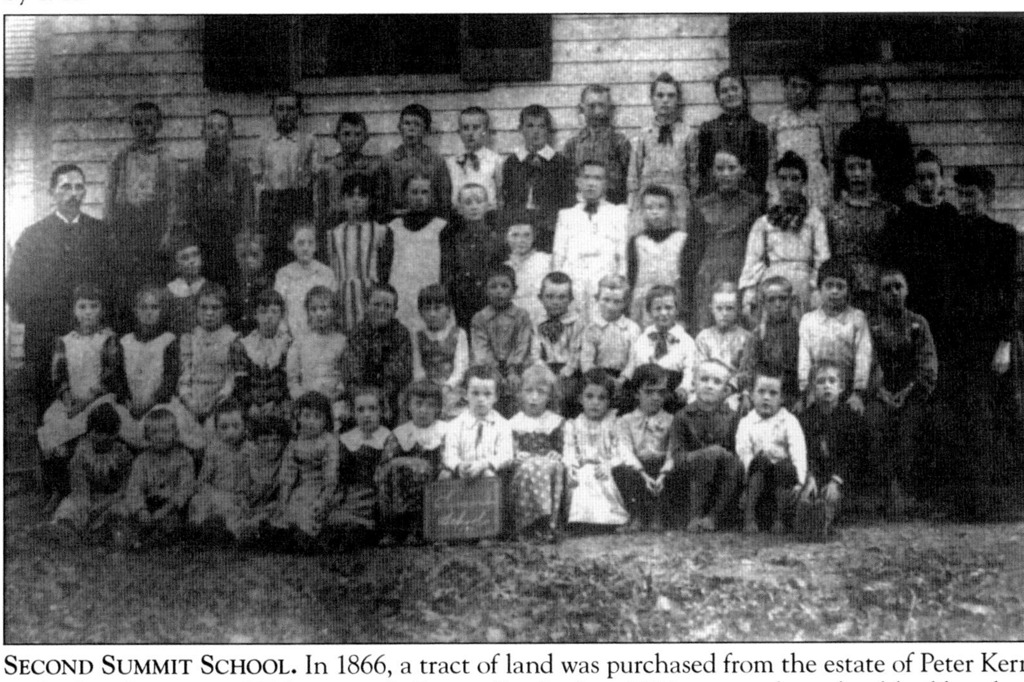

**Second Summit School.** In 1866, a tract of land was purchased from the estate of Peter Kern at Archer Avenue and Fifty-seventh Street. By the late 1800s, a wooden school building had been built. This image is of the Summit School class of 1891.

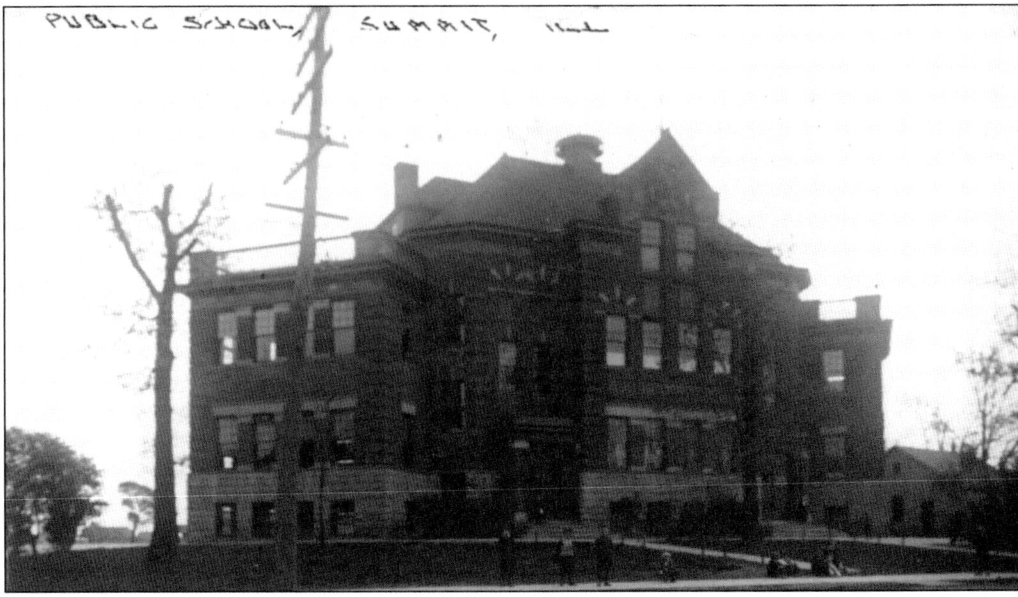


**THIRD SUMMIT SCHOOL.** In 1904, a new schoolhouse was built. Facing Archer Avenue between Fifty-sixth Place and Fifty-seventh Street, it was a hexagon-shaped brick building, which included a central hall and eight classrooms. Discontinued as a schoolhouse by the mid-1930s, the structure became a community building and youth recreation center called the Teen Inn. It was torn down in the 1950s. (Courtesy of the Paul Rush collection.)

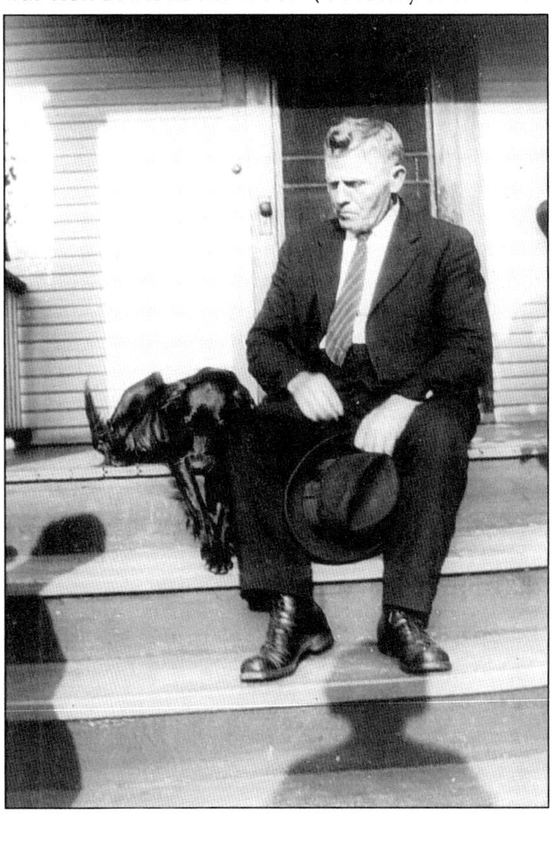

**JOHN D. WALSH.** The village's first police and fire marshal was John D. Walsh. He was also on the first public school board, serving from 1901 to 1934. To ease classroom overcrowding in 1929, the board built a new building behind the Summit School on the east side of the block and named it after him. The sixth, seventh, and eighth grades were then moved to the new Walsh School. (Courtesy of Celeste Johnstone.)

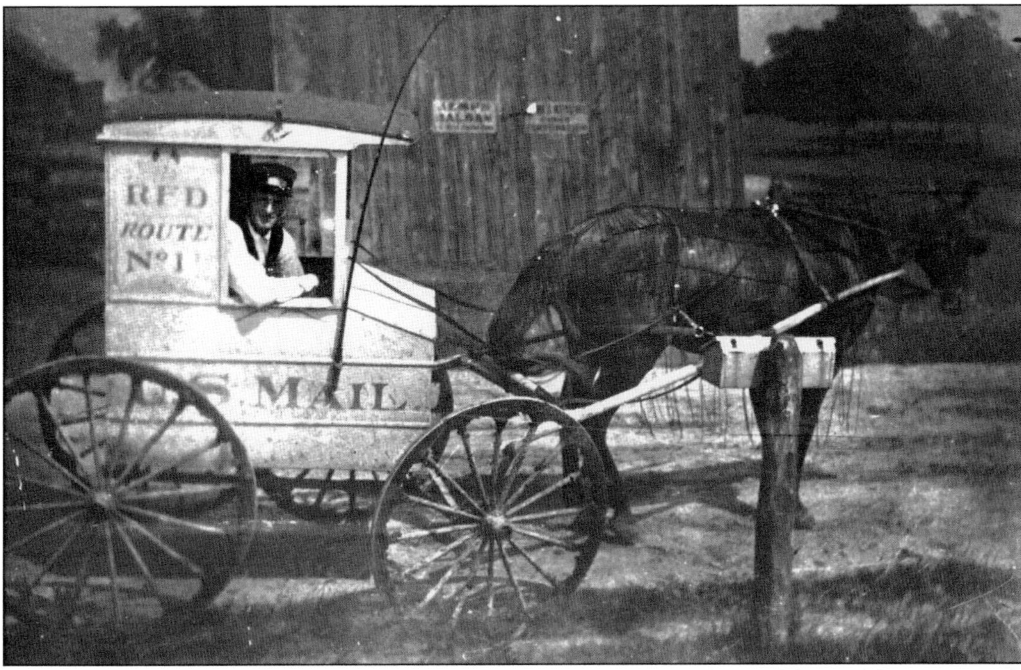


**MAIL RFD.** Summit had a post office as early as 1841, and mail was delivered by stagecoach. However, a rural free delivery (RFD) was available for those areas outside Summit's postal district. Nick Brouwer, seen here with his delivery wagon in 1907, served the RFD routes in unincorporated districts until 1915.

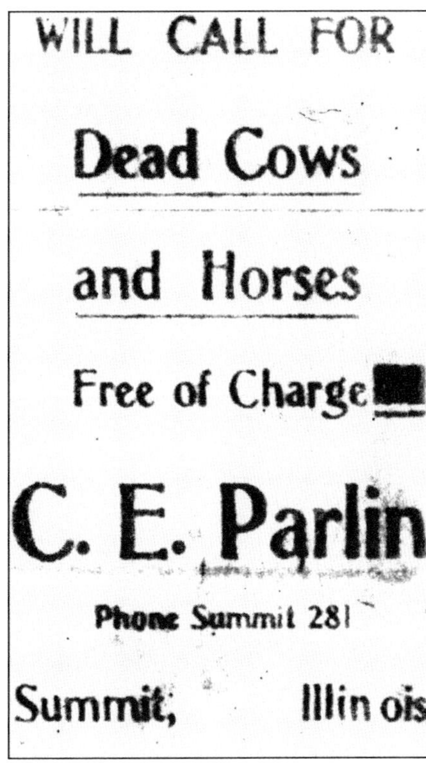


**PARLIN ADVERTISEMENT, 1912.** Cyrus E. Parlin, the owner of the old Wentworth estate, had many different business interests. Animal-rendering plants were common at one time but a health nuisance to small municipalities. Parlin would remove people's dead horses or cattle and resell the carcasses for rendering at a profit.

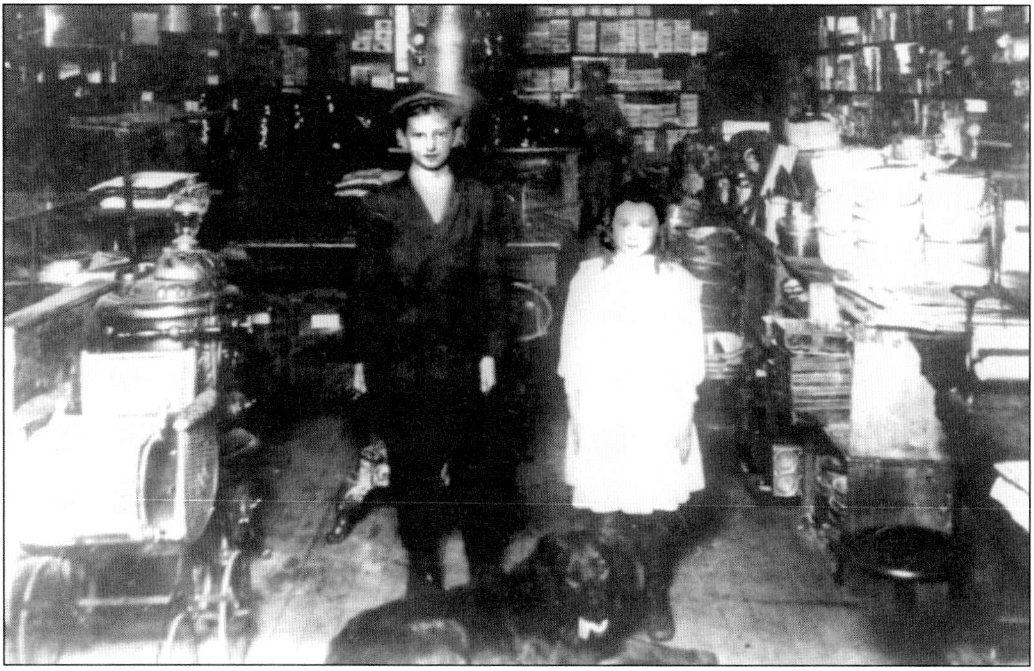

**KABAKER'S ON CENTER AVENUE.** The interior of Kabaker's General Store on Center Avenue is seen here around 1904. This image may have been taken just prior to its move to the top of the hill on Archer Avenue. Pictured here are Mary and Louis, children of pioneer merchant Solomon Kabaker.

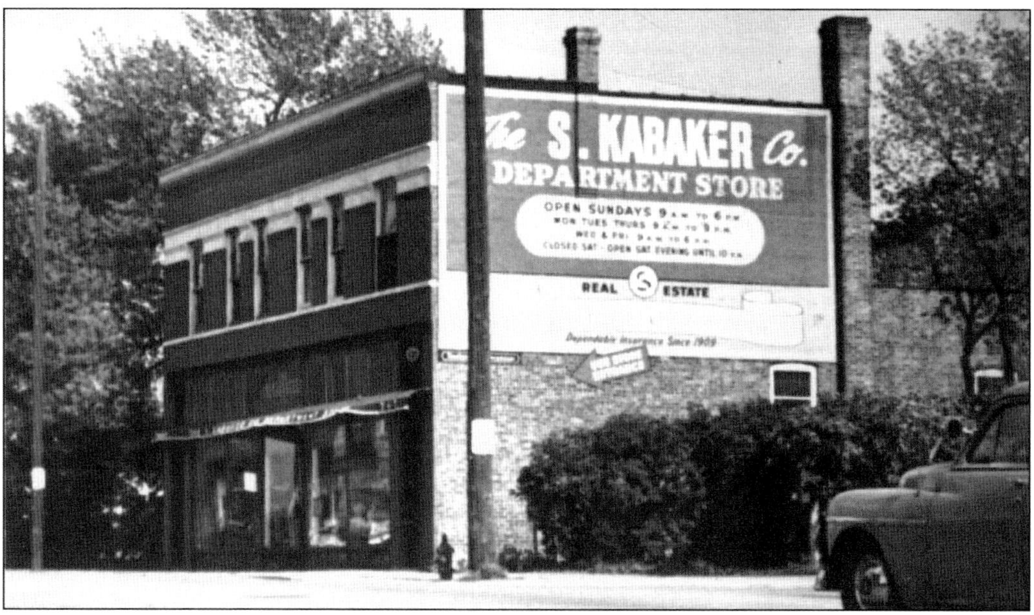


**KABAKER'S ON ARCHER AVENUE.** Solomon and Rey Kabaker came to Summit in 1897, opening a store at 5437 Center Avenue. By the end of 1904, they had moved to a new building at 7449–7451 Archer Avenue. The business remained until the Stevenson Expressway was constructed in 1964. The Kabakers lived in a large house behind the store and rented out the flats above this building.

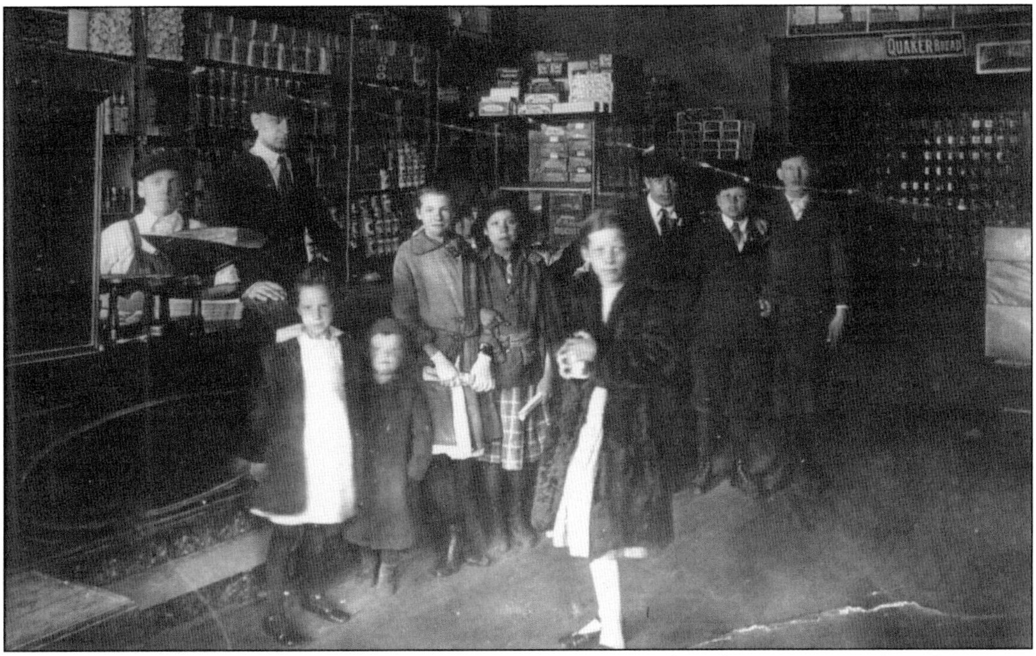

**MALOY STORE.** John Maloy came to Summit as a railroad worker about 1900. He later became a director of the Summit State Bank, a telephone exchange supervisor, a real estate developer, and a grocery store owner. His first store was located at Fifty-sixth Street and Archer Avenue, but by 1910, he had moved the store to 7432 Archer Avenue. He and his wife kept the Summit Post Office for over 20 years. Post boxes are seen here in the rear of his store around 1918.

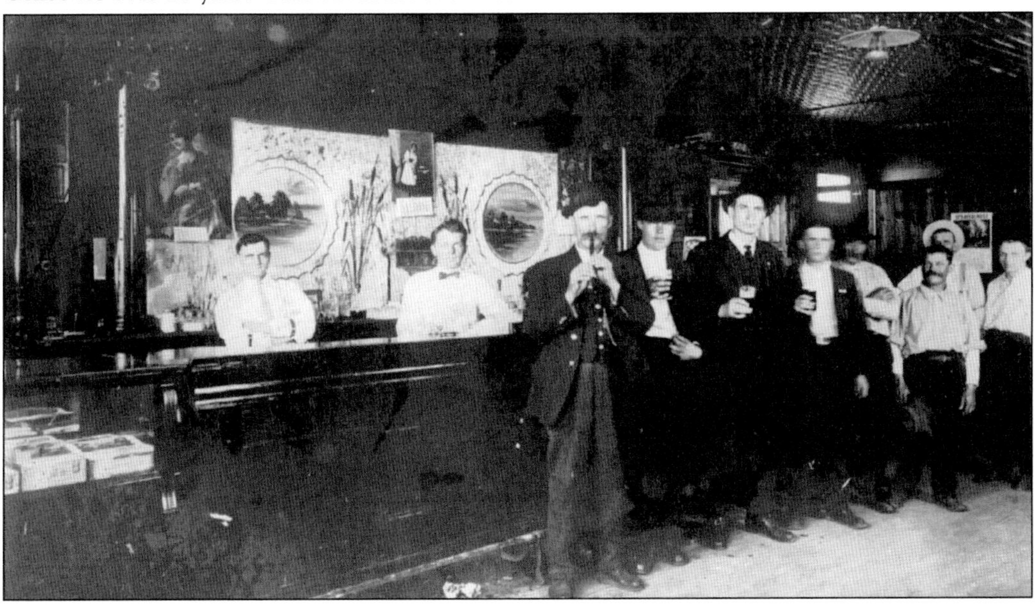

**POLICH TAVERN.** Yugoslavian immigrant Steve Polich and his wife came to Summit in 1907, at which time they operated a boardinghouse and tavern on Lawndale Avenue at the Des Plaines River. They catered mostly to the local quarrymen, but a few years later, they moved to what was last known as John Tomich's Tavern on Lawndale Avenue, just east of the Illinois and Michigan Canal. This is the interior of the Polich tavern around 1910.

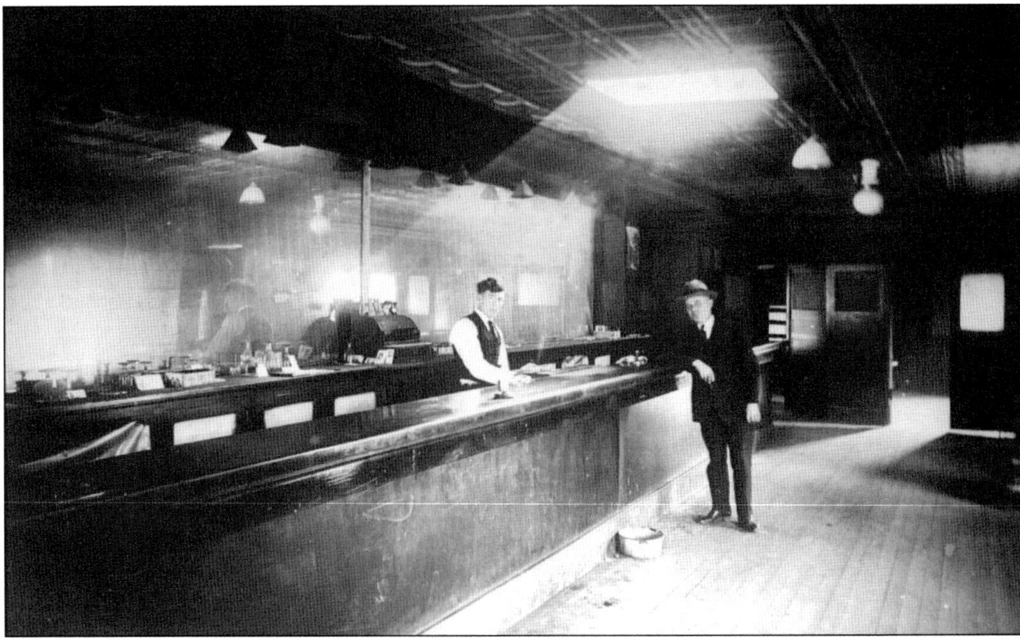

**JOHNSTONE TAVERN.** The Johnstone family in Summit dates back to 1871, when patriarch James came to work on the Wentworth farm. James was an early village clerk, having served from 1893 to 1913, the year he died. His son James Leslie took over the saloon of Mike Shanahan, located at 7445 Archer Avenue, in the early 1900s. He is seen here serving Andy Botz a frosty stein.

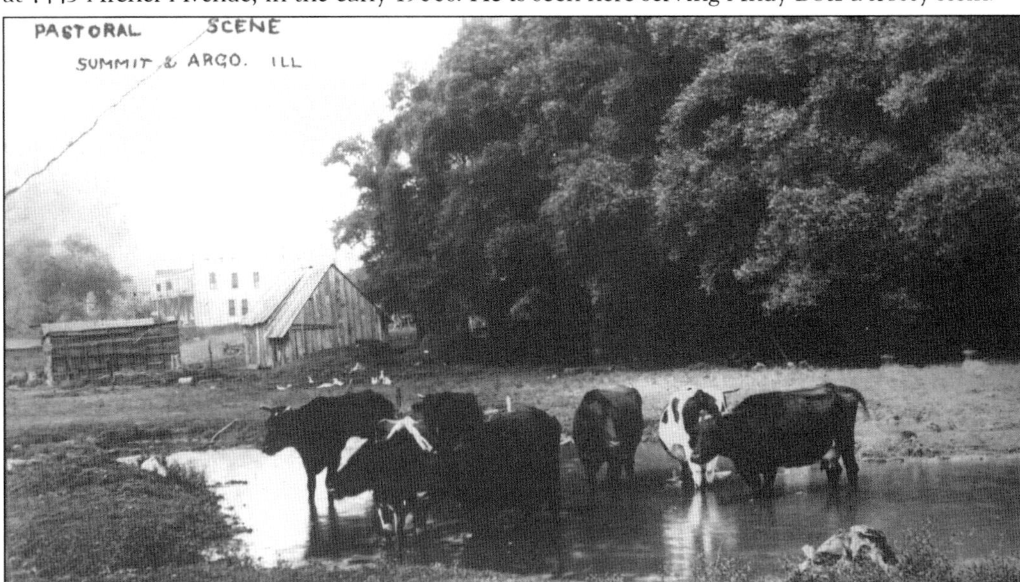


**MILLER'S FIELD.** Dick Vander Muil came to Summit in the late 1890s. He was an early pound master and a public works employee of Summit. He was known as Dick Miller, an Americanized version of his Dutch name. He farmed the land west of Archer Avenue between Fifty-ninth Place and Lawndale Avenue, the property now occupied by the Summit Park District. Seen here are a few of his cows and, in the background, the rear of the flat building located at Archer Avenue and Fifty-sixth Street.

# *Four*

# Transportation, Commerce, and Industry

Summit's topography was beneficial to economic growth on the southeast side of the Des Plaines River valley. The high ground, rising out of the surrounding wet prairies, offered valuable resources to inhabitants dating back to the aboriginal occupants.

Summit was the link that facilitated the success of Chicago. Commerce passing to and from the Mississippi River to Lake Michigan came through the Summit. The Chicago Portage was the earliest trade route. Archer Avenue, which roughly follows the ancient trail along the southerly ridge of the Des Plaines River valley, was a stagecoach route. Illinois and Michigan Canal construction commenced in 1836, but the canal was being used by early settlers before it was officially completed in 1848. A railroad following the southern bank of the Illinois and Michigan Canal came through Summit by 1857, offering its industrial benefits as well as commuter travel. By the 1890s, Summit had became the crossroads of no fewer then four railroads, and by 1900, the Chicago Drainage Canal was completed.

Summit's early industry centered around the local quarries and farming. Community growth remained stagnant, and the landowners had no plans of changing that fact. The southwest settlements were hindered in the fact that there was no way across the Chicago Drainage Canal between Lawndale and Kedzie Avenues until bridges were built for major thoroughfares in the late 1920s. (In fact, the Harlem Avenue canal bridge was not completed until 1933.) The lack of accessibility to the northerly communities significantly slowed community growth for those living on the southeast side of the valley.

Slow land development opened the door for railroad companies that bought up large tracts of land in unincorporated areas to lay out tracks. In 1889, the president of the Chicago and Great Western Railroad, A. B. Stickney, started construction of a massive railroad yard to the southeast of Summit in an area now known as Clearing. Although he was not initially successful, certain investors saw a sleeping giant in the wet prairies, waiting for the right time to erupt into an industrial boon. By 1903, the Chicago and Des Plaines Valley Electric Railway (later the Chicago and Joliet) was in full operation along Archer Avenue, offering interurban transportation from Lyons to Joliet. Summit and its canal town sisters were coming into an age of awakening that would change the landscape of the Point of Oaks forever.

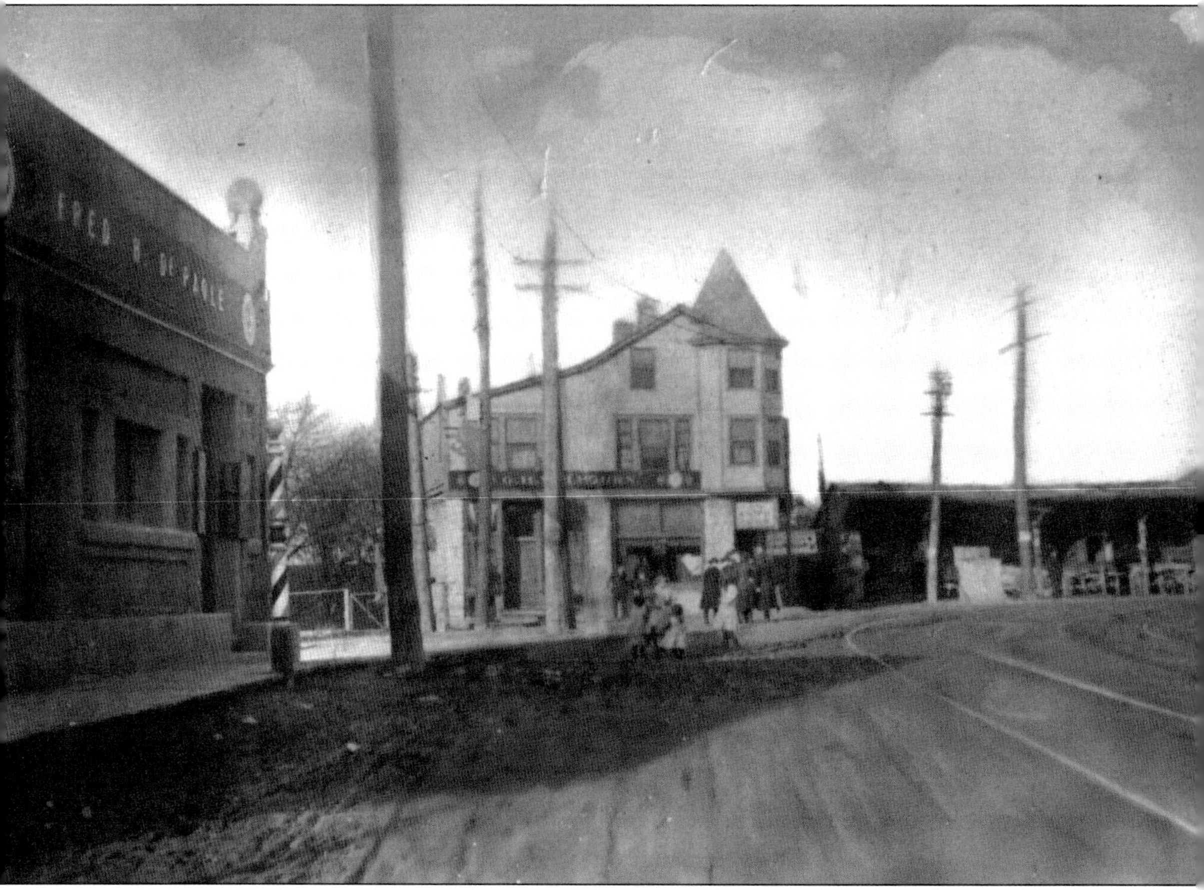

**THE STAGECOACH STOP.** The point in which Archer Avenue changes from a westerly direction to a southerly direction at Fifty-fifth Street extended is called the Summit Corner. The building in the center is the tavern of George Welbourn, with a hitching shed seen to the right (later Henry Keller's service station). George's father, John, bought this building and property from Denis O'Brien in 1893. It is the site of the original 1830s hotel and tavern used by the stagecoaches of Dr. John T. Temple and later Frink and Walker. Once owned by Russell Heacock, the property was acquired by O'Brien in 1845, and he ran the hotel while breeding horses on the adjoining land. The house was kept prior to 1845 by a host of names, some having kept hotels in early Chicago. The Welbourns raised the original wooden structure onto the foundation seen here in 1903. They also added the cupola at that time. The structure was made of beams cut from the oak trees that once populated Summit as far south at Fifty-ninth Street. George Welbourn, also an early mayor of Summit, sold the property to Anton Zopelis in 1912. This 1908 image was taken facing north on Archer Road and also shows Fred DePaole's building to the left. At this time, DePaole's was leased to Peter Gross, the Summit barber. The building was gutted by fire in 1928 and reconstructed with brick.

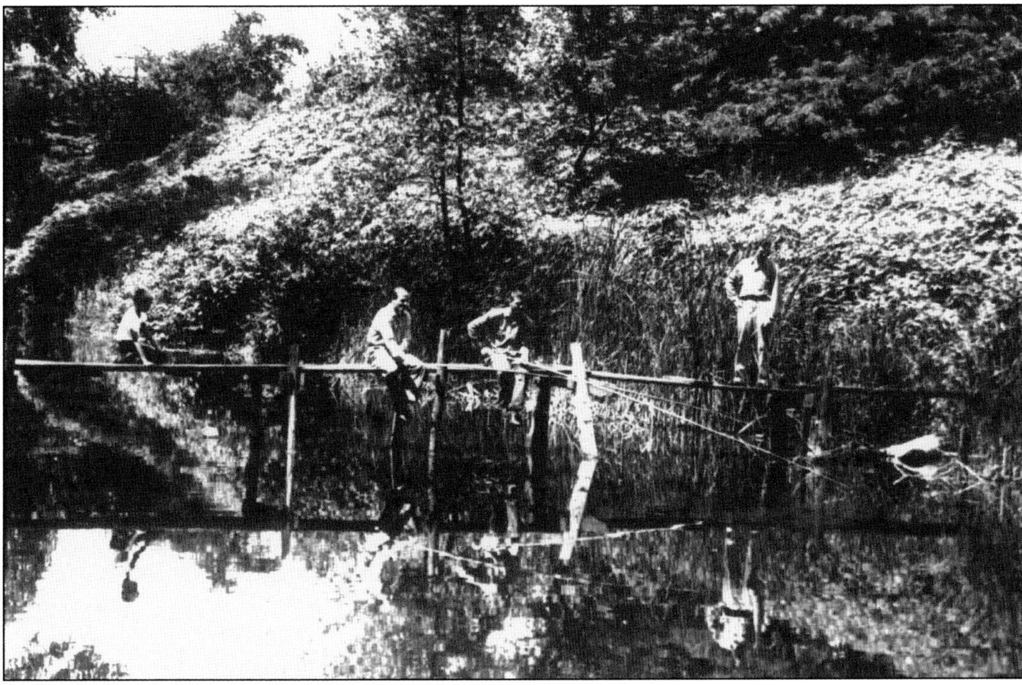

**ILLINOIS AND MICHIGAN CANAL.** The Illinois and Michigan Canal was responsible for turning Chicago into the Midwest industrial center it is today. After the completion of the Chicago Drainage Canal in 1900, the old Illinois and Michigan Canal fell into disuse and was abandoned. Seen here is a footbridge over the canal near the Janchenko farm in the 1950s or 1960s. The old tadpole ditch, as it was known, was filled in in 1974.

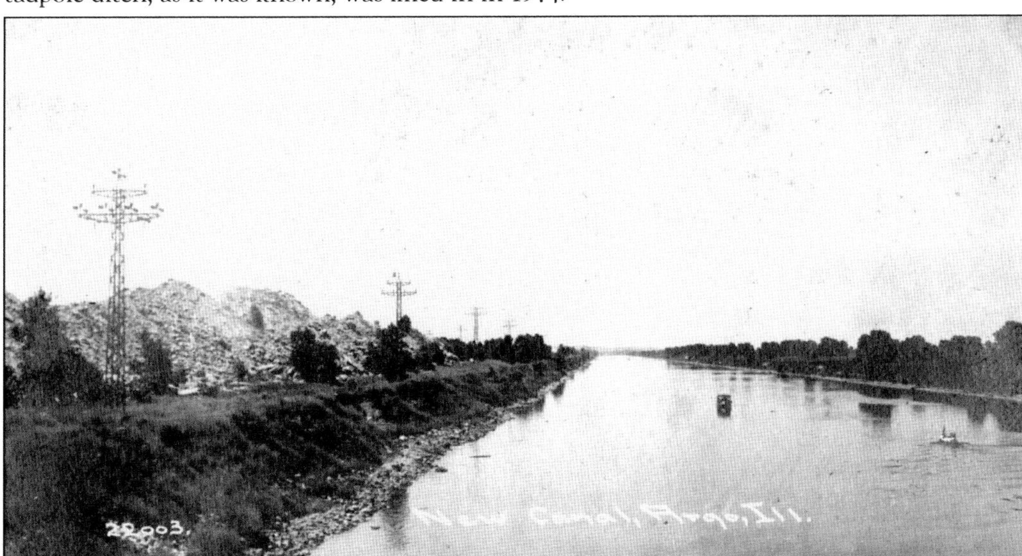


**CHICAGO DRAINAGE CANAL.** The rapidly growing city of Chicago found itself with a sewage disposal problem that overwhelmed the Illinois and Michigan Canal, which was too small and not designed to be used as a sewer to handle the needs of the city. In 1892, construction of a drainage canal commenced linking the South Branch of the Chicago River to the Des Plaines River at Lockport. (Courtesy of the Paul Rush collection.)

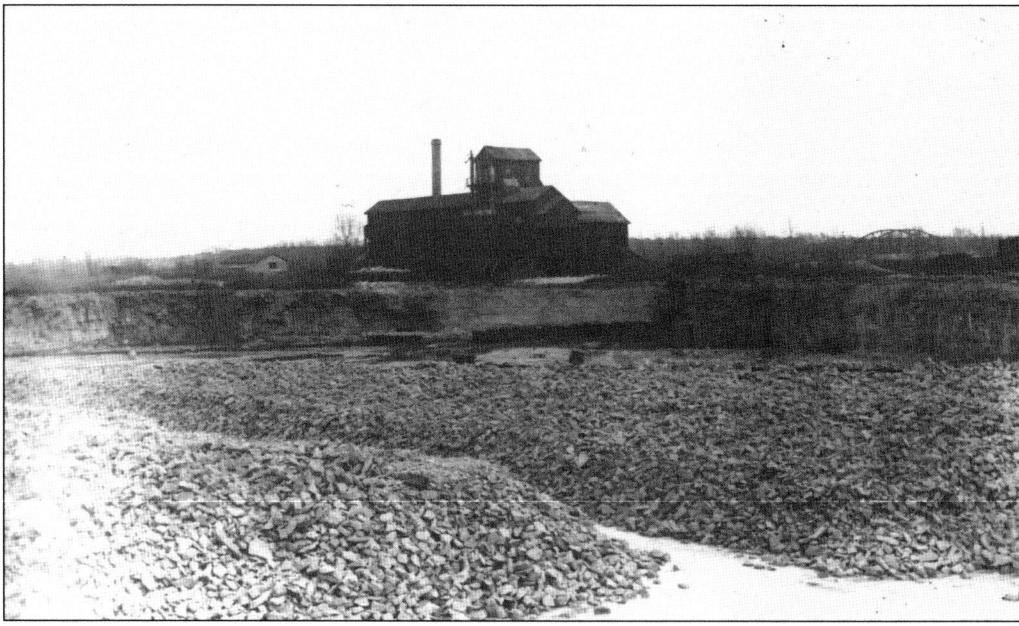

**CHICAGO CRUSHED STONE.** Located east of Lawndale Avenue, just south of the Santa Fe Railroad, was a quarry that dated back to the 1850s. The Chicago Crushed Stone Company plant closed in 1914, creating a swimming hole for local residents. By 1923, it was being used as a garbage dump for the city of Chicago. That same year, the Page Engineering Company built a foundry nearby but later build over the dump site. (Courtesy of the Summit Public Library Historical Archives.)

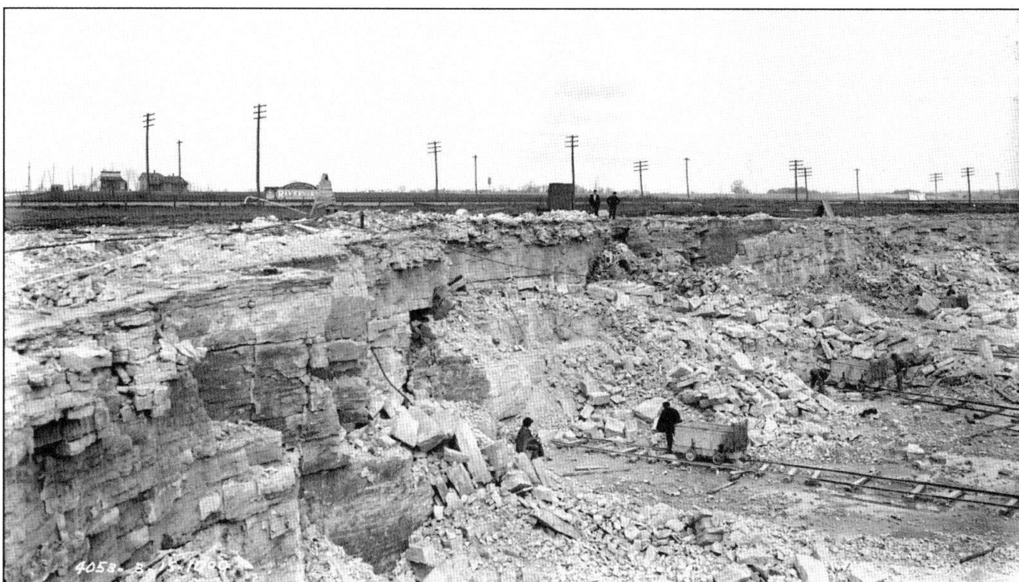

**CHICAGO CRUSHED STONE PIT.** This is a 1909 view of the Chicago Crushed Stone pit. Technically located in the village of McCook, this is the new northern 30-foot pit of the Summit-based company. The famous Green Corner tavern is seen to the left at Joliet Road and Lawndale Avenue. The Green Corner, also known as the Humph (1917), was a speakeasy and house of prostitution that burned in 1925. (Courtesy of the Summit Public Library Historical Archives.)

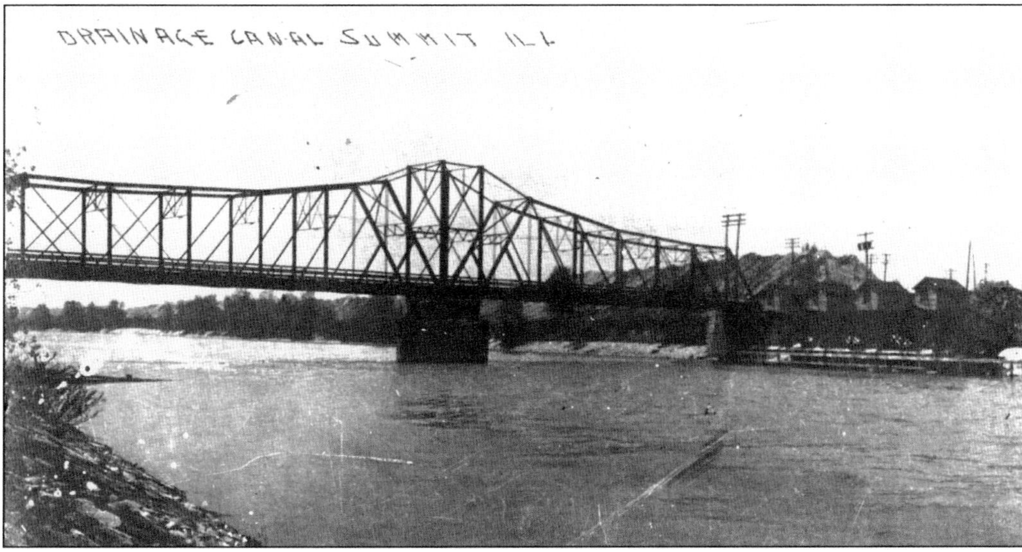

**Lawndale Bridge and Dock.** The local stone quarries utilized a dock facility on the north side of the drainage canal at Lawndale Avenue. Seen here are rail spur sheds where barges were loaded along a crude dock. When motor trucks commenced hauling quarry stone to the docks, traveling south on Lawndale Avenue from McCook and Lyons, the 1899 vintage bridge over the Des Plaines River came into constant disrepair.

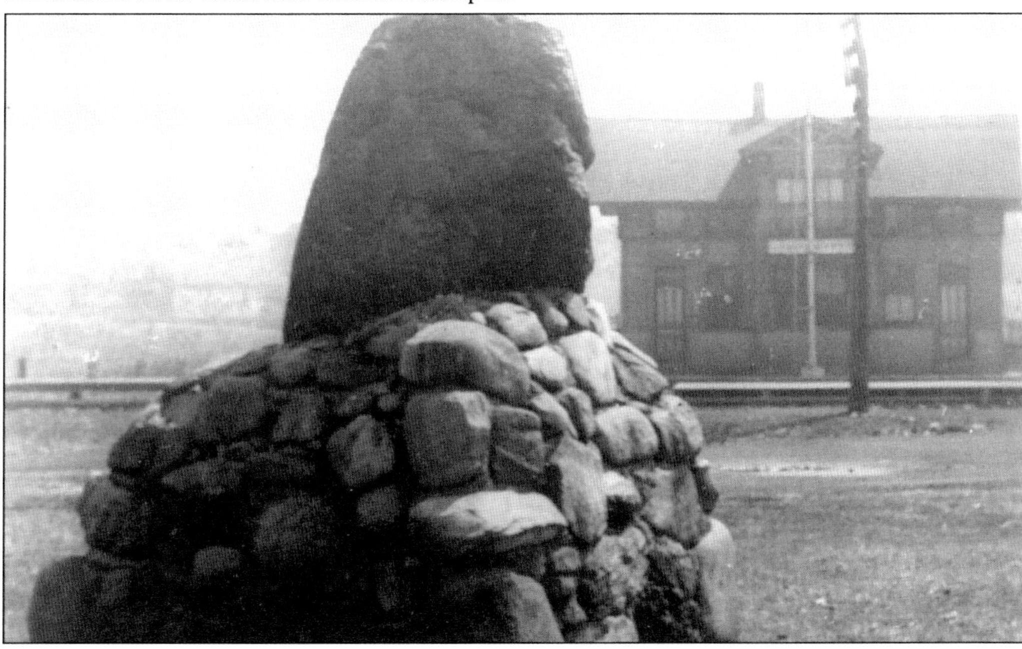

**Reminders of the Past.** Two historical structures that represented the birth and success of Chicago were located appropriately on the Summit: the 1895 monument commemorating Fr. Jacques Marquette's landing site in 1674–1675 and the Chicago and Alton Railroad station at Summit located across the tracks to the south. The monument was located between the Summit station and the Illinois and Michigan Canal on railroad property but was moved to Fifty-eighth Place and Archer Avenue in 1968. The station house was located roughly where the Metra platform is today.

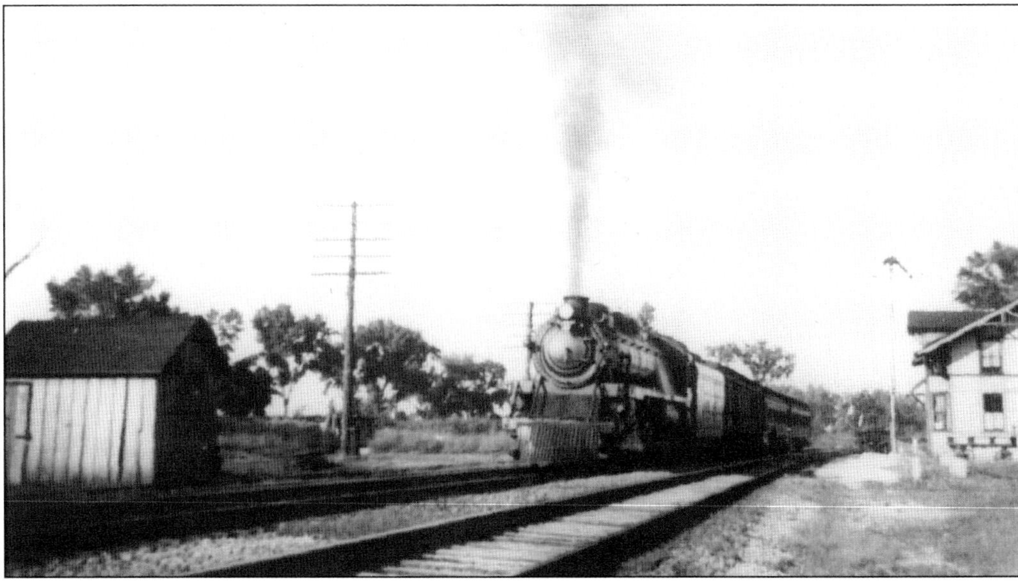

**CHICAGO AND ALTON TRAIN IN SUMMIT.** The Chicago, Alton and St. Louis Railroad (1857), later the Chicago and Alton Railroad (1862), employed Summit residents and transported products for the local industries. The Chicago and Alton was bought by the Baltimore and Ohio Railroad in 1931 and renamed the Alton Railroad Company. In 1947, it was acquired by the Gulf Mobile and Ohio Railroad. Merging with the Illinois Central Railroad in the 1970s, it is now known as the Illinois Central Gulf Railroad.

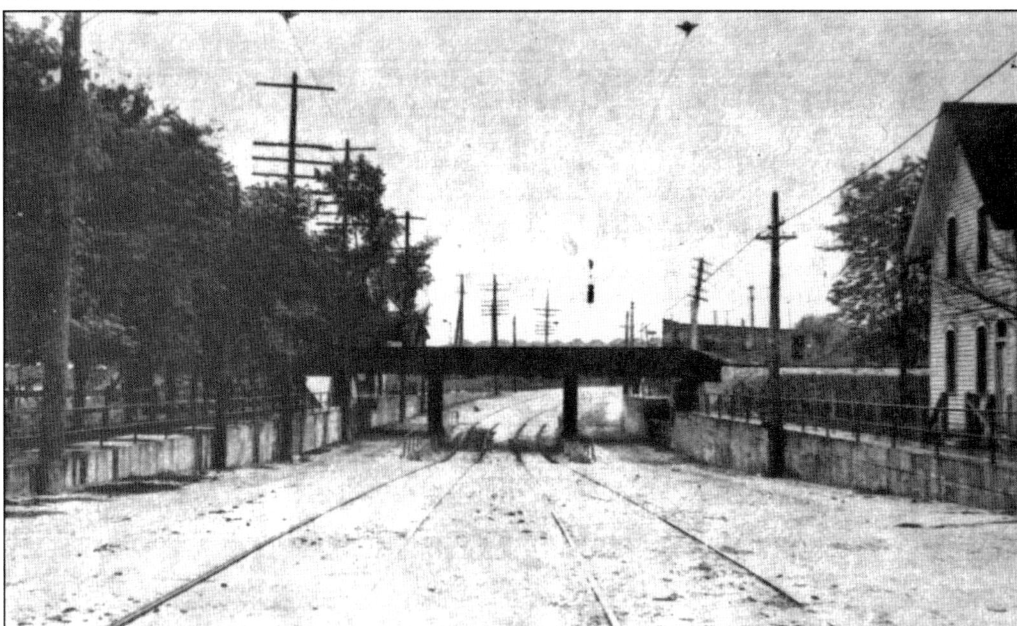

**CHICAGO AND ALTON OVERPASS.** When the Chicago and Des Plaines Valley Electric Railway came into Summit, it solved one of the village's early concerns: a flagman at the Lincoln Avenue crossing of the Chicago and Alton tracks. By a joint effort, the electric railway and the railroad company constructed this subway. After securing land from John F. Kirk and Moses Wentworth, this structure was completed in 1903.

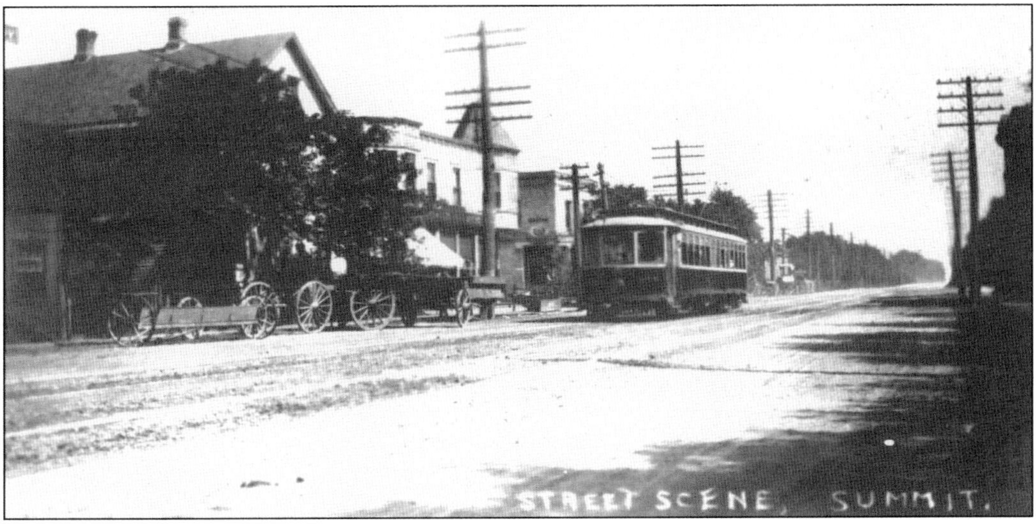


**ARCHER LOOKING EAST.** A Chicago and Joliet Electric Railway car heads west passing the corner grocery and post office of John Maloy in the early 1900s. Horse wagons line the side of the road, possibly waiting for the service of the man who lived in the house to the left of Maloy, John Greibler. His blacksmith shop is partially in view to the far left. Greibler was a Summit trustee first elected in 1898. (Courtesy of the Paul Rush collection.)

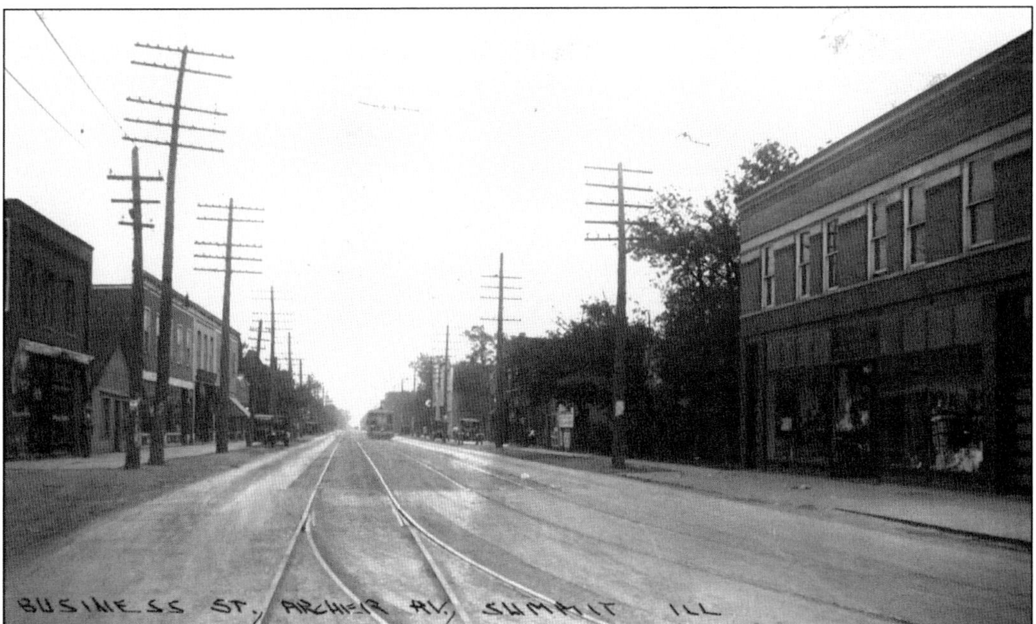


**EASTBOUND ARCHER, C. 1915.** The streetcar heads west from Harlem Avenue. The rails built into the center of the roadway start the turn to southbound at the Summit Corner. To the right are Kabaker's General Store, the Johnstone tavern, O. W. Keller's Grocery, the Summit State Bank, and the Greb buildings. To the left are the partially obstructed Pagni Confectionary, Spoto the shoemaker, the three stores of the Keller Hotel complex, and Greibler's blacksmith shop.

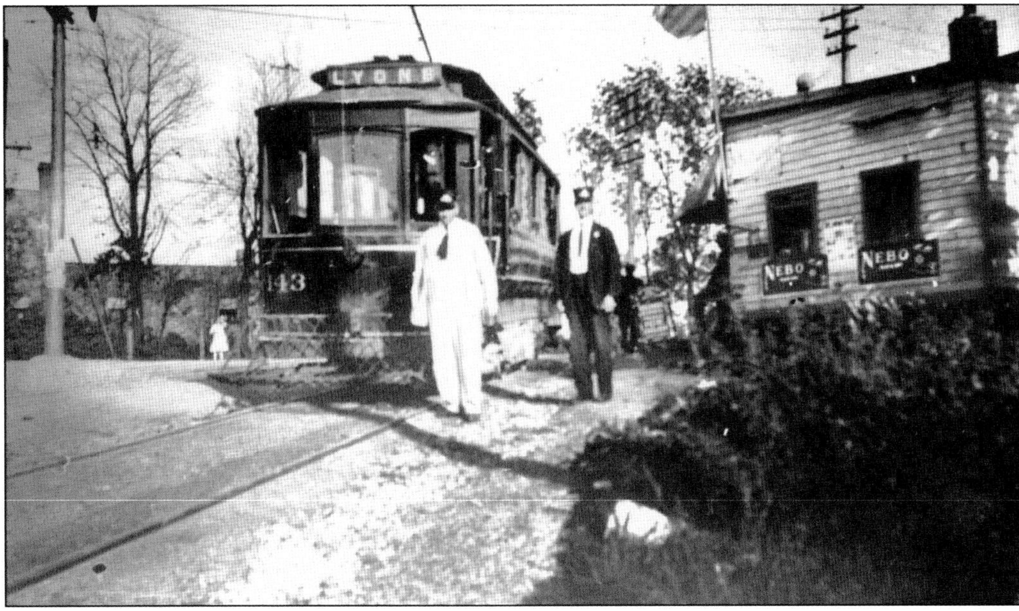


**THE TOP OF THE HILL.** The streetcar between Lyons and Summit traveled on Lawndale Avenue. In Summit, the car sat on an uphill grade at Center (Lawndale) Avenue at Archer Avenue, where it would wait until the main line car arrived. The layover was long enough at times that passengers could exit the car and have a quick drink or patronize the confectionary and tobacco shop that once existed on the southwest corner.

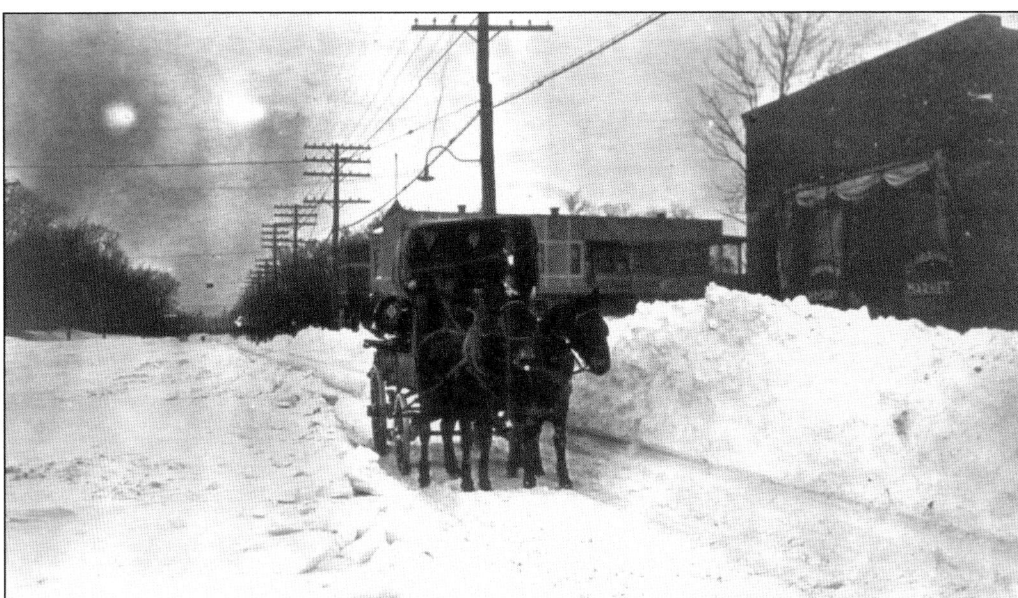

**HORSE AND BUGGY.** Automobiles did not come into prominence in Summit until the 1920s. The horse and buggy, seen here during the winter of 1917–1918, is southbound on Archer Avenue, passing Grahnke's Grocery located at 5735 Archer. In the background is Peter Berletich's saloon on the southeast corner of Fifty-seventh Place and Archer and on the northeast corner the 1912 poolroom of John J. Ruzich.

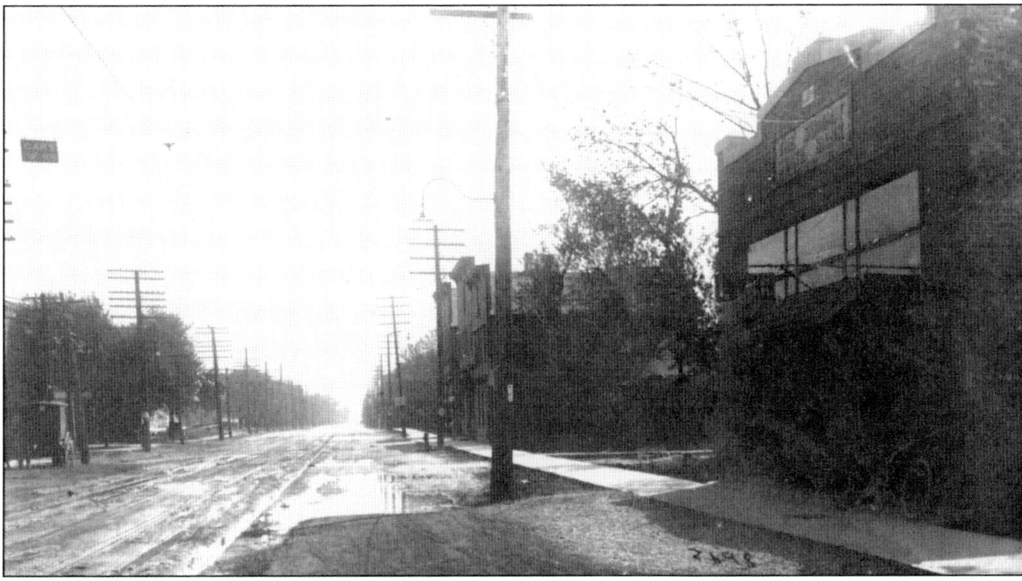

**SUMMIT STATE BANK, C. 1911.** Archer Avenue replaced Center Avenue as the main business street in the early 1900s. It is best symbolized by the Summit State Bank (far right). Organized in 1910 by Elias H. Wilson, Solomon Kabaker, Anton Zopelis, Cyrus E. Parlin, Otis P. Graves, John Maloy, Edward Barrett, and George Farrell, it was closed during the Depression. The building was leased by a number of businessmen until it was razed in the 1980s.

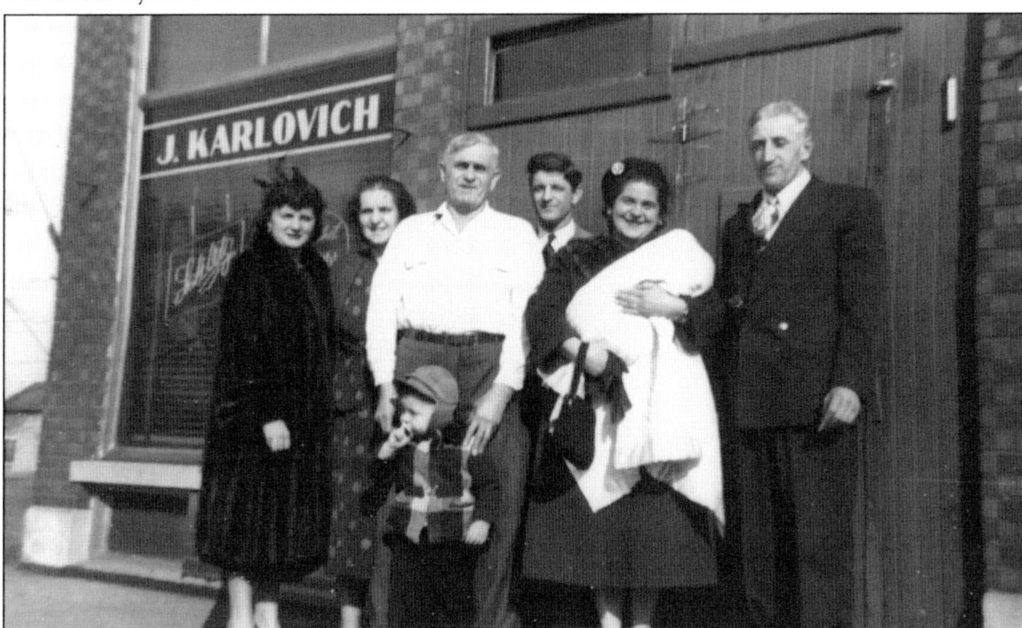


**KARLOVICH'S TAVERN.** The building at 5437 Center Avenue was built by William T. Welbourn and Ed Barrett in 1894. It was the original home of Kabaker's General Store (1897). The building burned in 1912 and was rebuilt by James Lusick. It is the Lusick building that stands to this day. Joe Karlovich (wearing the white shirt) bought it in 1933, and the later proprietors of the establishment have kept the Karlovich name even to the present date. (Courtesy of the Paul Rush collection.)

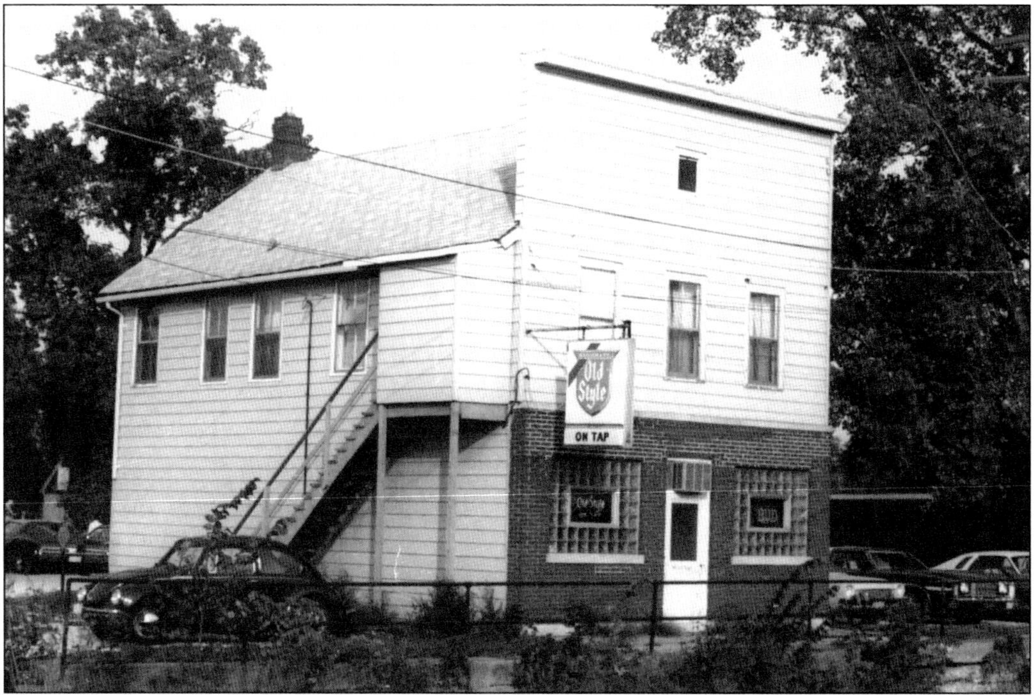


**TOMICH II, C. 1976.** John Tomich leased this old canal-era tavern at 7664 Lawndale Avenue from the Kirk family. It was once the location of Steve Polich's tavern in the early 1900s. Tomich II was so named because the tavern of a close relative named Matt Tomich occupied the old boardinghouse on the west bank of the Illinois and Michigan Canal just up the street. Both Tomich buildings are now gone.

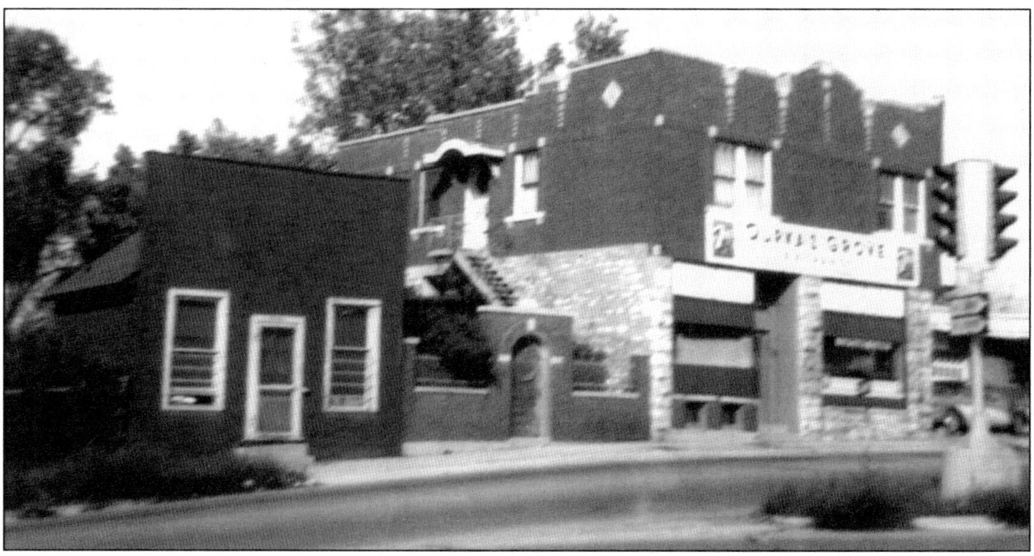

**BARBERSHOP.** Small frame structures were commonplace along the main streets of the old canal towns. Their simple design was easily recognizable as the site of a roadside merchant's stand or a barbershop. Located at 5475 Center Avenue, this building was at the top of the hill beside the Zopelis building (Durka's Grove here) and dates back to the 1890s. In 1940, it was Louis Knezevich's barbershop.

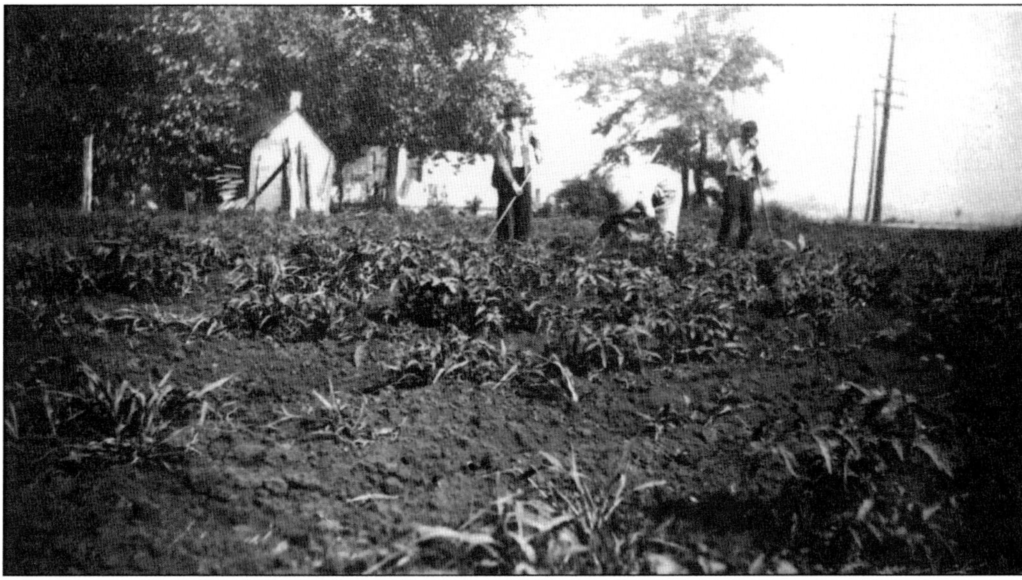

**WESTERHOFF FARM, 1920S.** The produce grown in Summit was famous in Chicago for its quality. Located in one of John Maloy's subdivisions of the Wentworth estate, bounded by Harlem Avenue, Seventy-fourth Avenue, Archer Avenue, and the Chicago and Alton Railroad tracks, were truck farms of six to nine acres in size. One of these farms was leased by the Westerhoff family. The truck farms stayed until the 1960s when they were replaced by apartment buildings.

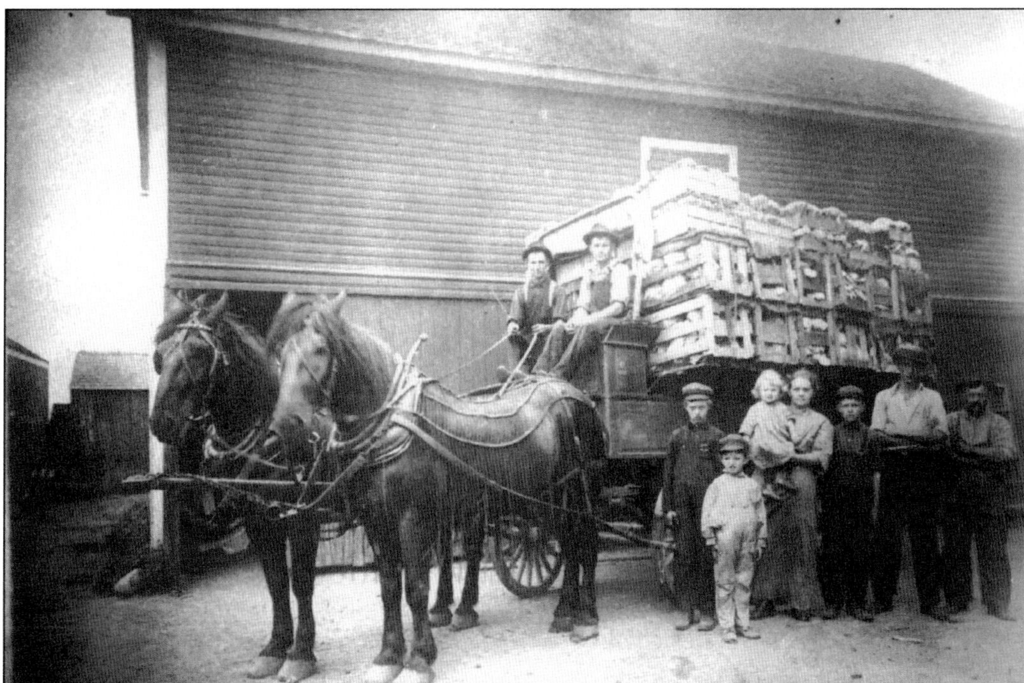

**VEGETABLE WAGON.** This undated photograph shows a truck farmer with a load of produce, possibly headed for Chicago. These farms generally produced great quantities of cabbage, cauliflower, tomatoes, and onions. Some of the past truck farmers in Summit were the Westerhoff, Grima, and Scholten families.

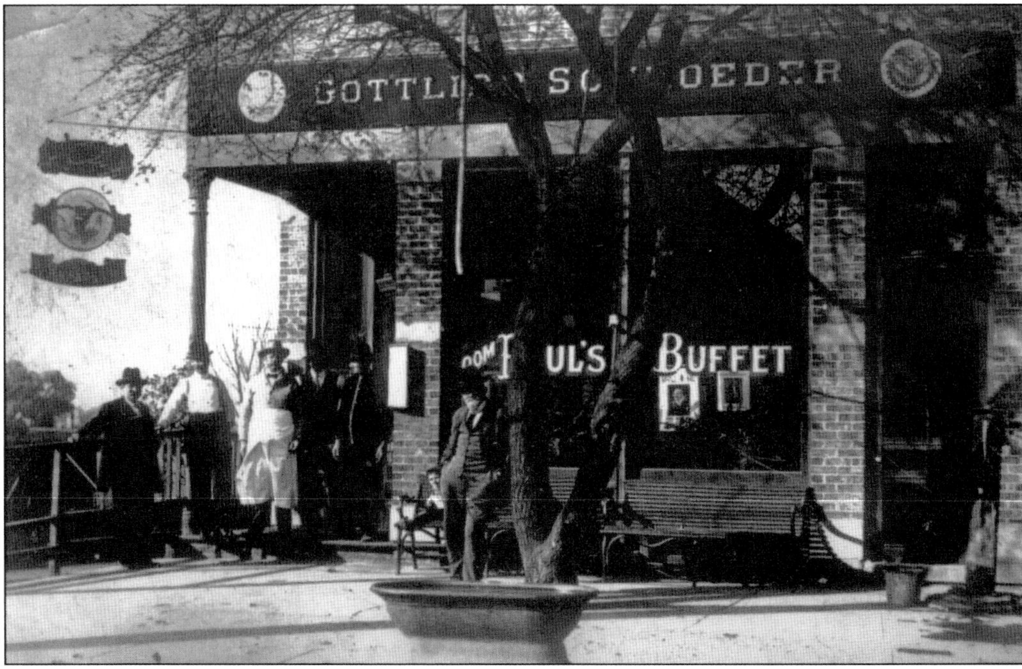



**DREWS BUFFET, C. 1913.** "Oom" Paul J. Drews occupied his father-in-law Gottlieb Schroeder's tavern at 7424 West Archer Avenue until 1916. The property was owned by village trustee Charles Vehmeyer (who died in 1896) and bought by Schroeder in 1901. It was home of Beigel's Pharmacy from 1924 to 1938 and Bell's Pharmacy into the 1940s. The building still stands to this day but had an extension added to the front face at some point.

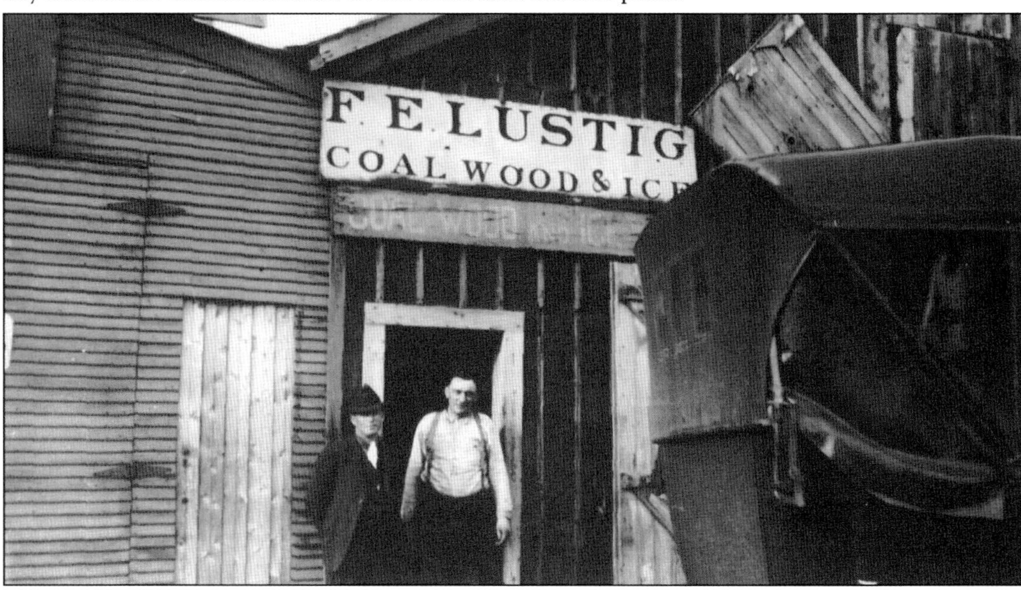



**LUSTIG COAL AND ICE.** Coal, ice, and wood merchants were commonplace up until the mid-1950s. The ice was cut from the river or a quarry and stored in large sheds. Frank Lustig bought the ice and coal business of Anton Zopelis in 1913. Lustig (right) is seen here at his horse barn at 7460 Archer Avenue, adjacent to the Zopelis building. Lustig sold the business to the Raddatz Brothers in 1922.

# *Five*

# The Twin Cities of Summit and Argo

In 1906, E. T. Bedford, president of the Corn Products Refining Company, sought a location to build a corn-milling plant for his newly incorporated glucose combine. A 100-acre tract was purchased within the western landholdings of the Chicago Transfer and Clearing Company (CT&C). The CT&C was planning an undivided industrial district spanning from its rail yards at Central Avenue to the drainage canal. The availability of rail and water transportation in this area of unincorporated Cook County offered a prime location for the construction of the Corn Products Refining Company.

In 1907, engineer George Chamberlain went to the tract south of Sixty-third Street to survey the land and design the new refining plant. It was Chamberlain who used the name Argo for this new industrial district. Argo was a brand name that was utilized by a refining company in Nebraska that had been absorbed into the new Corn Products combine.

Corn Products was the first industry in what was to become the Clearing Industrial District. Although the location south of Summit was ideal for the corn-milling industry, it lacked a labor force. A rail spur was built to accommodate construction of the plant, and the Chicago Surface Line extended down Sixty-third Place to bring in laborers. Most of the men who worked on the construction of the plant stayed in barracks within the fenced Corn Products property, while residential and commercial lots were sold within the unincorporated section of CT&C-owned land, south of Sixty-third Street, in what was known as the Corn Products Subdivision, which was incorporated into Summit on September 12, 1911.

The Fifty-ninth Street railroad tracks divided the municipality into halves. The north is traditionally called Summit, while the south is Argo. In 1924, John Kott wrote to the *Des Plaines Valley News* with the suggestion that "Twin City" be used as a pet term for Argo, as he had given the name Twin City Inn to his new restaurant at Archer Avenue and Sixty-first Street. Even to this day, some residents still think of Argo and Summit as separate villages.

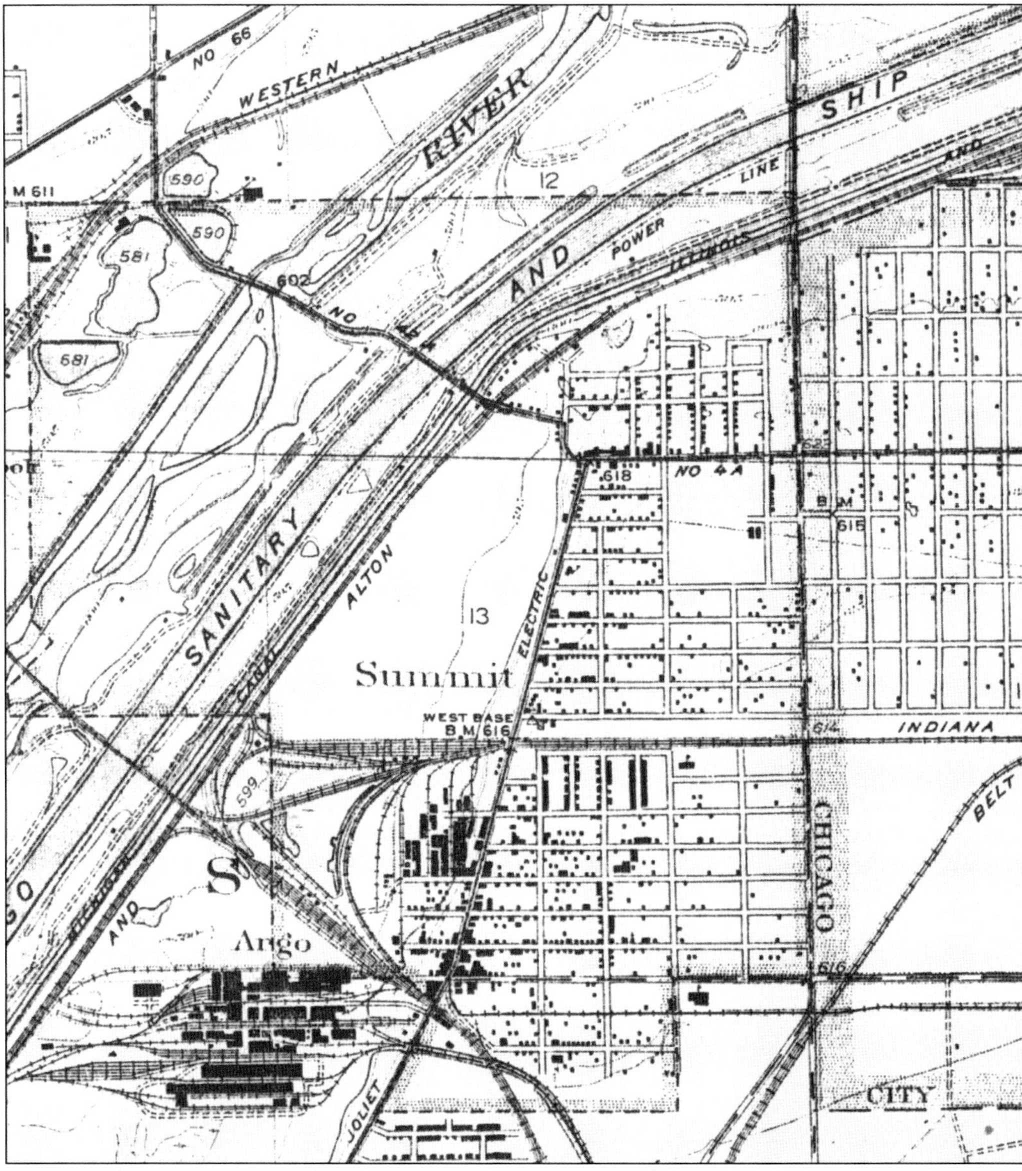


**FEDERAL SURVEY MAP OF SUMMIT-ARGO, 1928.** In April 1908, an advertisement appeared in the *Chicago Tribune* stating, "Opportunities of Business and Investments at Argo opposite the new Corn Products Plant. F. W. McKinney and S. H. Hodge. 1350 First National Bank Building, Chicago and 63rd Street and Archer Ave, Argo." McKinney and Hodge had a frame real estate office near the southeast corner of Sixty-third Street and Archer Avenue. They were brought in by the CT&C to develop its industrial interests in Argo. Backed by bankers such as Ira Cobe, McKinney had acquired an option on the available land south of Fifty-ninth Street to Sixty-third Street, and from Harlem Avenue to the Chicago and Alton Railroad tracks. A regulated community was to be built to cater to the labor force of the Corn Products Refining Company and any future industries that were to come. McKinney built business blocks for lease to retailers, hotels, saloons, a theater, and a savings bank to accommodate the community to come. Investors from the north end of town even built in Argo, but the real boom was yet to come. (Courtesy of the U.S. Geological Survey.)

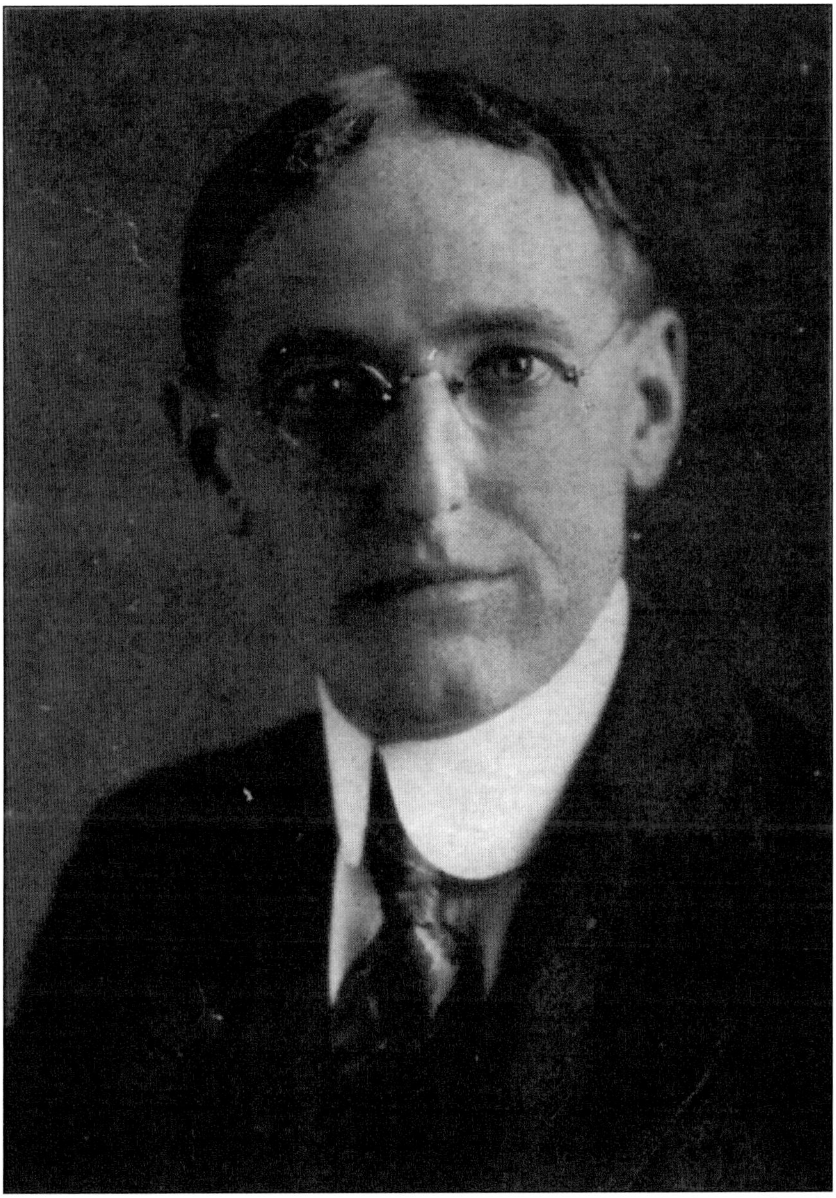

**W. G. KNOEDLER.** Shortly after F. W. McKinney came to Argo, he brought his two brothers-in-law to assist. William G. and Philip L. Knoedler of Augusta, Kentucky, were already established bankers and investors when they took over the management of the Argo Commercial and Savings Bank. The Knoedler brothers bought out all remaining land interests held by McKinney in 1913 and opened their own real estate business. William resided in the community and managed their properties, while enticing new industry to move to Argo. William was involved (usually as president) in most of the community organizations. He and his wife Eva were charter members of the Argo Congregational Church. He was charitable and well loved by his fellow residents. He fought to bring about the community high school and served on its first board. William was the treasurer of the Elgin Motor Car Company, which he brought to town, but moved to Riverside after the company's failure in 1923. William was always there for his community and truly is the father of Argo.

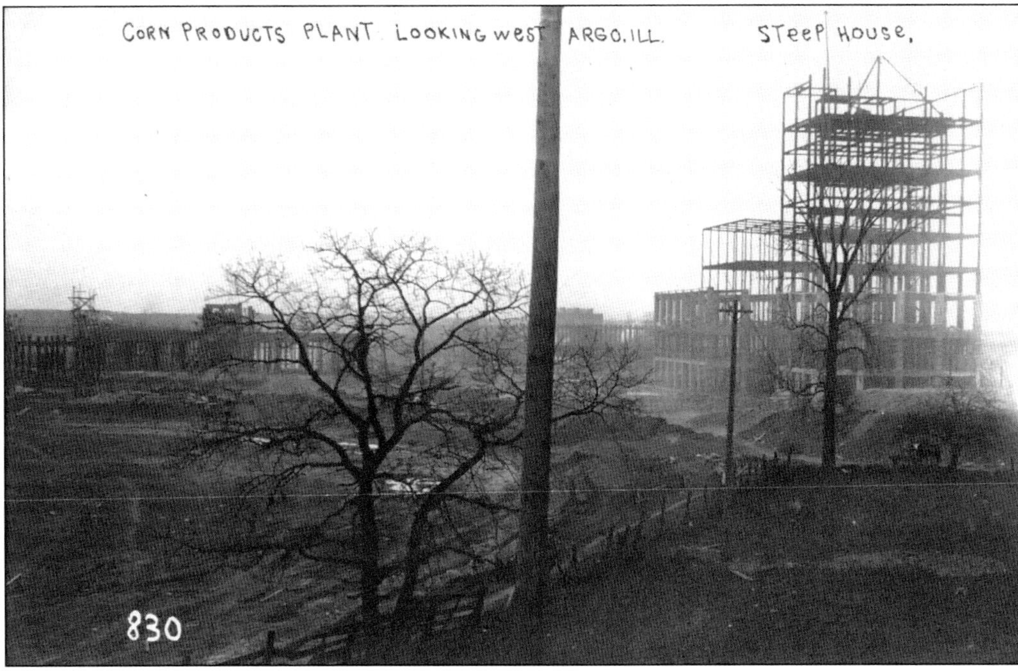


**CORN PRODUCTS CONSTRUCTION.** Construction of the Corn Products Refining Company plant commenced in 1907, with the first operational unit completed in 1910. It was this facility that employed thousands of people in the surrounding suburbs. Corn Products facilitated community clubs, plant bowling and shooting teams, dances, yearly picnics, and more. By 1965, there were some 2,900 employees, but by 2008, the number had dwindled to about 400 due to automation.

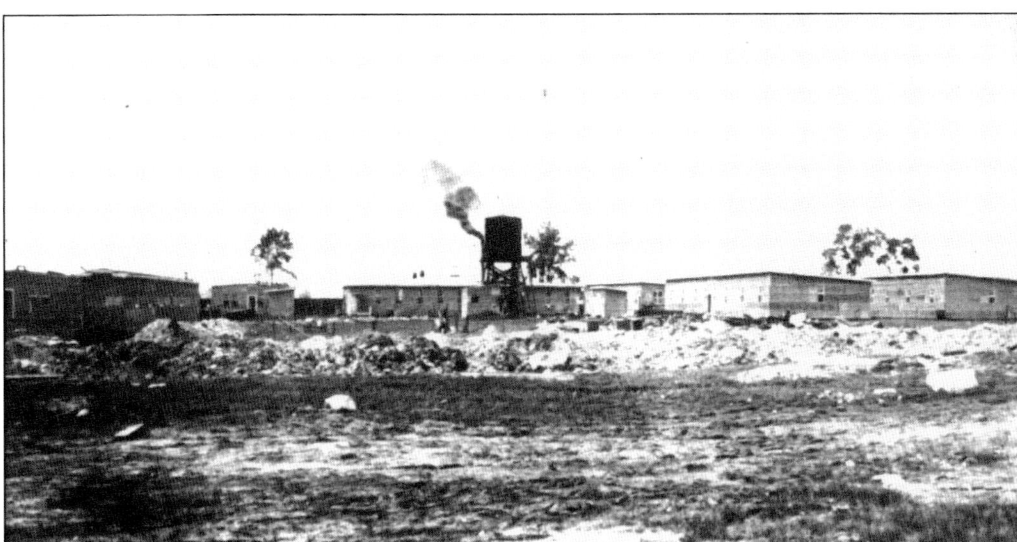

**CONSTRUCTION BARRACKS, 1908.** Wooden structures built to house the labor force brought in to construct the Corn Products plant were enclosed within a stockade fence built around the property. Men had to buy their supplies and personal sundries from a commissary located within and were not allowed to leave the compound unless their bills were fully paid. This practice caused some labor unrest but was found to be legal.

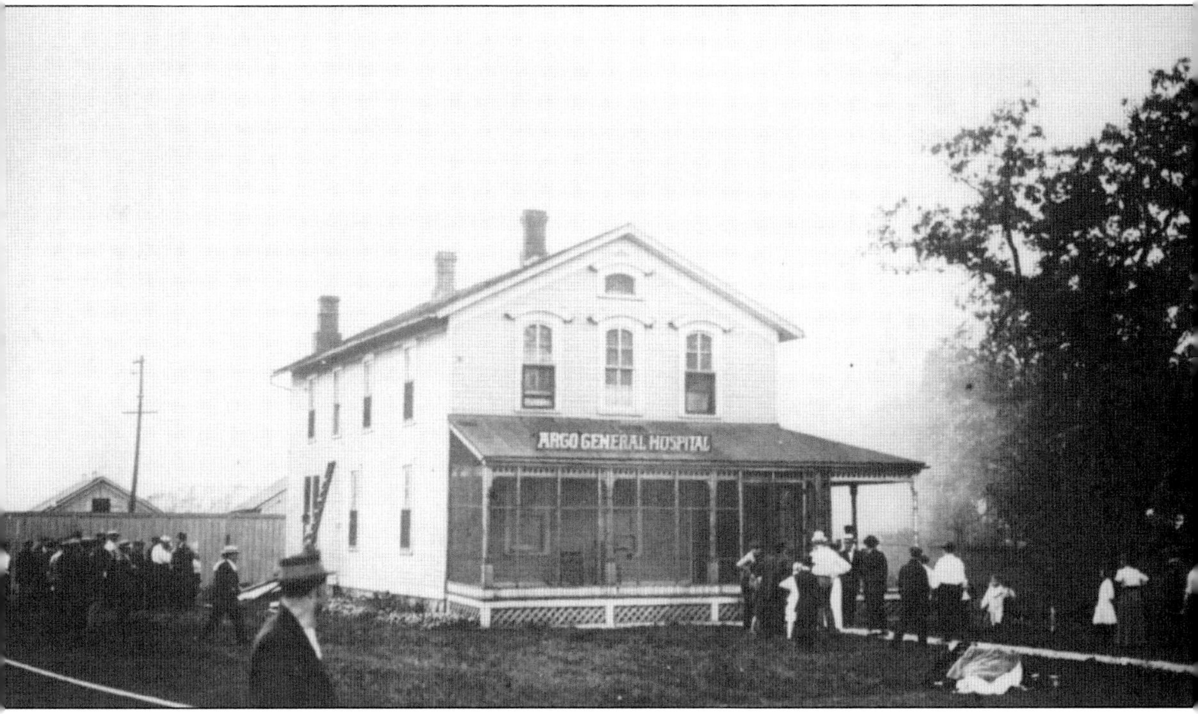


**ARGO GENERAL HOSPITAL.** Corn Products utilized an existing farmhouse adjacent to its property for the construction superintendent. After the superintendent was moved to the bank building in 1909, the house was used as an emergency hospital. By 1913, it was the busiest emergency facility in suburban Cook County. After a fire caused considerable damage in August 1915, it was discontinued for medical use and leased out to a farmer. The house remained until the Indiana Harbor Belt Railroad (IHB) underpass was built in 1940.

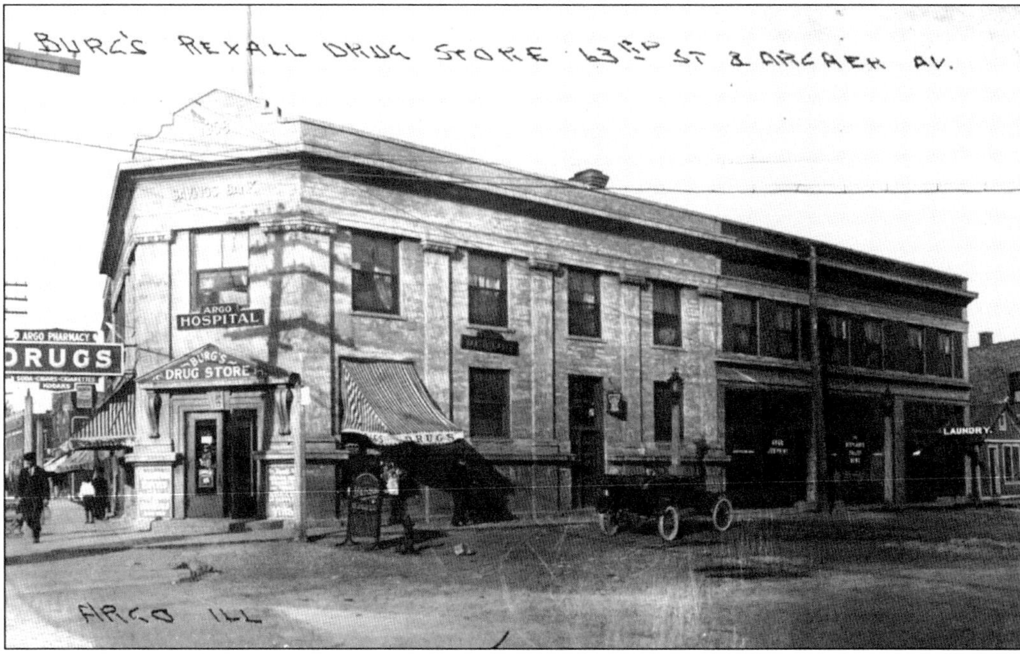


**ARGO COMMERCIAL AND SAVINGS BANK, 1915.** In this view looking north from Sixty-third Street at the south face of the 1908 savings bank building, Burg's has moved into the corner space after the bank moved across the street. The *Des Plaines Valley News* and Tom Wah's Chinese Laundry occupied the rooms facing on Sixty-third Street. The news office would eventually share this space with the Argo Post Office. The second floor was the Argo Hospital, managed by Rose DeKrauze. (Courtesy of the Paul Rush collection.)

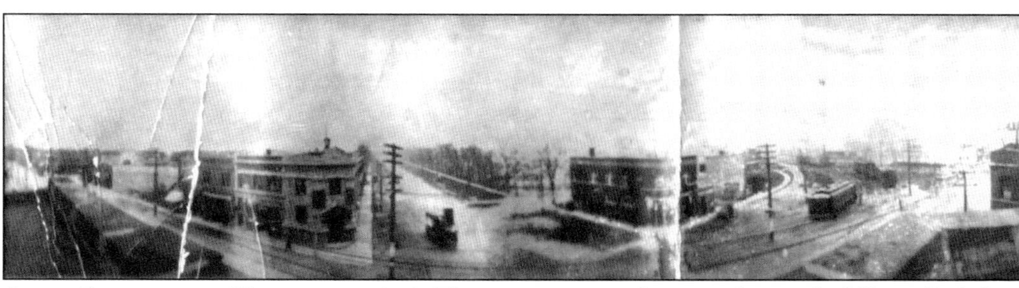

**ARGO PANORAMIC, NOVEMBER 1914.** This image was taken on the roof of Knoedler's Real Estate in the Terminal Building at Sixty-third Street and Archer Avenue. Distorted because of the lens, the Argo Theater is visible to the right as well as the savings bank block, and the 1913 Herzog and O'Heran building is on the opposite corner at 6301 Archer Avenue.

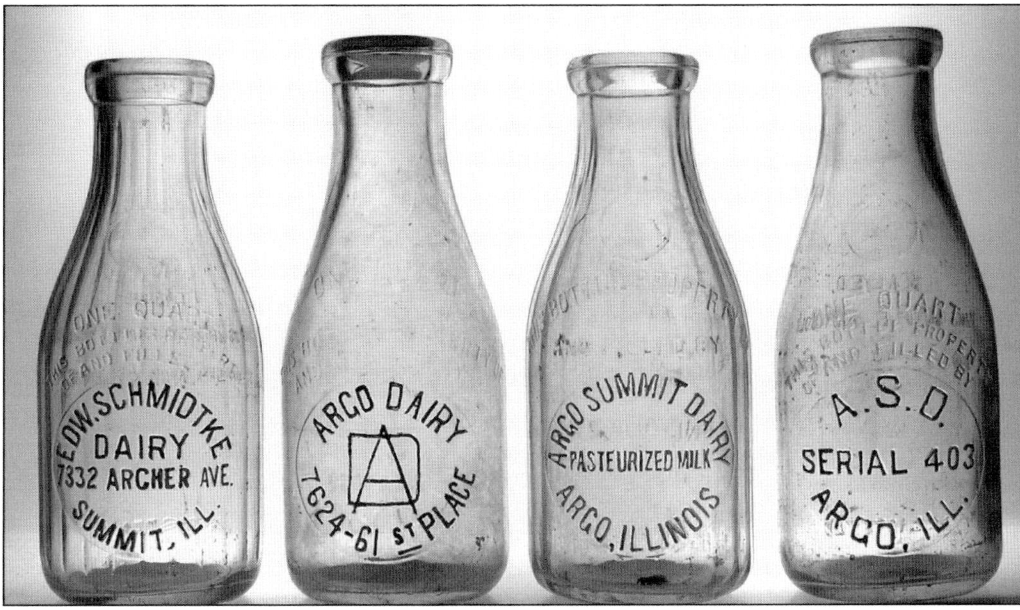


**MILK BOTTLES.** Summit and Argo had many milk merchants through the years. These are 1920–1935 examples of bottles from the Argo Dairy, the Argo Summit Dairy, and the Edward Schmidtke Dairy of Summit. Some Summit residents still recall collecting milk bottles as children and cashing them in for deposits to buy candy.

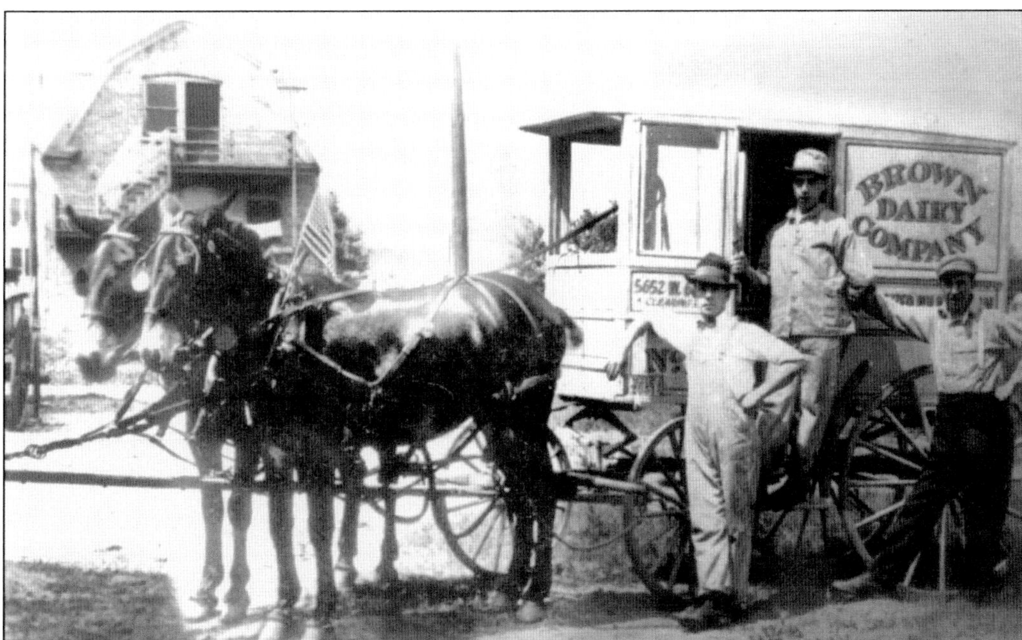


**BROWN DAIRY.** The longest-lasting dairy business in the village was that owned by William H. Brown Sr. Brown started delivering milk in Clearing but in July 1912 took over the Werner Dairy at 7717 Sixty-second Place, and the Argo Summit Dairy was born. The business name changed to Brown Dairy Products in the 1930s. Three generations of the Brown family worked for the dairy until business ceased in 1971.

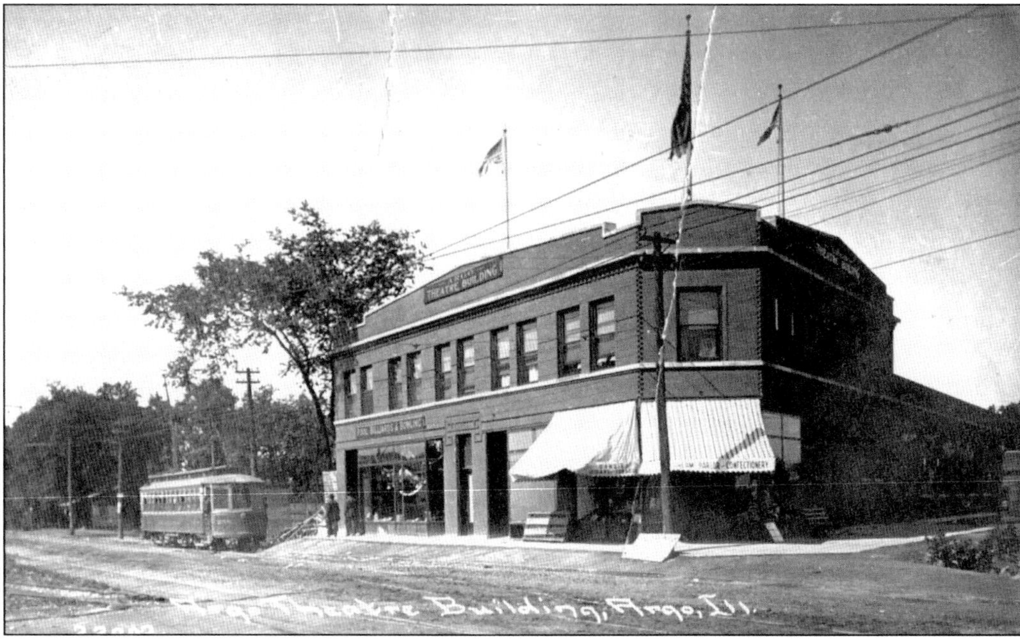


**ARGO THEATER BUILDING.** Argo's original theater was built in 1911 at the southwest corner of Sixty-third Street and Archer Avenue. The building also housed the Argo confectionery and streetcar stop, a pool hall, the offices of the Elgin Motor Car Company, and later Nettie Pease's Blue Rose Café. Within a decade, the theater became outdated and was relegated to hall rentals and sporting events. Plagued by mysterious fires, the building burned for the last time in 1928.

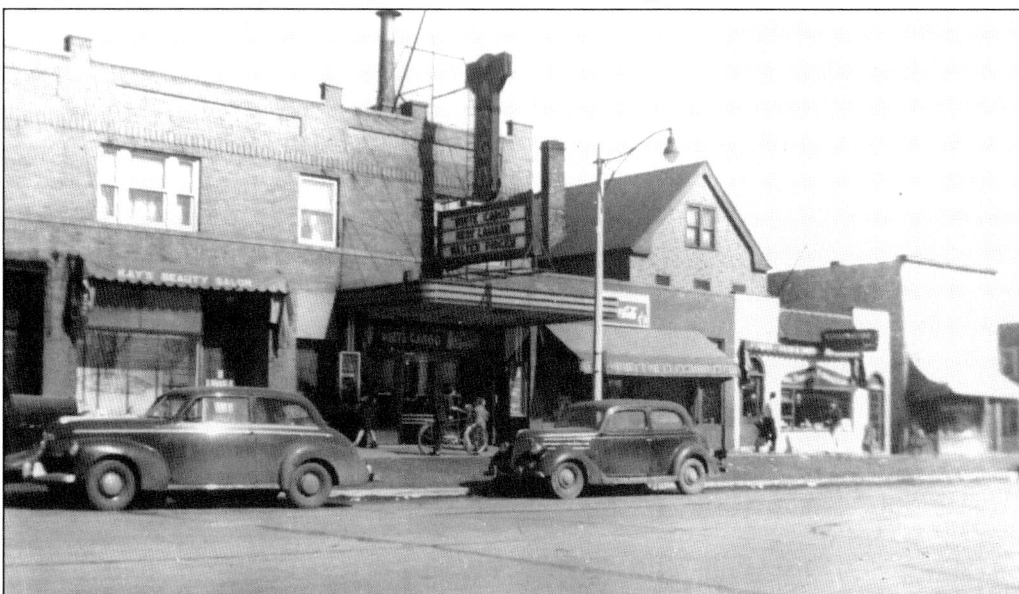

**ARGO GRANDE THEATER, 1942.** In 1916, Edward Hope replaced his three-store business block with a theater complex at 7666 West Sixty-third Street. The Argo Grande was popular for movies and also community events. The theater was managed by a number of people, but from 1919, J. B. Learner leased it. Learner bought it in 1929. He operated it until 1959 when it was sold, then demolished in 1961 for the Service Savings and Loan building.

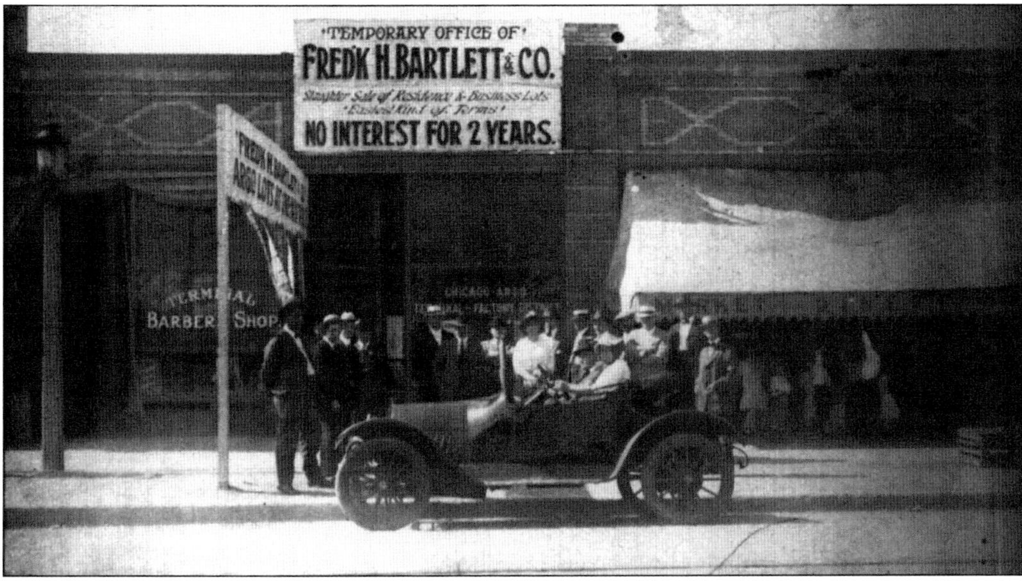


**TERMINAL BUILDING.** In 1910, F. W. McKinney built a business block at the northwest corner of Sixty-third Street and Archer Avenue in his Argo second addition to the Summit subdivision. The structure housed many memorable businesses, including Dineff Brothers Bakery and Grocery, Frederick H. Bartlett's real estate office (the first Summit-Argo Library location in 1917), Mike Metska's barbershop (Terminal Barber Shop), R. P. Lambert's tavern (out of view on the corner, later the Gorlis Restaurant), and the Terminal Hotel upstairs.

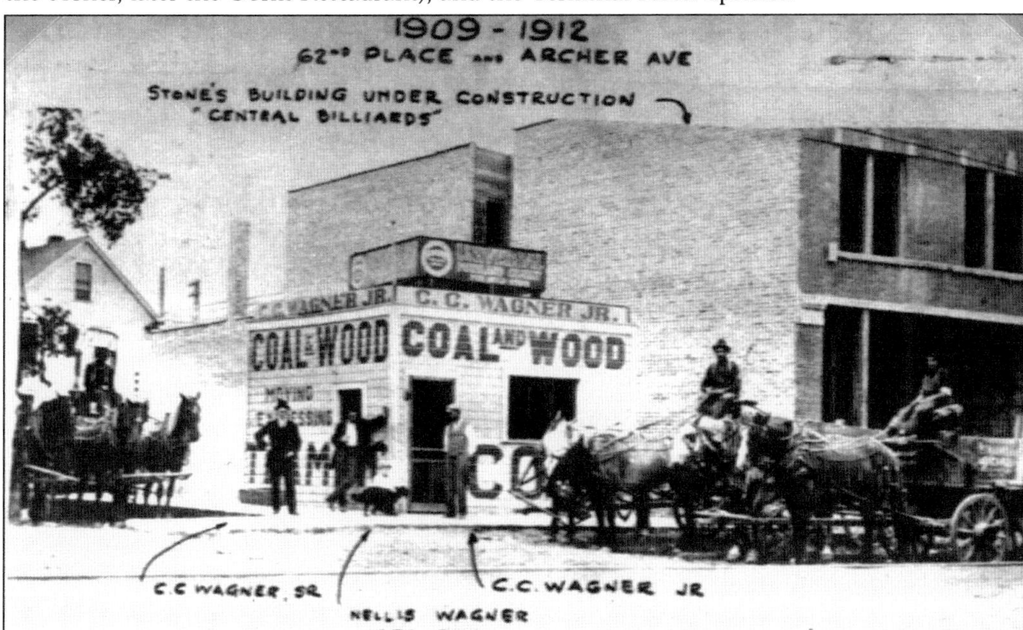


**WAGNER AND STONE, 1910.** Pioneer merchant C. C. Wagner Jr. operated his coal and building supply business office out of this wooden stand at the southeast corner of Sixty-second Place and Archer Avenue from 1909 to 1912. To the right is the uncompleted Stone Department Store located at 6237 Archer Avenue. This would be Stone's third location in Argo. (Courtesy of the C. C. Wagner Company.)

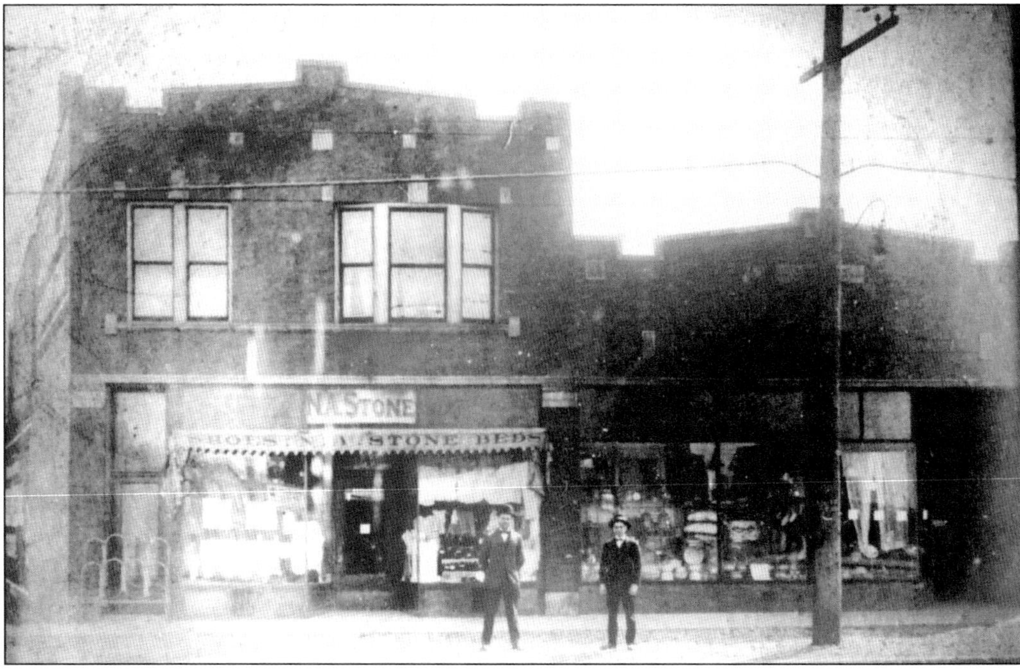


**STONE DEPARTMENT STORE.** Nathan A. Stone came to Argo in 1907 and by the next year was leasing space for a dry goods and grocery store in the first retail business structure erected in Argo. Shortly thereafter, Stone moved to 6217 Archer Avenue but then constructed the building seen here at left in 1910. His second expansion (right) was built next door in 1912 at 6239 Archer Avenue.

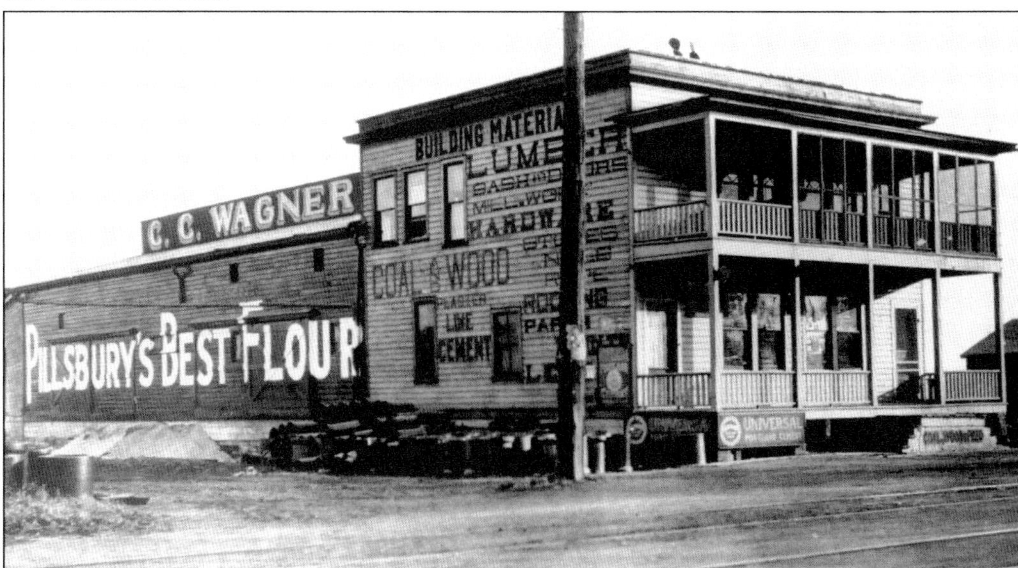


**WAGNER LUMBER.** C. C. Wagner Jr. came to Argo in 1907 and was bookkeeper in this building at 6401 Archer Avenue, under the Peabody Coal Company. In 1912, Peabody lost the lease, and Wagner took over the building. The C. C. Wagner Company bought out Schenk Lumber in 1955 and later consolidated to this site. A family business passed down through the generations of Wagners, it celebrated 100 years in 2008. (Courtesy of the C. C. Wagner Company.)

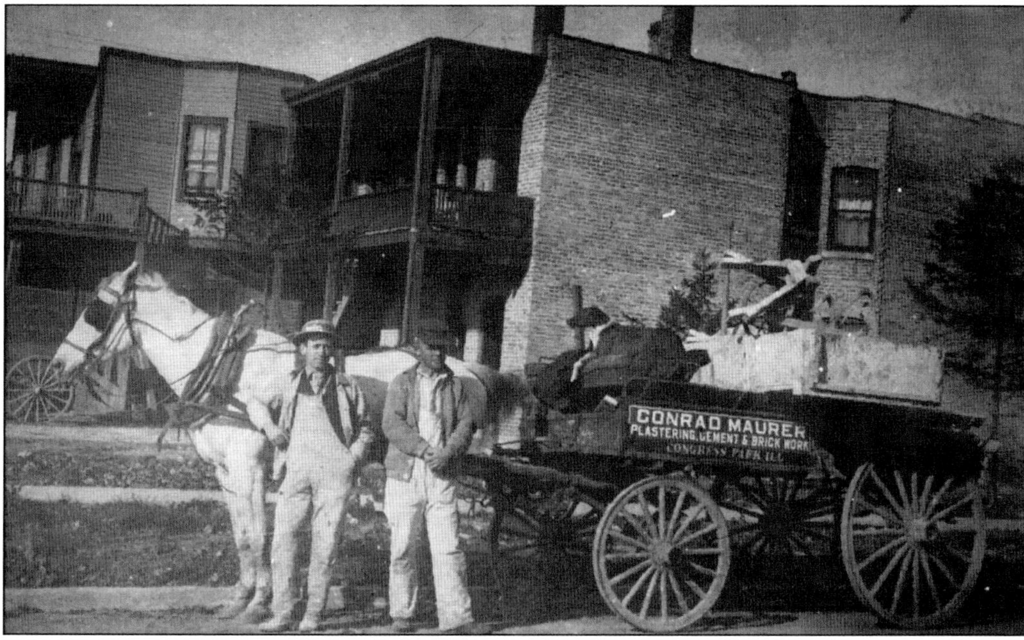


**WORK WAGON.** Local merchants and peddlers utilized horse teams before the wide use of automobiles. Wagon salesmen and peddlers were a common sight. Villages created license fees for mobile businesses such as these, and Summit-Argo had its share. Snake oil salesmen, gypsy fortune-tellers, and the rag and metal collectors plying the streets and alleys are still remembered by senior residents.

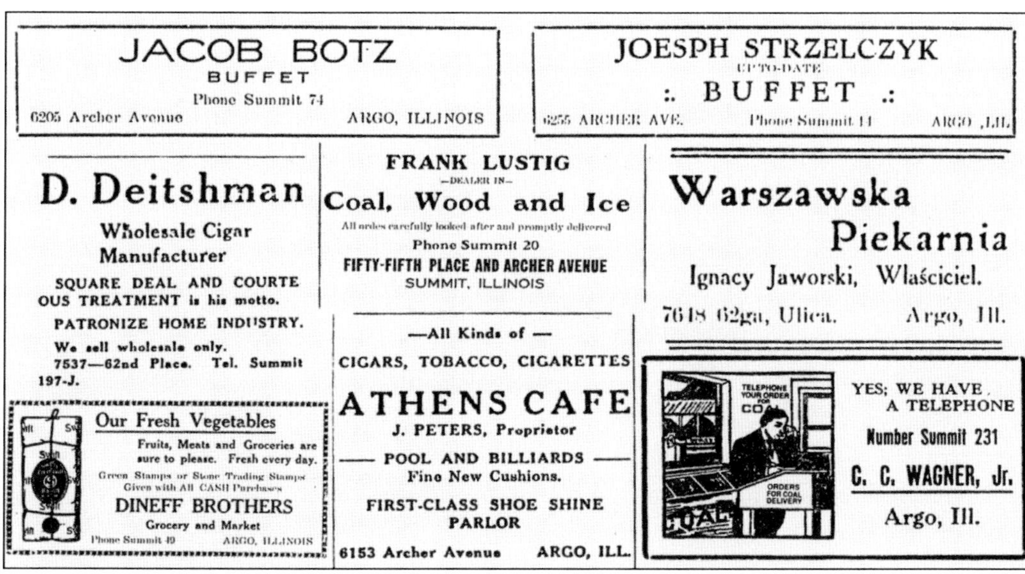


**ARGO BUSINESS ADVERTISEMENTS.** Shown here are a number of pre–World War I advertisements as seen in the *Des Plaines Valley News*.

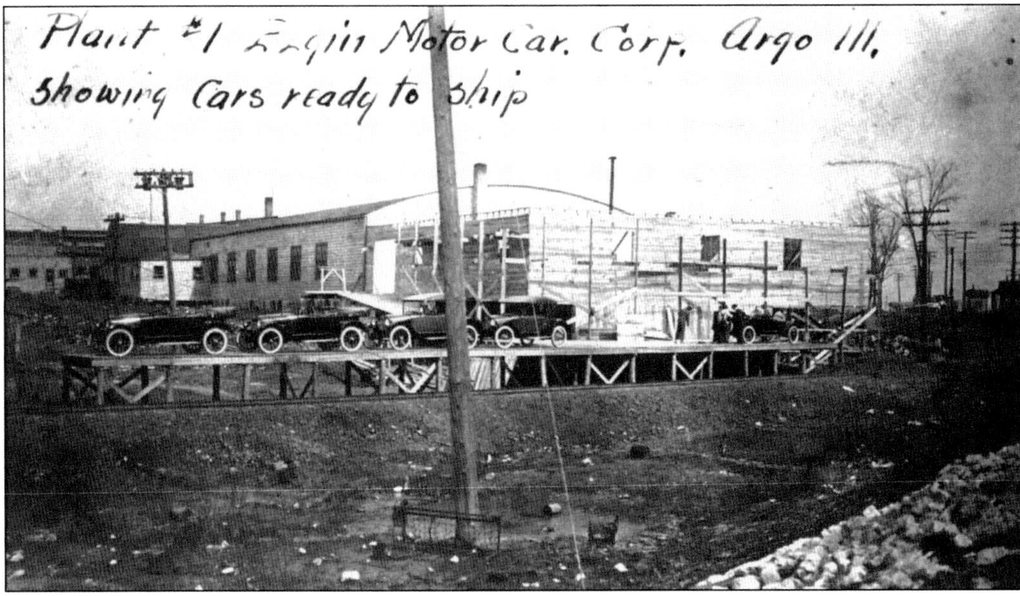


**ELGIN MOTORS.** In 1915, the Elgin Motor Car Company used the converted Argo Skating Rink as its first factory, located on the north side of Sixty-third Street west of Archer Avenue. This view is facing east from the IHB tracks. A shipment of cars wait on the platform of the rail spur extended from the line servicing the Argo-Summit Lumber Company. The company offices were located on the second story of the Argo Theater building.

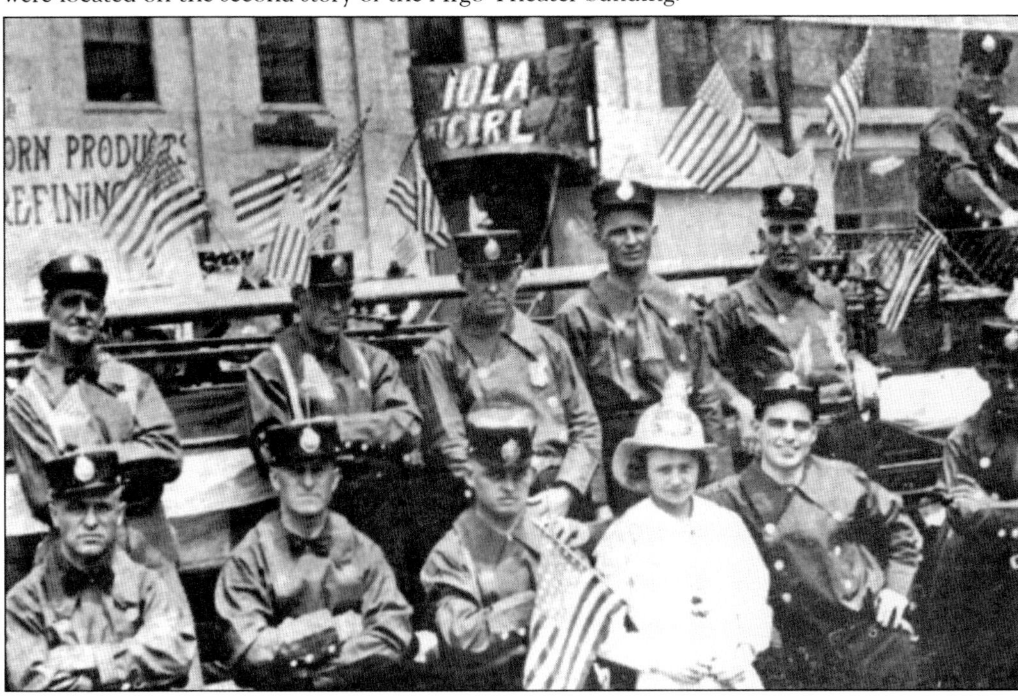


**SUMMIT'S *IOLA*.** Summit's first gas-powered fire engine, *Iola*, arrived in October 1918. A July 1917 fund-raiser in the form of a three-day carnival featured a burlesque dancer whom the new engine was named after. Pictured is the volunteer fire department during the carnival sitting atop a horse-drawn fire apparatus.

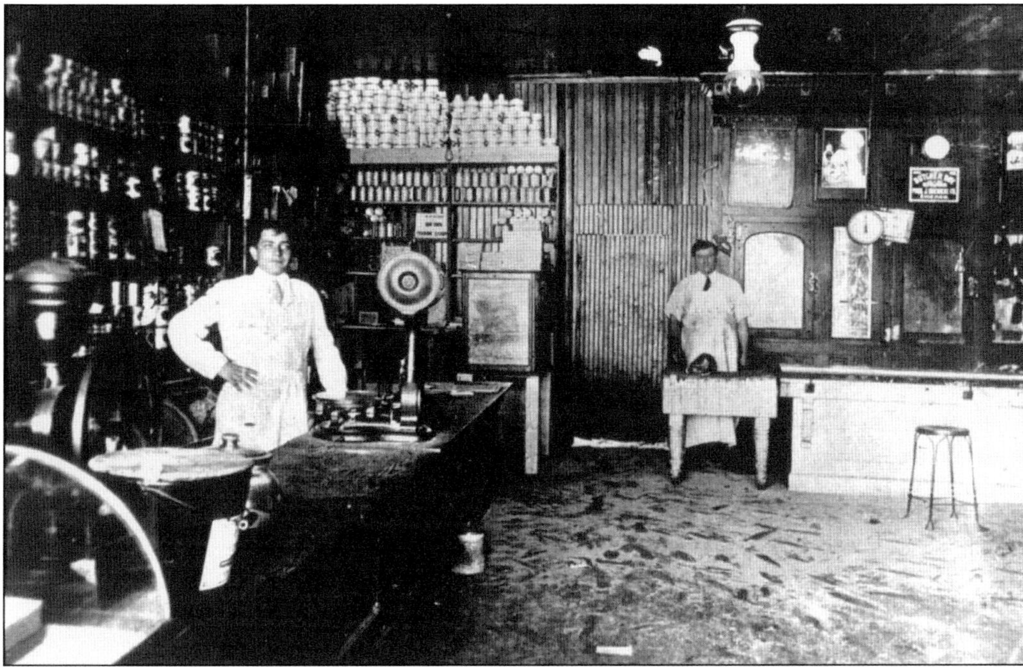

**RONCZKOWSKI GROCERY.** Argo pioneer merchant Stanley Ronczkowski came in 1908. In 1912, he opened his first store at 6217 Archer Avenue in the Maloy building. He moved to 6155 Archer Avenue in 1920 and later opened a service station (1926) at 6200 Archer Avenue. He is seen here with his brother-in-law Stan Kaput (left) in his grocery at 6155 Archer Avenue. Ronczkowski's children still live in the Summit area to this day. (Courtesy of Ted Ronczkowski.)

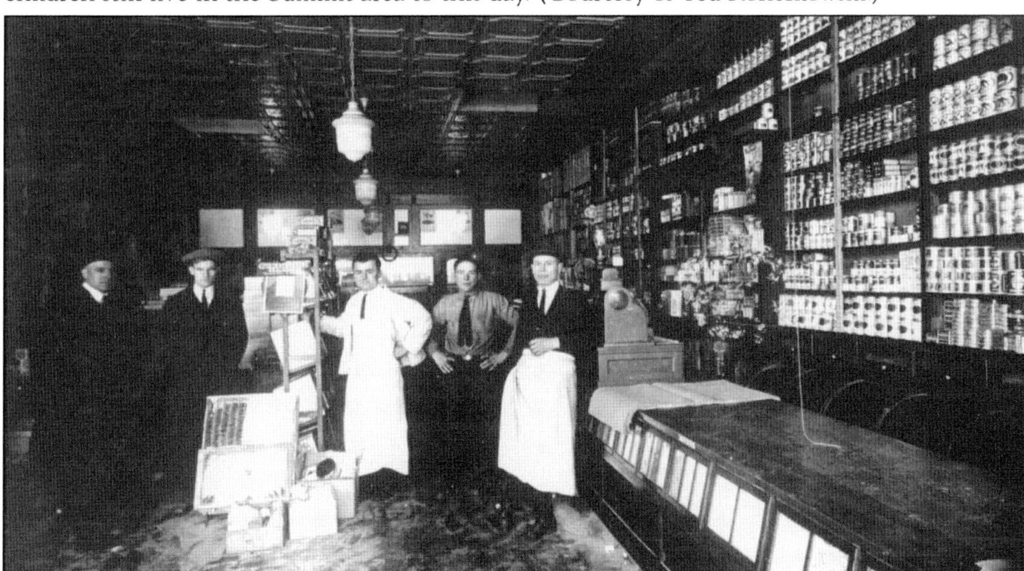

**DINEFF BROTHERS.** Lazarus (Lazo) Dineff bought out the interests in his brother Chris's bakery at 7660 Sixty-third Street in 1913. By 1915, Dineff Brothers was running a grocery at 6254 Archer Avenue. Lazo would later bring two of his sons to America from Macedonia, one being Christ, who became a real estate man, banker, and politician. The Dineff store was leased to A&P in 1930.

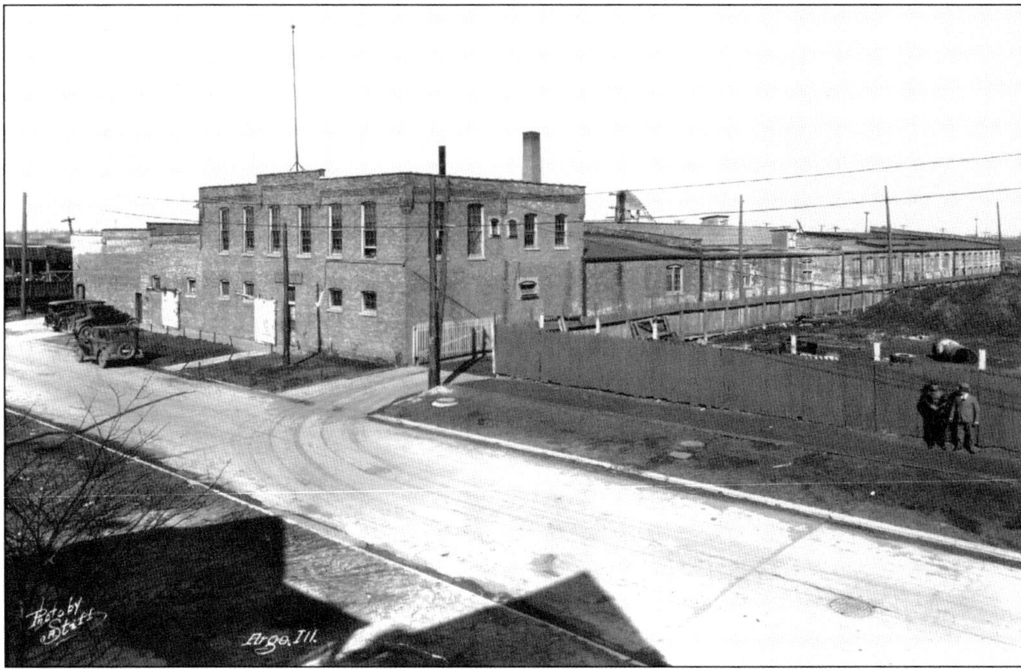


**BECKMAN-DAWSON ROOFING.** These buildings located at the western end of Sixty-first Place belonged to the Winthrop Asphalt Shingle Company from 1910 until about 1917, when the facility became Beckman-Dawson Roofing. In 1928, the facility became a division of the Flintkote Company, which manufactured fire-resistant felt sheets, among other things. Due to asbestos concerns, Flintkote ceased manufacturing in the 1980s.

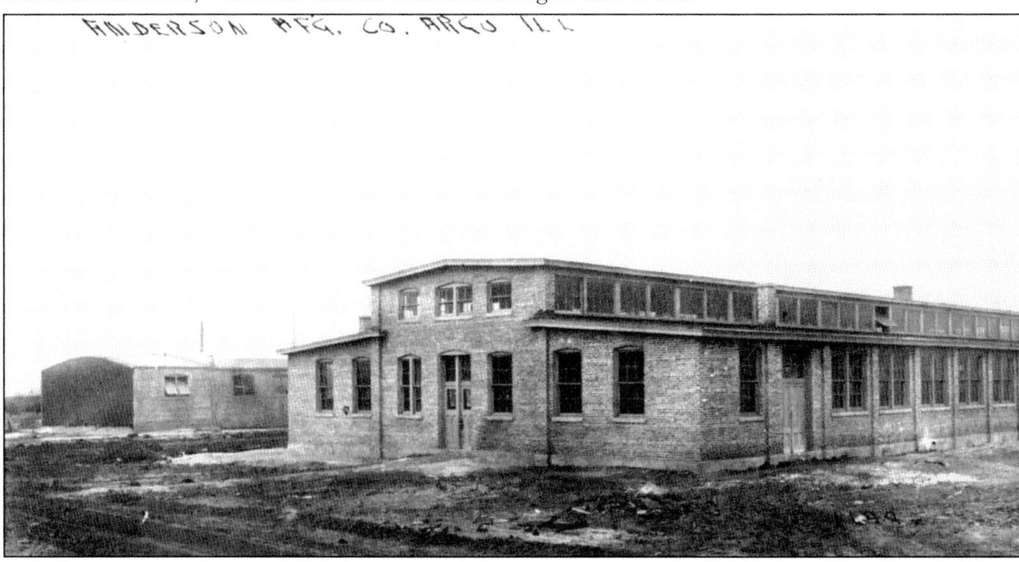


**ANDERSON ENGINEERING COMPANY.** In 1912, a gasoline engine manufacturing plant was built on Sixty-first Place, west of Archer Avenue, next to the Winthrop Asphalt Shingle Company. Anderson Motors was from Shelbyville. Connecting to this building was a grinding plant of the U.S. Kellastone Company (1913), which manufactured a resilient construction coating used for stucco. Kellastone moved out in 1917, but the motor company's fate is unknown. (Courtesy of the Paul Rush collection.)

# *Six*

# TUMULT OF THE 1920s

The 1920s and Chicago bring images of Prohibition and Al Capone. Summit had speakeasies and illegal distilleries also, the most elaborate within the block garage at 5448 Hunt Avenue, but the 1920s also brought on a development boom for Chicago's suburbs.

After World War I, many local farmers began selling land to subdividers. The main thoroughfares to the suburbs were being paved. The Cook County Forest Preserve District, established in 1914, had bought thousands of aces of land. By the mid-1920s, it had built the Swallow Cliff Ski Jump and the Maple Lake recreation area in the Palos area. It shipped in live buffalo for an attraction at Eighty-seventh Street and Kean Avenue. Bridges were erected to span the drainage canal at California, Crawford, and Cicero Avenues, and the municipal field (Midway Airport) opened.

The Corn Products Refining Company and the Clearing Industrial District brought in so many people to Summit that the infrastructure almost collapsed. To help assist in housing for its labor force, Corn Products bought property between Sixtieth and Sixty-first Streets for its Argo Homes Subdivision. In 1919 and 1920, it sold lots and homes to its employees. Corn Products also bought land across from the plant for company houses intended for supervisors. This was called Argo Manor, later Bedford Park.

The village nearly went bankrupt trying to keep up with the population increase that nearly tripled within 10 years. The water systems were horribly outdated, and even when pressure was good, it would not supply a second story. Streets were in bad shape, and paving was expensive. The grade schools were overcrowded and the high school too far away. Summit saw the greatest increase in building construction in the 1920s. Summit saw the quarries of the Chicago Crushed Stone Company get filled with garbage in 1923 and later the quarry of the Artesian Stone and Lime Company across the street. In 1926, a petition was brought forth for a public vote to annex Summit into Chicago, but a county judge threw it out before it went on the ballot. The seeds were planted for the next few decades to come.

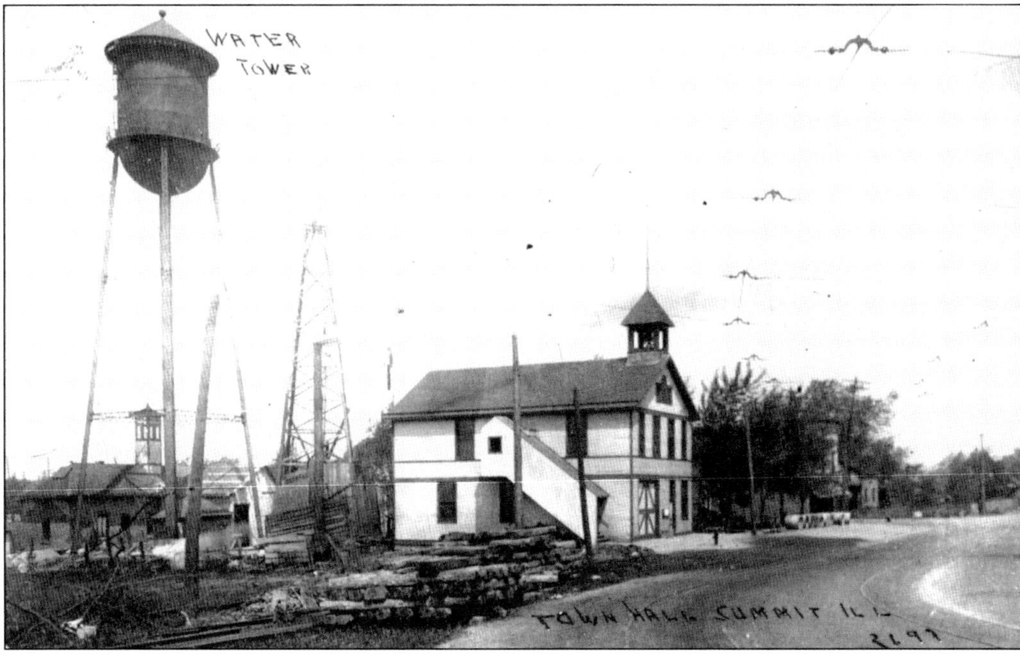


**VILLAGE WATER.** Summit's water supply was provided by three deep wells located behind the old village hall on Center Avenue. With residential, industrial, and municipal needs for water increasing, the old well arrangements became outdated by the 1920s and continuously malfunctioned. This image shows the village hall and water pump house while drilling of a third well is underway in 1913. (Courtesy of the Summit Public Library Historical Archives.)

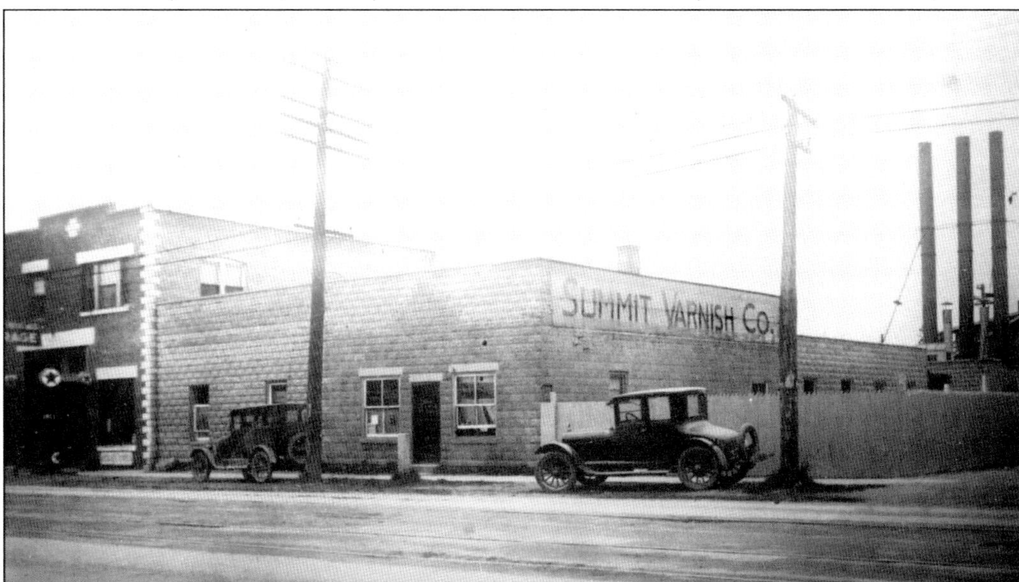


**THE SUMMIT VARNISH COMPANY.** Organized in 1920, the Summit Varnish Company started in an old frame building having a very small cement back building for an office. In 1923, a second addition was erected with the intention of an added second story. Also added were three stacks to take off the fumes, but they were soon after raised because of complaints of local residents. The Summit Varnish Company became the Archer Paint and Varnish Company in the 1930s.

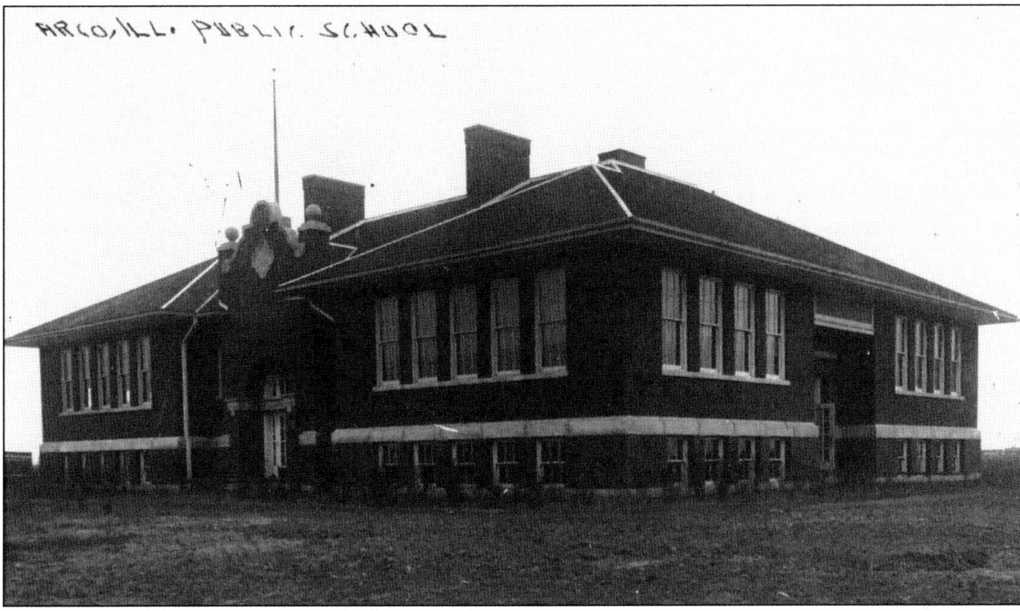


**ARGO SCHOOL.** Now the Donald Wharton Elementary School, the Argo School was the first grade school in Argo. School District No. 104 purchased the land from the CT&C in 1911, and the school opened in August 1912. Many additions were made to the school over the years to accommodate population increases, including a second floor. It is seen here as it originally was built. (Courtesy of the Summit Public Library Historical Archives.)

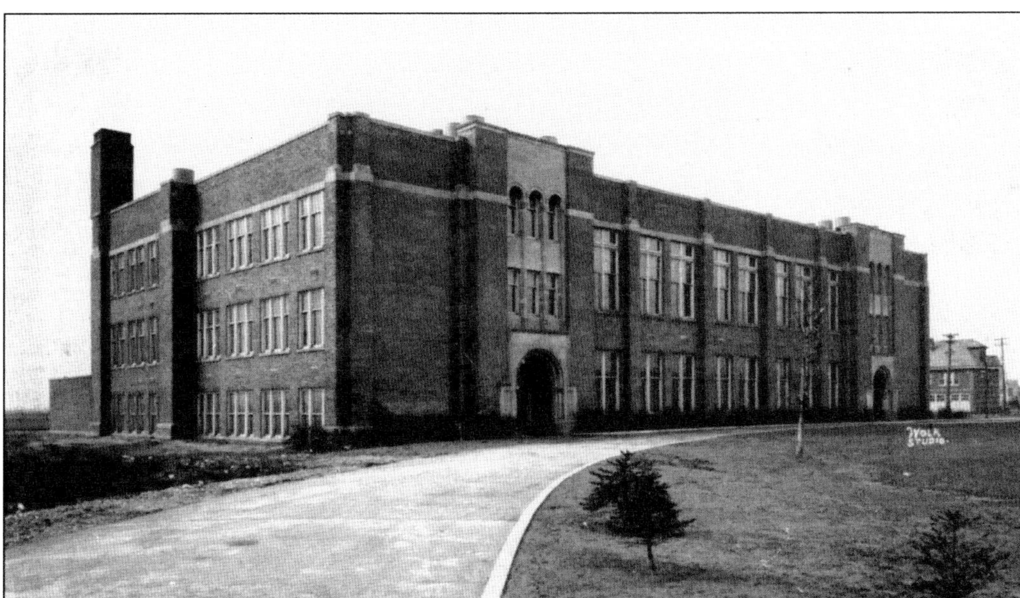

**ARGO COMMUNITY HIGH SCHOOL.** Summit's students attended Lyons Township High School in LaGrange prior to 1920. Those who lived southeast of the river had to travel to school by horse until the electric line in 1900. When the trolley came, they had to pay six car fares and walk two miles to get to school. The severe winter of 1917–1918, taxation, and contempt for the Lyons Township School Board led to the construction of the community high school in 1923.

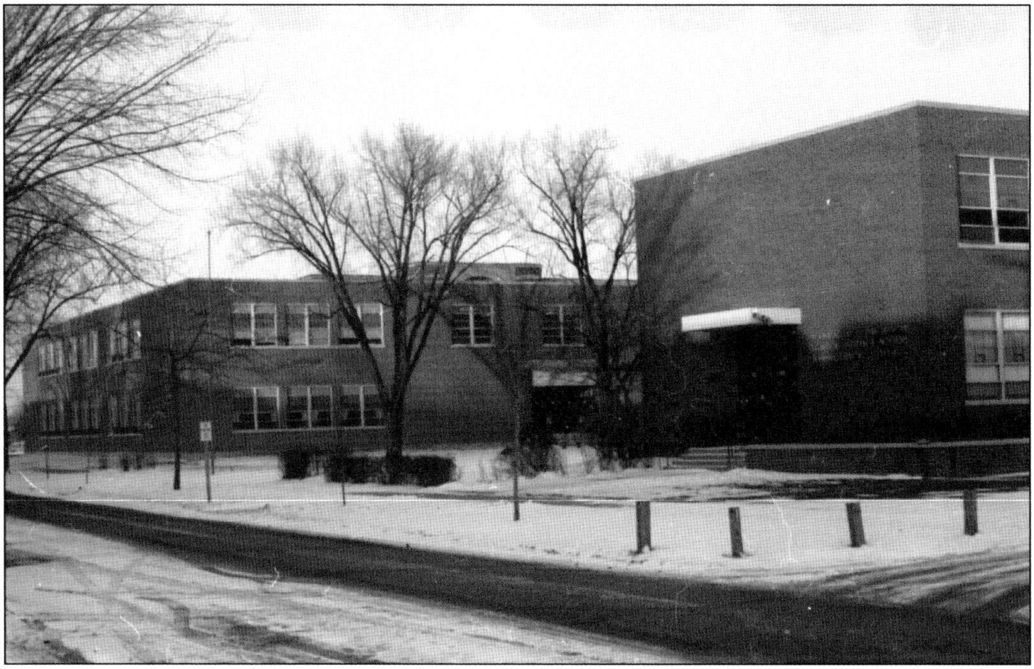

**GRAVES SCHOOL.** Otis P. Graves School was built in 1924 to alleviate overcrowding. It is located across the street from the Argo Homes Subdivision at 6021 South Seventy-fourth Avenue. The original school structure once faced on 7336 Sixtieth Street, but future additions caused a vacation of the roadway. The administration building was named after James C. Wrenn in 1986.

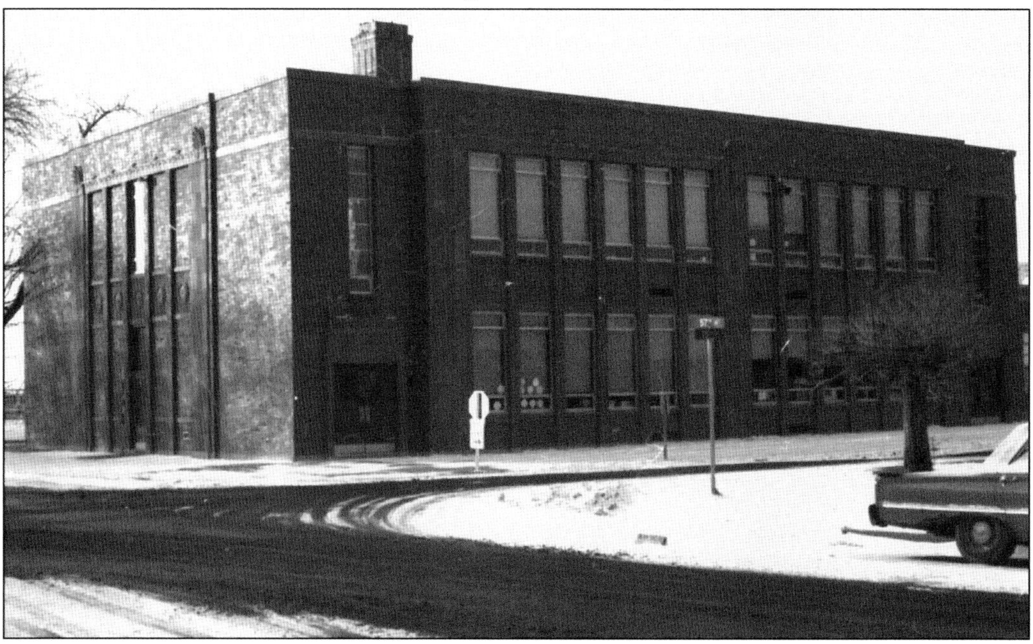

**JOHN D. WALSH SCHOOL.** Right after Otis P. Graves School was completed, the school district was once again faced with overcrowding and the issue of children having to cross the Fifty-ninth Street tracks from the Summit section of town. In 1929, John D. Walsh School was built to supplement the original Summit School located on the west end of the property.

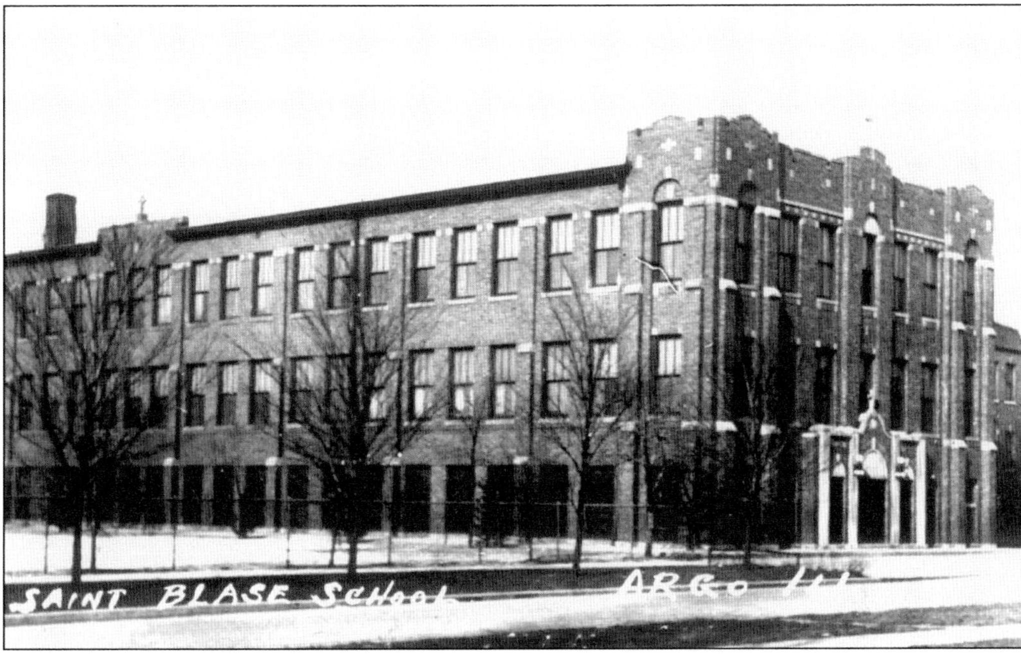


**ST. BLASE SCHOOL.** St. Joseph's, the Catholic congregation in Summit, erected a school in 1918 at 7438 Sixty-first Place, the same year its church burned. The school hall was used for church services afterward. The congregation split in 1924, and the school stayed with the newly formed St. Blase, while St. Joseph's built a new school on its block located at Seventy-second Court and Fifty-sixth Street in 1925. (Courtesy of the Paul Rush collection.)

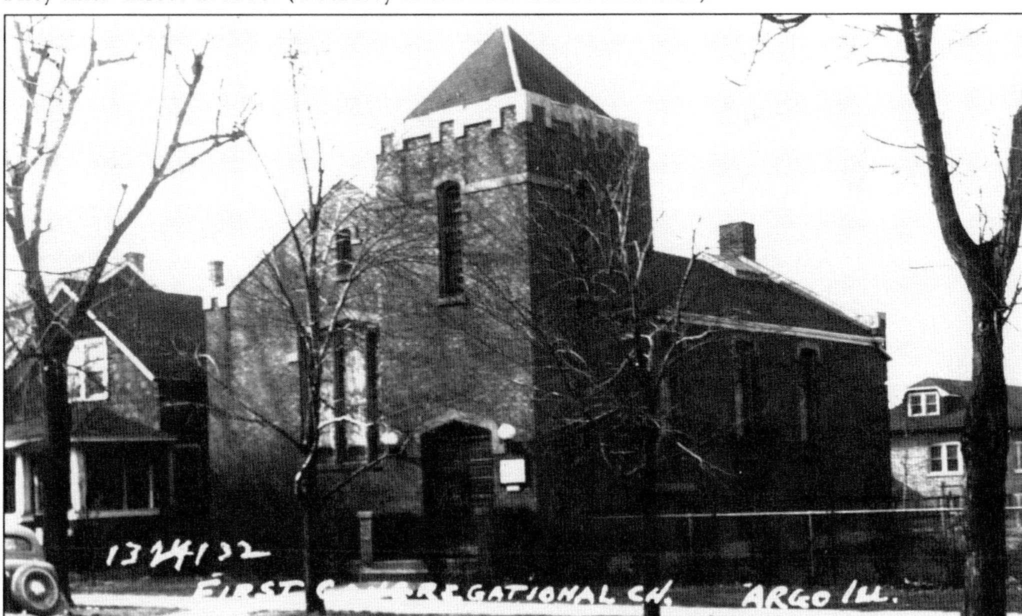


**ARGO CONGREGATIONAL CHURCH.** The Ladies Society of Argo, formed in 1911, was instrumental in causing the creation of the Argo Congregational Church. Initially the services were held at Knoedler's Hall at 6227 Archer Avenue until the church at 7438 Sixty-second Place was built in March 1913.

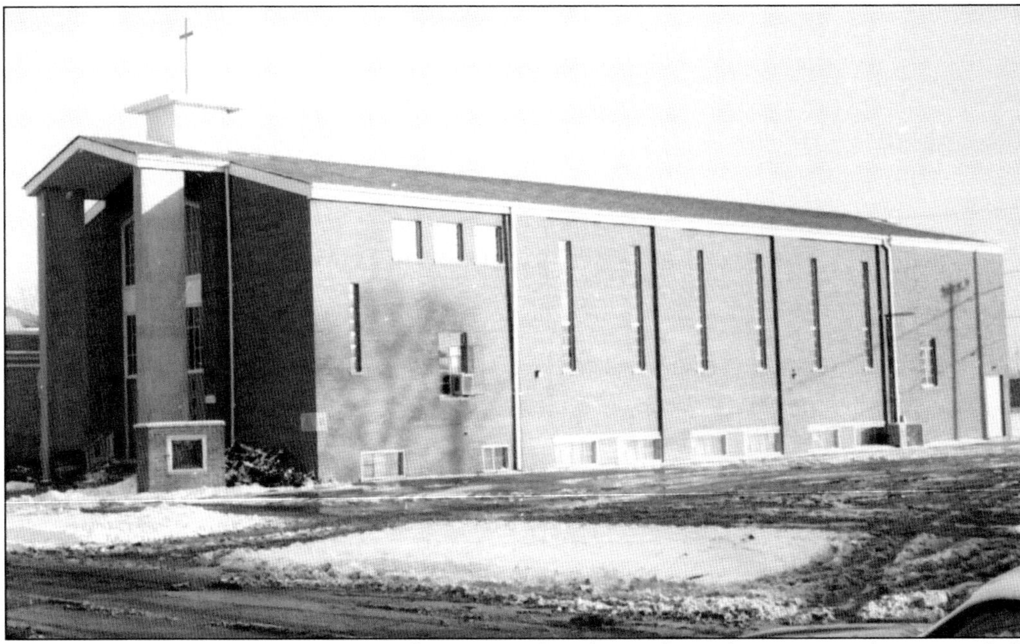

**ANTIOCH BAPTIST CHURCH.** Antioch Baptist Church was formed in 1919, with services held at the Argo Elementary School. In September 1921, the church was reorganized under William Fowler (later a pastor). The first church was built at 7519 West Sixty-fourth Street in May 1924 but burned in December 1925. A new church was built next door in 1926, but in 1929, there was found to be a property discrepancy so the structure was moved back to the original lot. A new church was again built in 1963 and remains to this day.

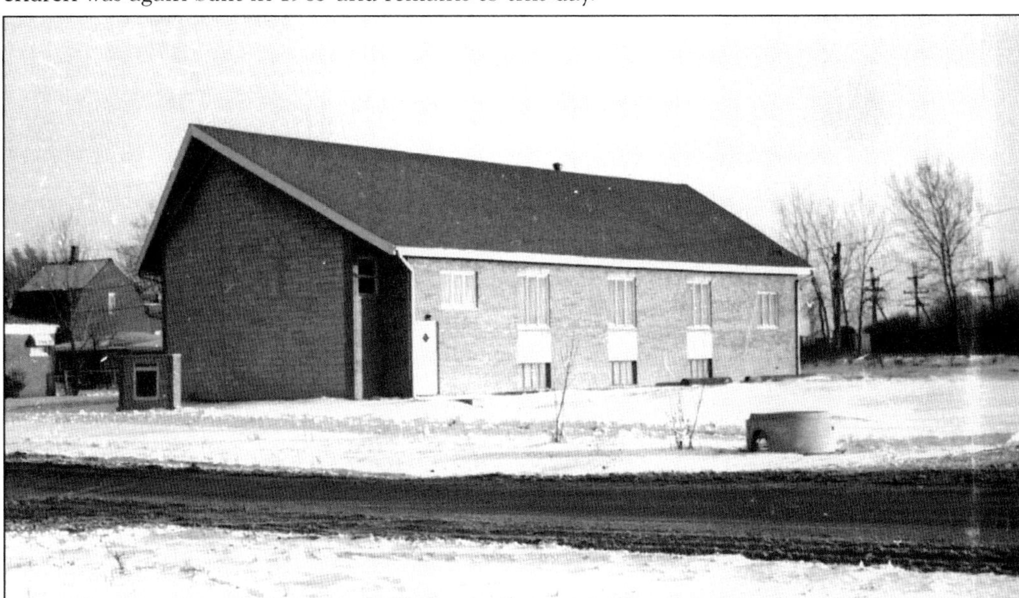

**SHILOH MISSIONARY BAPTIST CHURCH.** Beginning in 1924 under Rev. William Coleman, Shiloh Missionary Baptist Church was located at 7444 West Sixty-fourth Street where it remained for 44 years. On November 10, 1968, the new church pictured here was completed at 7661 Sixty-third Place.

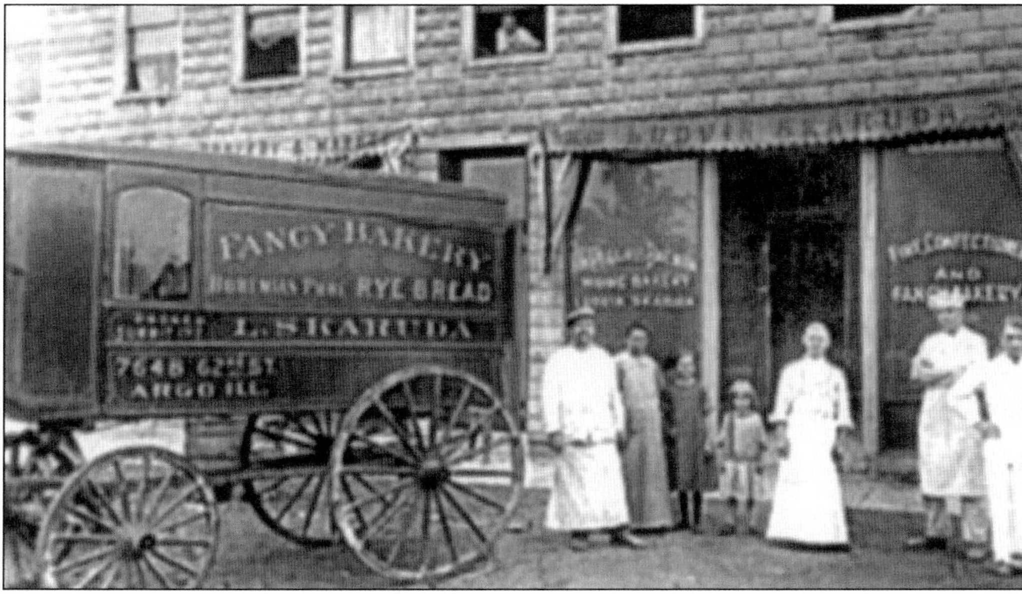


**SKARUDA BAKERY, 1909.** Coming to Argo in 1909, Ludwig Skaruda leased the east half of the Tomaszewski building for his bakery. He remained until his own building at 6136 Archer Avenue was completed in 1915. This building at 7648 West Sixty-second Street was home to many bakers such as Jaworski, Kolias, Nicklson, and the Peters Brothers. It later was a used furniture store and was a prior home of Ed Spadoni's electronics store.

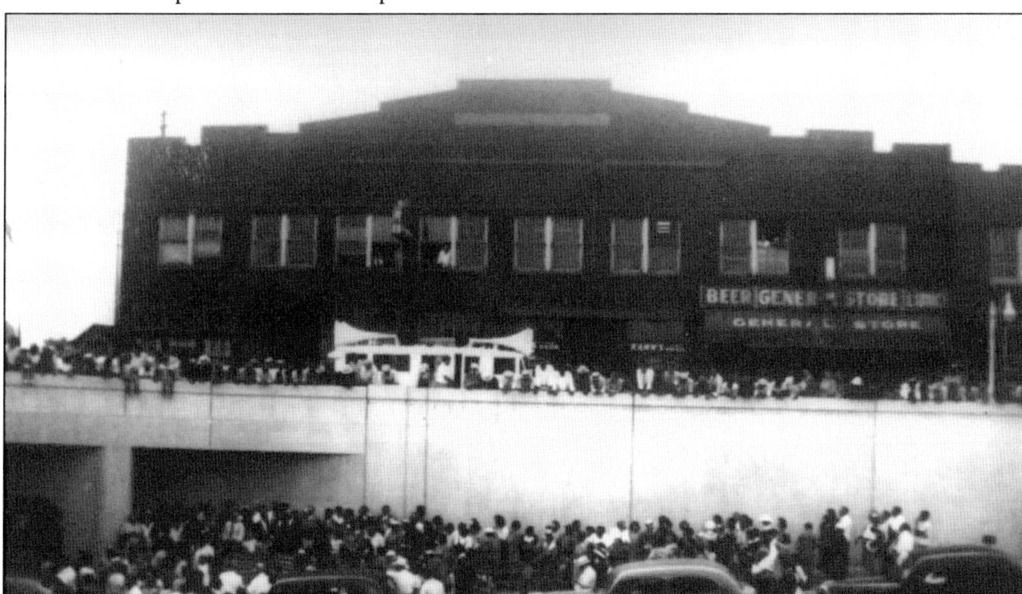

**TIMES SQUARE BUILDING.** In 1921, Lazo Dineff built this structure abutting the south side of the Argo Theater on the west side of Archer Avenue, just north of the railroad crossing. The building contained the Times Square restaurant, a confectionary store, and a hall on the second floor. The second floor was converted to bowling alleys in 1924. Located at what was known as the "Horseshoe" after the Archer Avenue viaduct was built in 1940, the structure served the community until it burned in 1967.

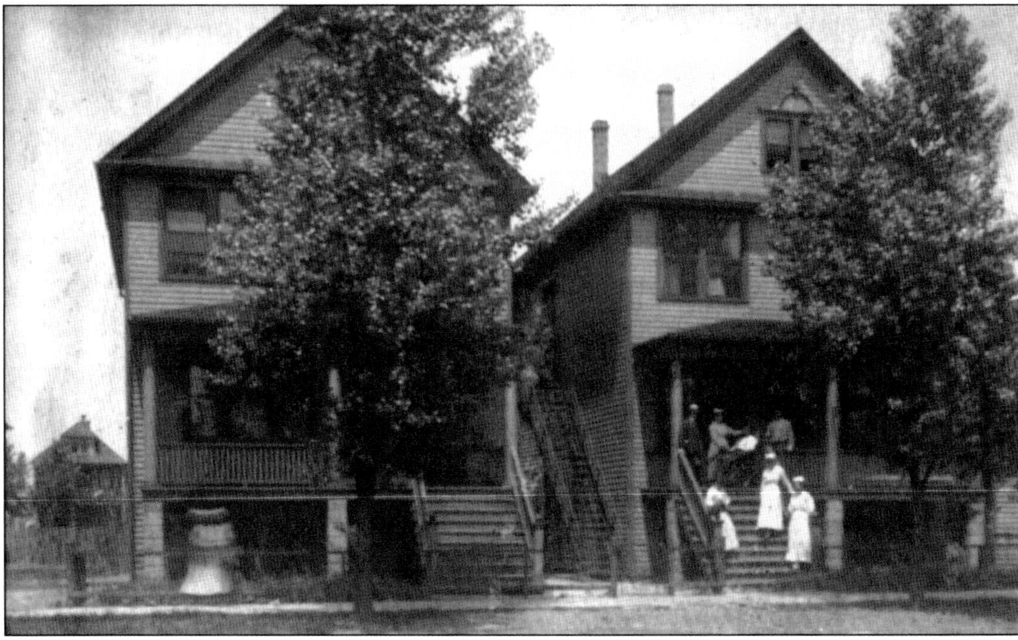

**PROVIDENCE HOSPITAL.** Housing for female employees was erected by the Corn Products Refining Company in 1913 at 7540 Sixty-first Street. Under the direction of the Sisters of Nazareth, one floor was used for St. Joseph's school. The building next door at 7538, also part of the complex, was converted into a hospital managed by the nuns in 1918. The hospital closed in 1920 when the nuns were reassigned. Both structures were sold by Corn Products in 1922.

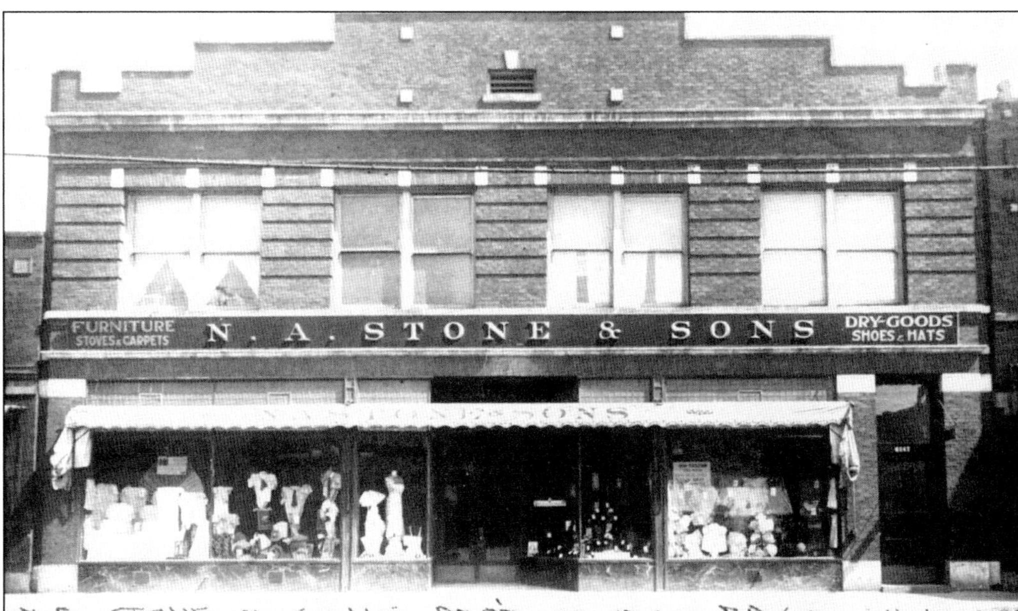


**STONE MOVES AGAIN.** Nathan A. Stone built his largest and final store at 6247 Archer Avenue in 1922. Sons Harry and Saul ran the store for most of its existence, passing it on to their children, who then sold to Adam Novosad in 1975. The second floor held offices, and from 1925, it was also the site of Archer Hospital. Stone's closed its doors for good in 1987.

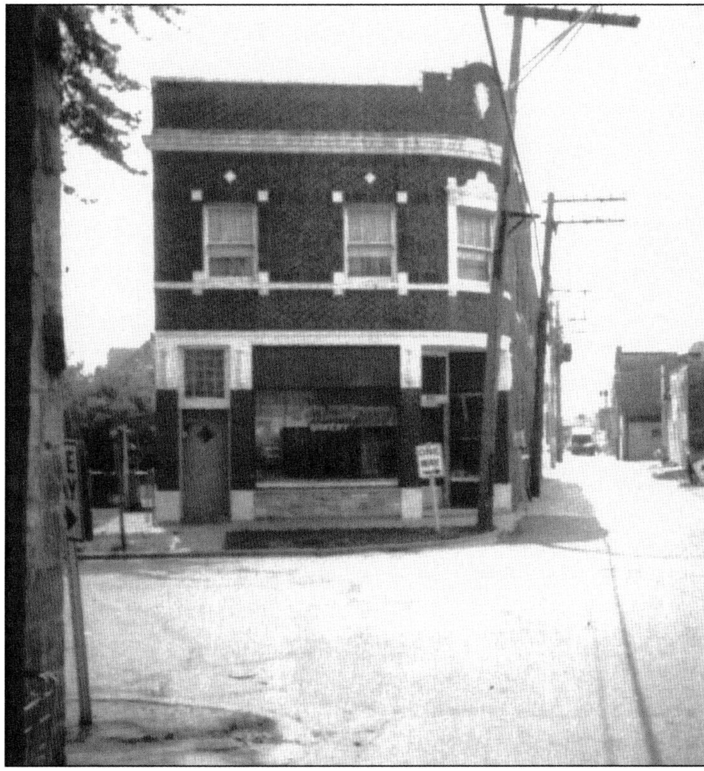

**ARGO SANITARY BAKERY, 7651 SIXTY-SECOND STREET.** As a testament to Summit's ethnic diversity, this Polish bakery was built by the Lyznicki Brothers for I. Jaworski in 1926. A Greek bakery was right across the street, both serving their respective ethnic customers. Jaworski soon traded bakeries with Chicago-based Anton Kowalski in the early 1930s, who in turn ran a bakery out of this building for over 50 years.

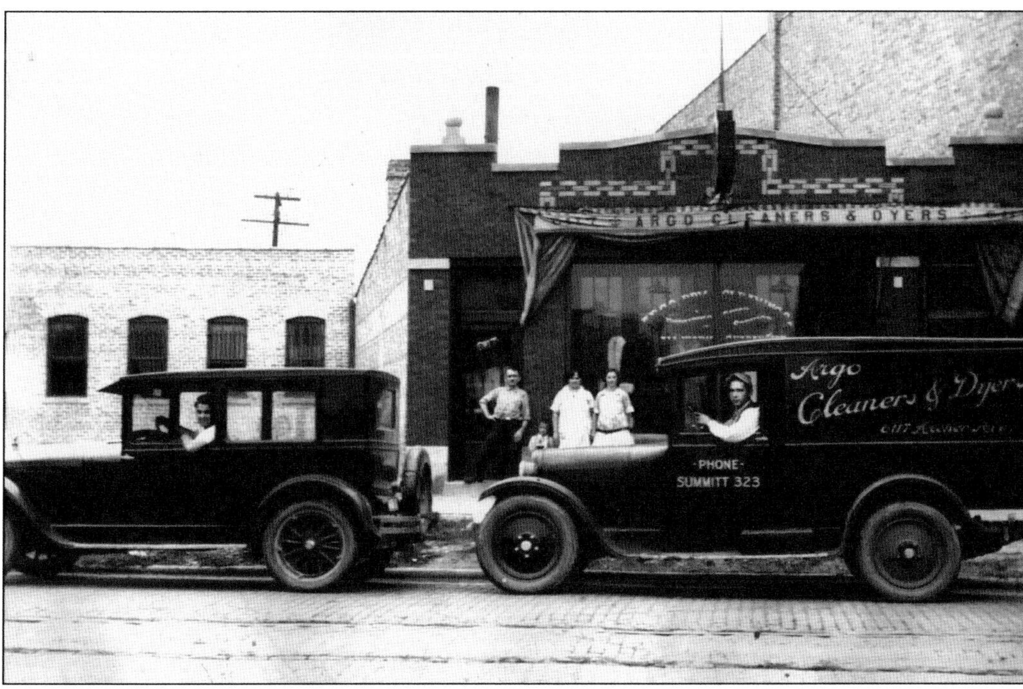


**ARGO DYEING AND CLEANING.** Dry cleaners were abundant in Summit-Argo. This building, located at 6115–6117 South Archer Avenue, was constructed in 1924 by Charles Demitriu. Located next door to the *Des Plaines Valley News* office, the cleaners stayed in business until 1975.

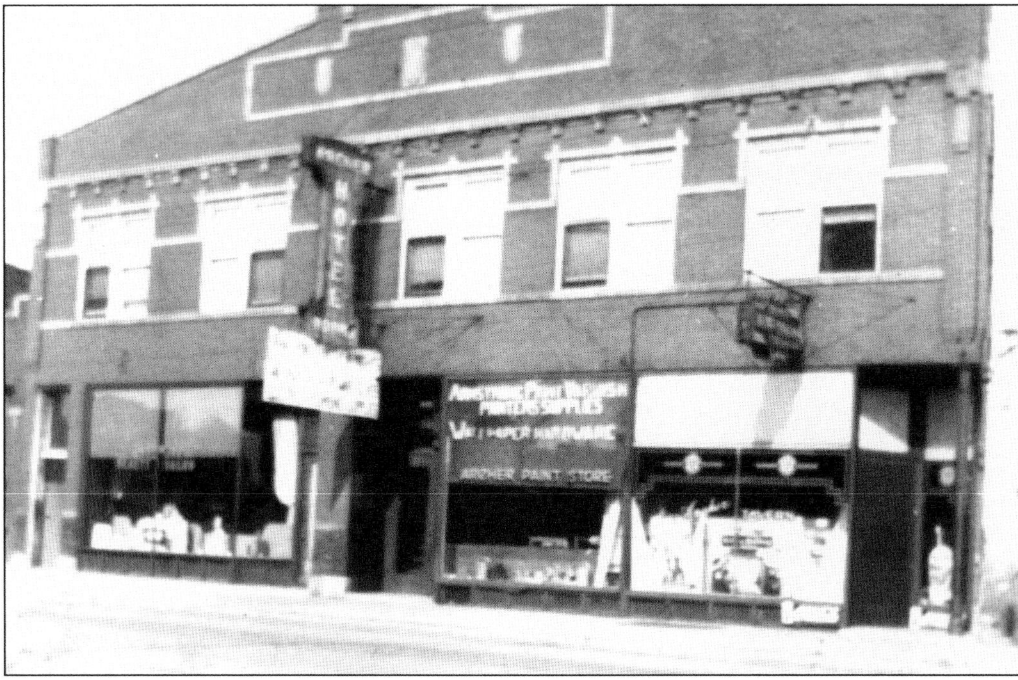


**TOMASHUNAS.** Built by Ludwig Skaruda in 1914, this structure consisted only of the north half of the present building at 6136 Archer Avenue. It was a bakery (corner) with rental storefront (south end). Stanley Tomashunas bought the building in 1922. The south portion of the building at 6138, with the Archer Hotel on the second floor, was added in 1926. Since the 1980s, 6136 Archer Avenue has been the home of El Faro, originator of the famous football-size burrito.

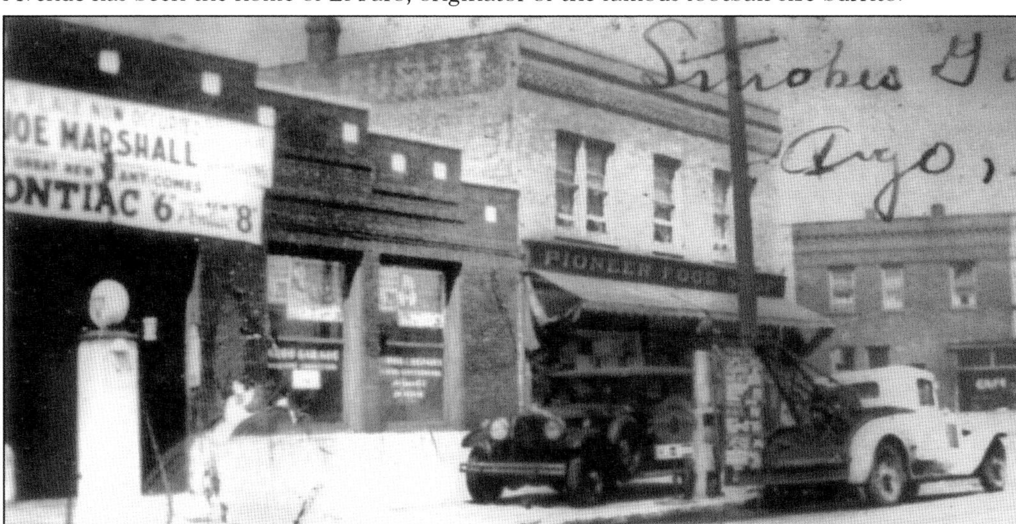


**PIONEER MARKET AND SMOKE'S.** The corner building of 6134–6136 Archer Avenue, built in 1909, originally consisted of a tavern (corner) and rental storefront (south end). The second floor was the Olympia Hotel. John Puchalski operated the Pioneer Market from 1925 to 1975. It is now the Esquire Barber Shop. The building next door at 6240–6242, built in 1920, was Southwest Auto Sales, later Smoke Martin's Argo Garage. It is more commonly remembered as Lambert's Bowling Alley, a popular spot in the 1940s and 1950s.

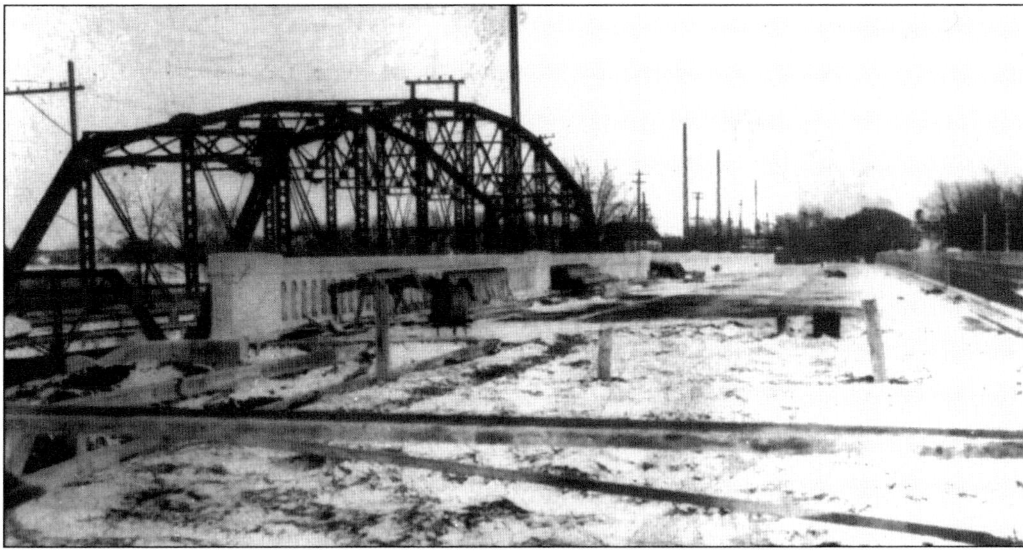

**DES PLAINES RIVER BRIDGE.** With the coming of age of the southwest suburbs in the 1920s, the need for bridges across the canals and Des Plaines River was a requirement. Lawndale Avenue was bridged over the Des Plaines since the 1830s. A steel bridge was built by the sanitary district in the 1890s, but within a few decades, it would fall into constant disrepair. The state finally built a new concrete bridge for Summit as is seen here in 1925.

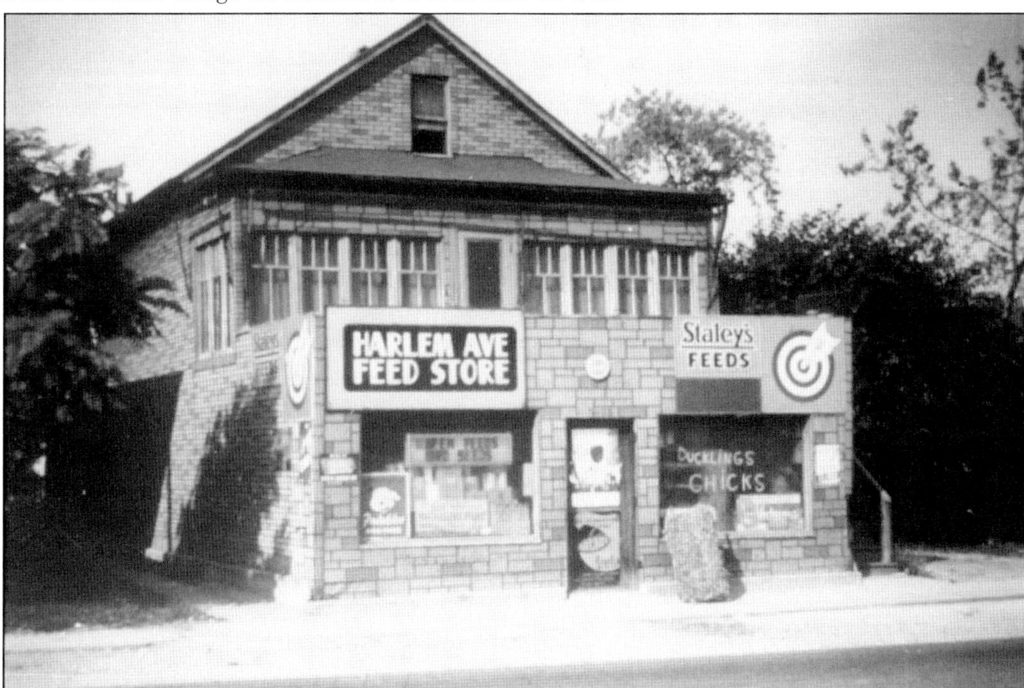


**HARLEM FEED STORE.** Paving Harlem Avenue helped to open the suburbs to commerce. Investors bought up lots fronting Harlem Avenue for future development. This structure, located at 5408 South Harlem Avenue, was built about 1925. It was once Charles Cima's Grocery and Meats but was converted to a feed store by Joe and Rudy Bestwina in 1948. In an updated brick building, the feed store is still in business to this day.

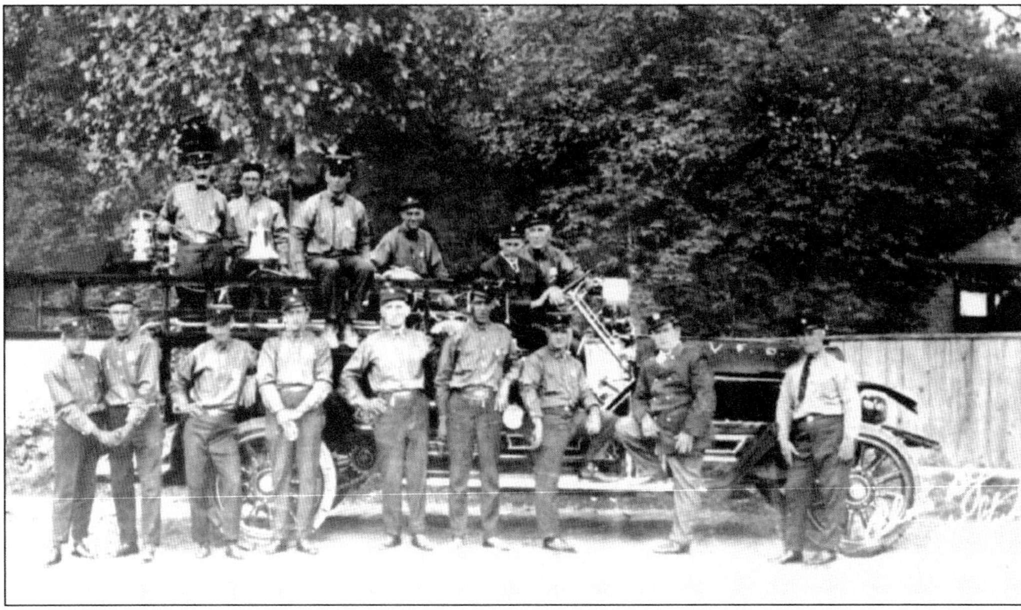

**LaFrance.** Because of increasing fire outbreaks and rising insurance costs, Summit's firemen instituted a fund-raising drive for a new fire engine in 1922. After the community pitched in, and with a large contribution from the Corn Products Refining Company (with the stipulation that the engine must also be used for Bedford Park), a new American LaFrance fire engine arrived in Summit in July 1924. The volunteer firemen posed with it, and the photographs were sold from the *Des Plaines Valley News* office on Archer Avenue.

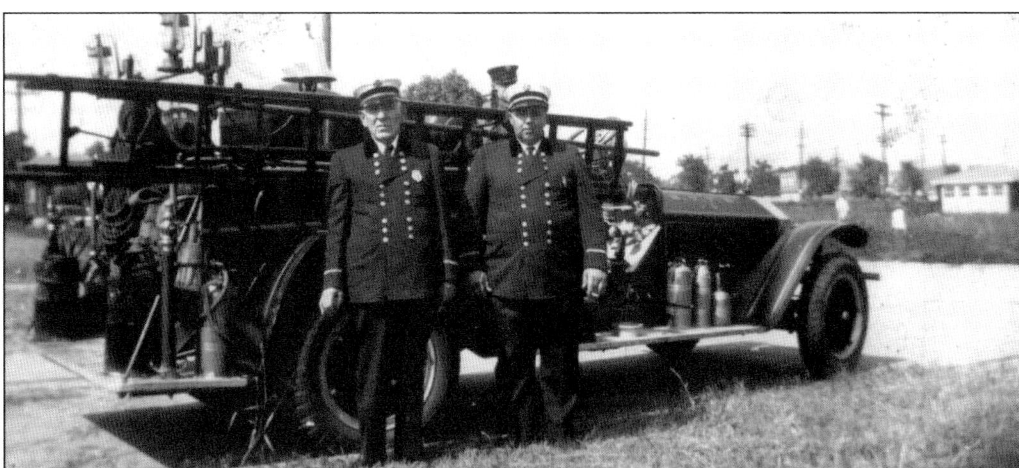

**William W. Walker.** The Summit Fire Department had organizational problems for years, but they were rectified with the appointment of William W. Walker as chief in 1917. Walker was a long-standing member of the school board and involved with other organizations. The Bedford Park school is named after Walker. He is seen here at left standing next to Ben Schmidtke in 1938 in front the American LaFrance. (Courtesy of Kay Kalaga.)

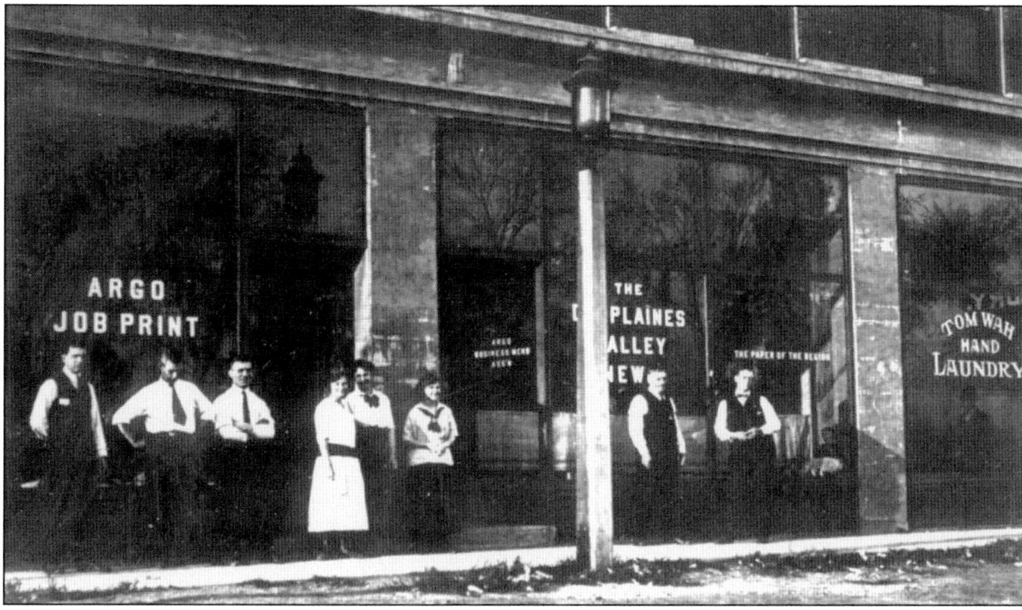


**DES PLAINES VALLEY NEWS, c. 1915.** The *Des Plaines Valley News* came to Argo from Lemont in 1915, under control of W. F. Walkowiak. Originally located on Sixty-third Street in the savings bank building, it moved to 6121–6123 Archer Avenue in 1919. Walkowiak was an influential community activist in the 1920s and helped bring about the community high school. The newspaper has changed ownership through the years but is still in business to this day.

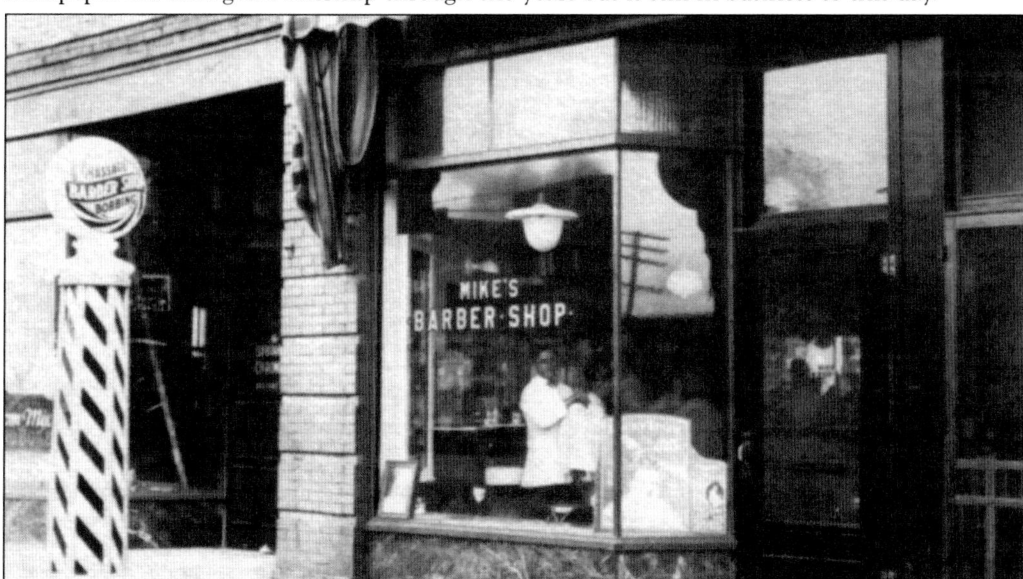


**MIKE METSKAS, 1926.** In 1914, a young Macedonian came to Argo to work as a barber at 6258 Archer Avenue. In 1922, Mike Metskas constructed the building at 6305 Archer Avenue that he leased out to other businesses. He cut the hair of Al Capone on occasion when he was passing through town. He remained in Argo and worked cutting hair for 66 years, retiring in 1980. He was well loved by the community. (Courtesy of the Summit Public Library Historical Archives.)

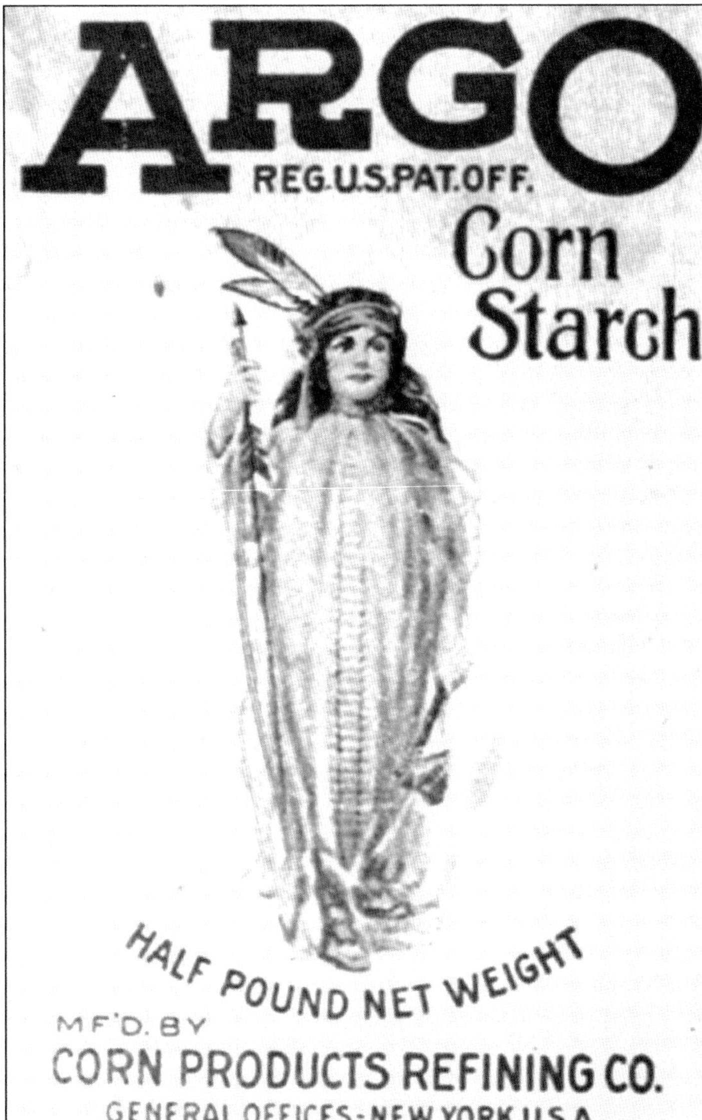


**ARGO CORN STARCH.** Argo Corn Starch remains a symbol of the factory that paved the way for the growth of Summit and the surrounding communities. The Corn Products Refining Company seeded the Clearing Industrial District, Elgin Motor Car Company, Electro-Motive Division of General Motors, and a list of other firms that tapped the labor force in the southwest suburbs. Corn Products even created housing for its employees. The original Corn Products Subdivision of 1911, south of Sixty-third Street, settled mostly by African American employees, was overpopulated and landlocked. In 1918, the plant purchased lots from Frederick Barrett and created the Argo Homes Subdivision at Sixtieth Street, as well as Argo Manor (later Bedford Park). Employees were offered easy terms for newly constructed houses between 1919 and 1920. The plant employed diverse ethnicities that gave Argo-Summit its distinct melting pot character. There were Irish, Dutch, Polish, Italian, Greek, Lithuanian, Slovenian, Albanian, Serbian, Russian, Croatian, German, African American, and Latino enclaves within the community (and these sometimes clashed). The year 1929 brought the Depression, and Corn Products was there to help make the hard times a bit easier.

# *Seven*

# Depression and War Years

October 29, 1929, brought the Great Depression. Summit did not feel the crunch right away, but by 1930, the local merchants who owned buildings with adjacent rental storefronts were having problems finding tenants to meet their mortgages. The Argo Summit Health Center was active in community wellness under the direction of nurse Robina Lyle. Community activist Rose DeKrauze took part in the Parent-Teacher Association day camps and soup kitchens. The government provided municipalities with Works Progress Administration (WPA) money, and communal gardens were farmed on vacant lots. The land that is now Summit Park was used to grow feed during the Depression era. Land and seeds were provided to residents as a means of maintaining nutrition during this difficult time.

Argo State Bank, which had moved from the corner of Sixty-third Street and Archer Avenue to 6252 Archer Avenue in 1914, felt the crunch of the Depression. An investment company affiliated with the Corn Products Refining Company began buying stock in the bank in December 1931 to save it from failure. Although Corn Products had little to lose if the bank closed, it was concerned about its employees' money. Company president George Moffett made a drastic move and made cash advancements to the bank. Moffett received criticism for doing this, but he secured the savings of his employees and saved the bank from going under.

The Depression was also the final straw for the Chicago and Joliet Electric Railway, which discontinued its Archer Avenue service in 1933. That year also saw the forced closing of Summit State Bank on Archer Avenue. Christ Dineff, son of Lazo, had taken to real estate in 1934 and bought up much of the business property that closed.

The year 1941 changed everything. The residents of Summit had sprung back to life but were rationing their basic needs not for lack of money, but for a war. Summit sent its boys off to fight and took losses as any other community. Summit also had war heroes, such as Nick Fryziuk, who survived the Bataan Death March in 1942. The year 1943 saw the burning of the original village hall on Center (Lawndale) Avenue, which perhaps marked the end of an era.

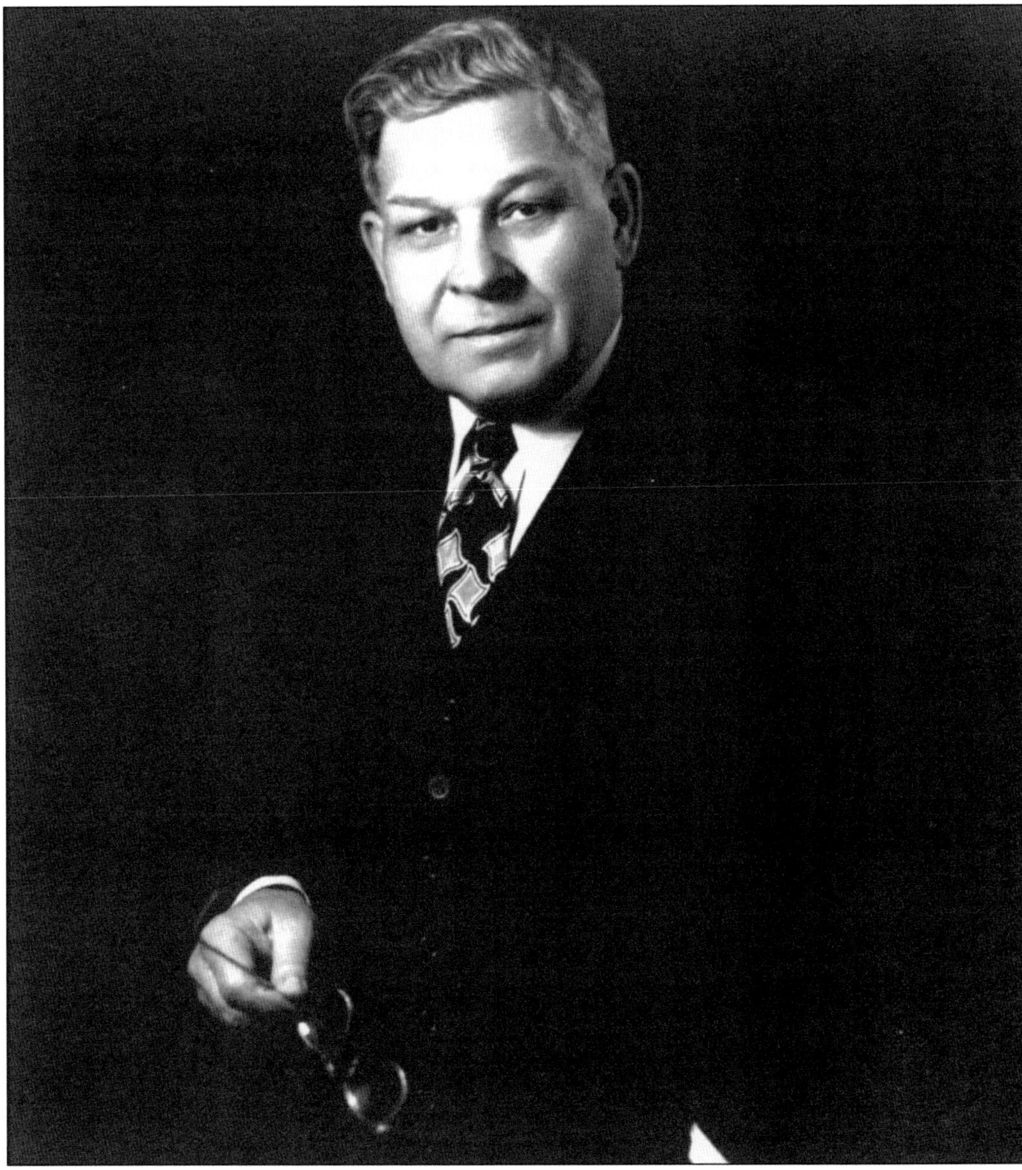

**DR. PAUL RUSH (1890–1986).** Dr. Paul Rush was an outstanding physician who served the Summit region and was known for his 50-plus-year involvement in civic affairs. His credo was "When something needed doing, I got in and did it." He was medical director at the Corn Products Refining Company plant for over 43 years and also a school board, draft board, and charter Lions Club member. He was an organizer and activist who championed such causes as Depression soup kitchens, the formation of Argo Community High School District No. 217, the Summit Park District, the Des Plaines Valley Community Health Center, and also the Des Plaines Valley Community Center. From Dr. George M. Fox in the 1850s through today, many good doctors have served the people of Summit. Among them are Drs. Shanahan, Lundeen, Barclay, Valentine, DeKrauze, Cox, Cannon, Geehan, Napieralska, Mahan, Gold, Kogan, Scott, Frisbie, Nienow, Mann, Schleuter, Allison, Jacula, Woods, Dwan, Zitek, Bolino, Gogan, Kolomicjew, Arseneau, Breakey, Rathbone, Plucinski, Sullivan, and Gilman. (Courtesy of the Paul Rush collection.)

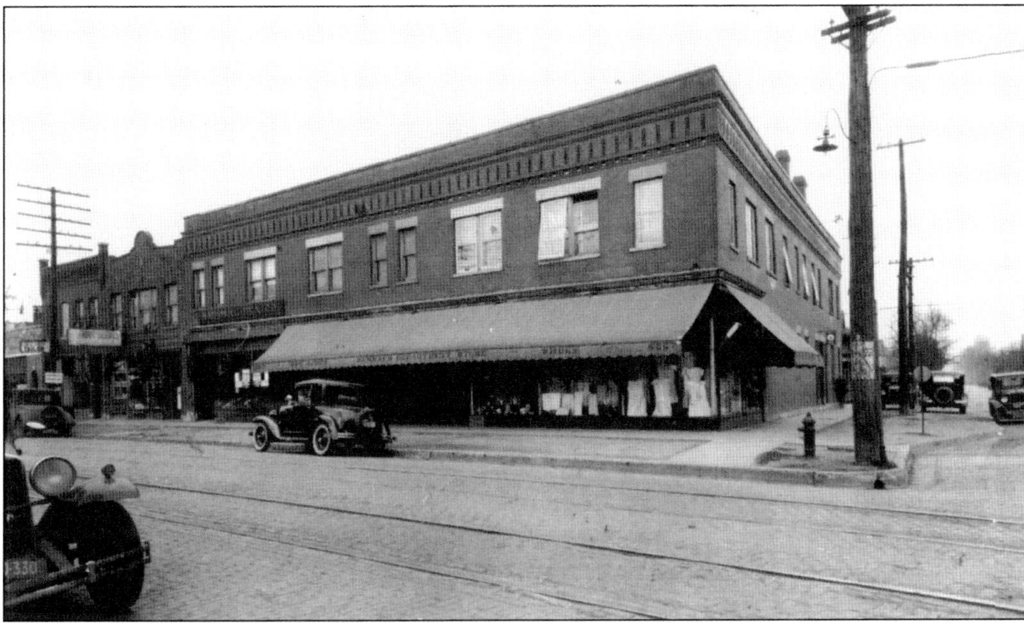

**NEWMAN'S DEPARTMENT STORE.** Taken in 1931, this image shows Newman's Department Store at 6225–6227 Archer Avenue, which was later Goldstine's. The second floor was once Knoedler's Hall, but the telephone company leased the south side at this time at 7662 West Sixty-second Place. Next door to the left are National Tea Company at 6221, Service Electrical Company at 6219½, the "K" Cigar Store at 6219 with the Knights of Columbus hall on second floor, and Charlie's Tailor Shop at 6217.

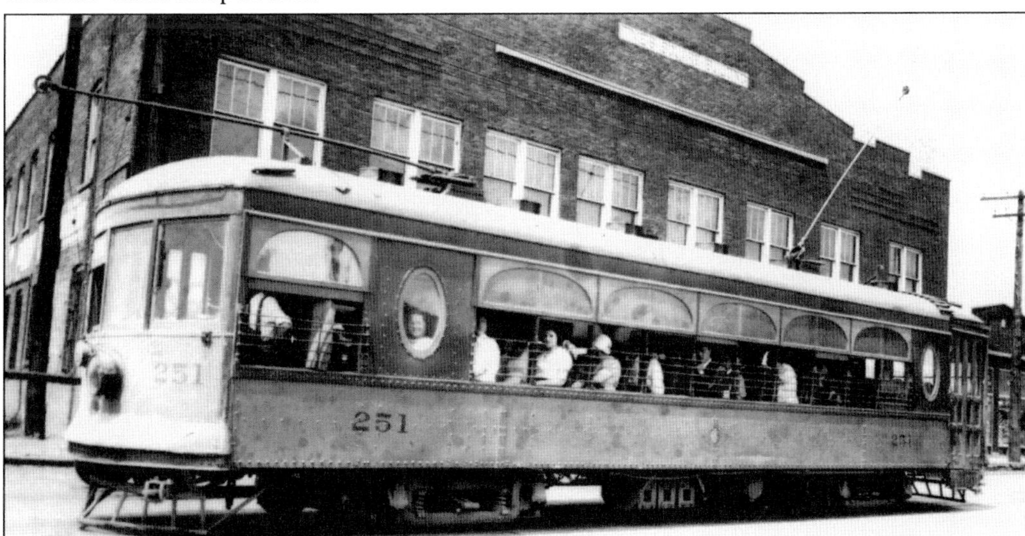

**CHICAGO AND JOLIET'S LAST YEAR.** This photograph is from Sunday, July 23, 1933. The Chicago and Joliet Electric Railway streetcar is loaded with passengers passing in front of the Times Square Building on Archer Avenue. The first floor of the building held a confectionery, which was the Argo ticket office for the Chicago and Joliet after Vitalakis's Argo Confectionery burned down a few years before. The interurban service would be discontinued by November of this year and replaced with buses.

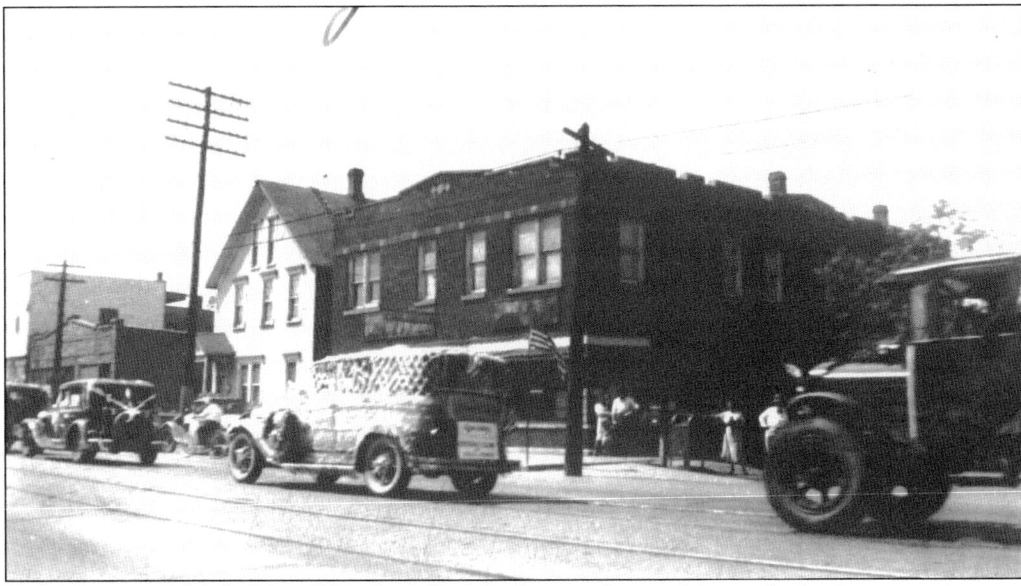

**J. E. MALOY, 1934.** In May 1934, the village had a parade to celebrate the businessmen in town. In this scene the parade heads westbound past J. E. Maloy's Grocery.

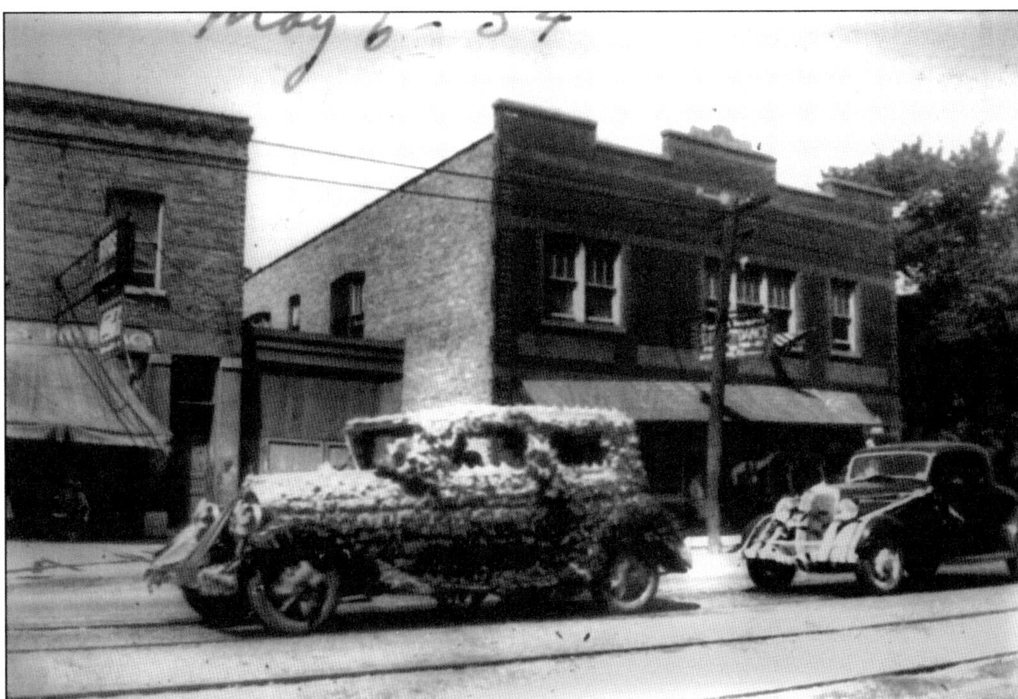

**GUSTAV GRIMM.** Cars from the 1934 businessmen's parade pass the building of Gustav Grimm at 7420 Archer Avenue. Grimm was a bricklayer and champion wrestler who came from Lyons to Summit to build this two-story store and flat building in 1925. He leased the business for a time to Walter Shulfer. The Depression caused Grimm to lose most of his investments, except for this building in Summit.

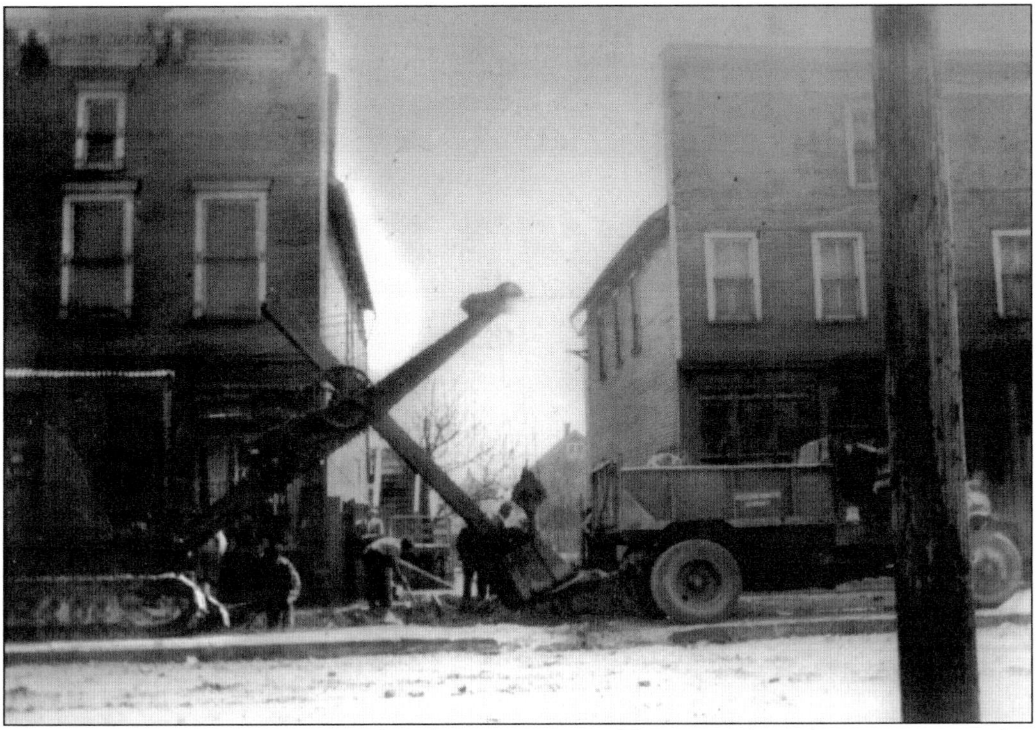

**ARCHER REPAVING.** The paving of Archer Avenue in 1935 was significant because it was at this time that the roadway was completely reconstructed and the old streetcar tracks were covered over. Pictured here are Carl Greb's general store at 7423 Archer Avenue (left) and Carl Greb's rental building at 7427 Archer Avenue (right).

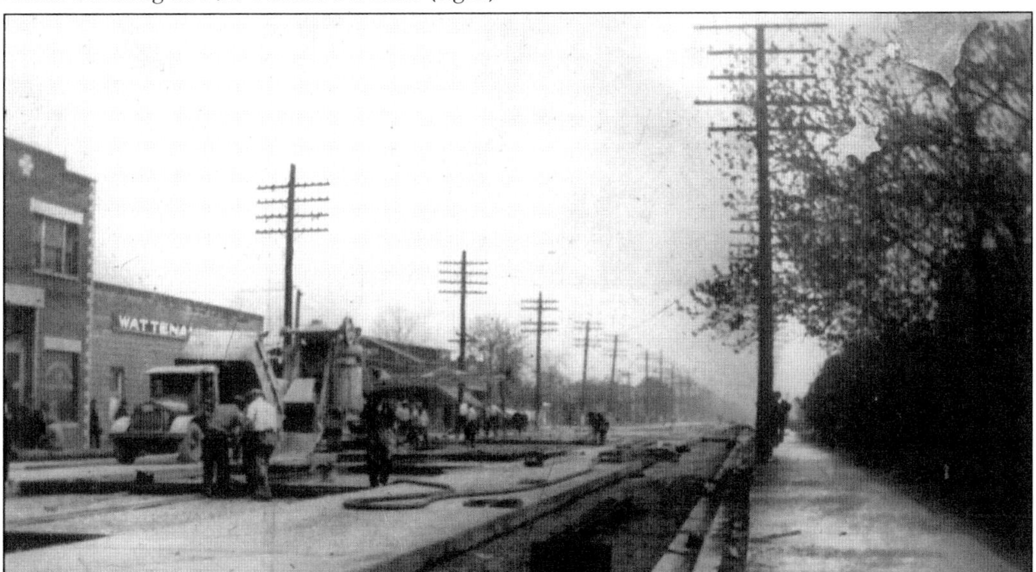

**ARCHER REPAVING, WATTENAMEL.** This photograph of the repaving of Archer Avenue in 1935 shows the Wattenamel Company (the old Summit Varnish Company) at 7400–7402 Archer Avenue, with E. M. Watts as proprietor. To the left and adjoining is Summit-Argo Motor Sales, which in 1934 was called the Parwood Garage.

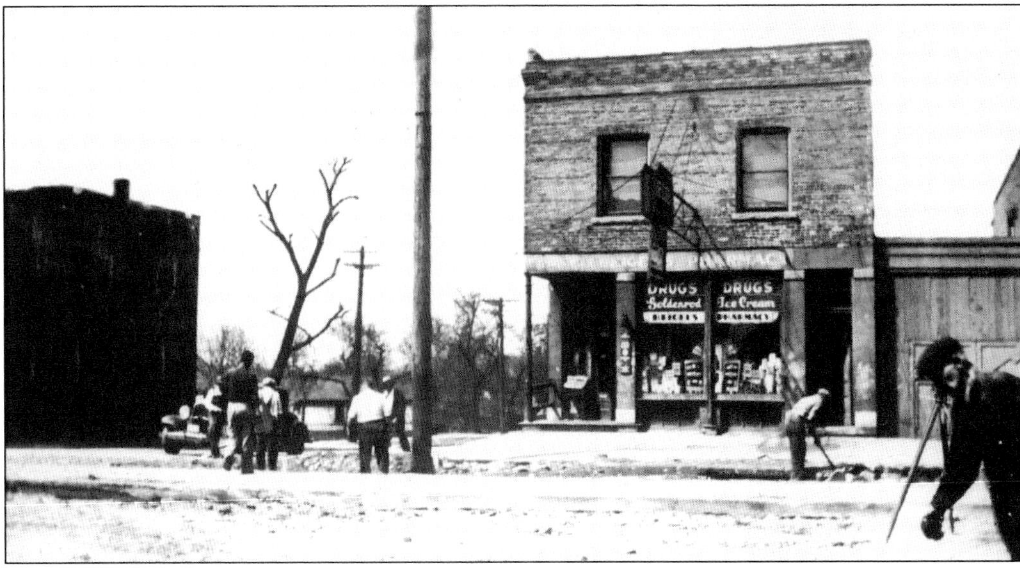

**BEIGEL'S PHARMACY.** Many of the older residents of Summit remember going to Beigel's Pharmacy at 7424 Archer Avenue for ice cream and have fond memories of the drugstore. Charles Beigel leased the building from Carl Greb, son-in-law of the late Gottlieb Schroeder. Beigel died in 1938. It then became Bell's Pharmacy into the mid-1940s. John Maloy's building is partially seen to the left on the corner of Hunt and Archer Avenues.

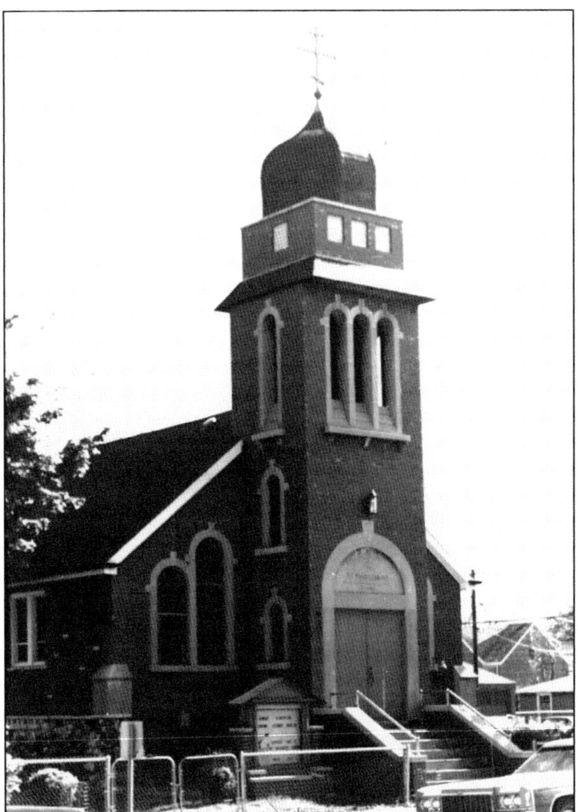

**ST. PANTELEIMON RUSSIAN ORTHODOX CHURCH.** This Russian Orthodox congregation was founded in 1938. The first services were held in the First Congregational Church of Summit building. In June of that year, the congregation rented out the old administration building of the Elgin Motor Car Company at 6100 Archer Avenue. In 1939, it purchased the old Nazarene church at Seventy-fifth Avenue and Sixty-first Place where it remains to this day.

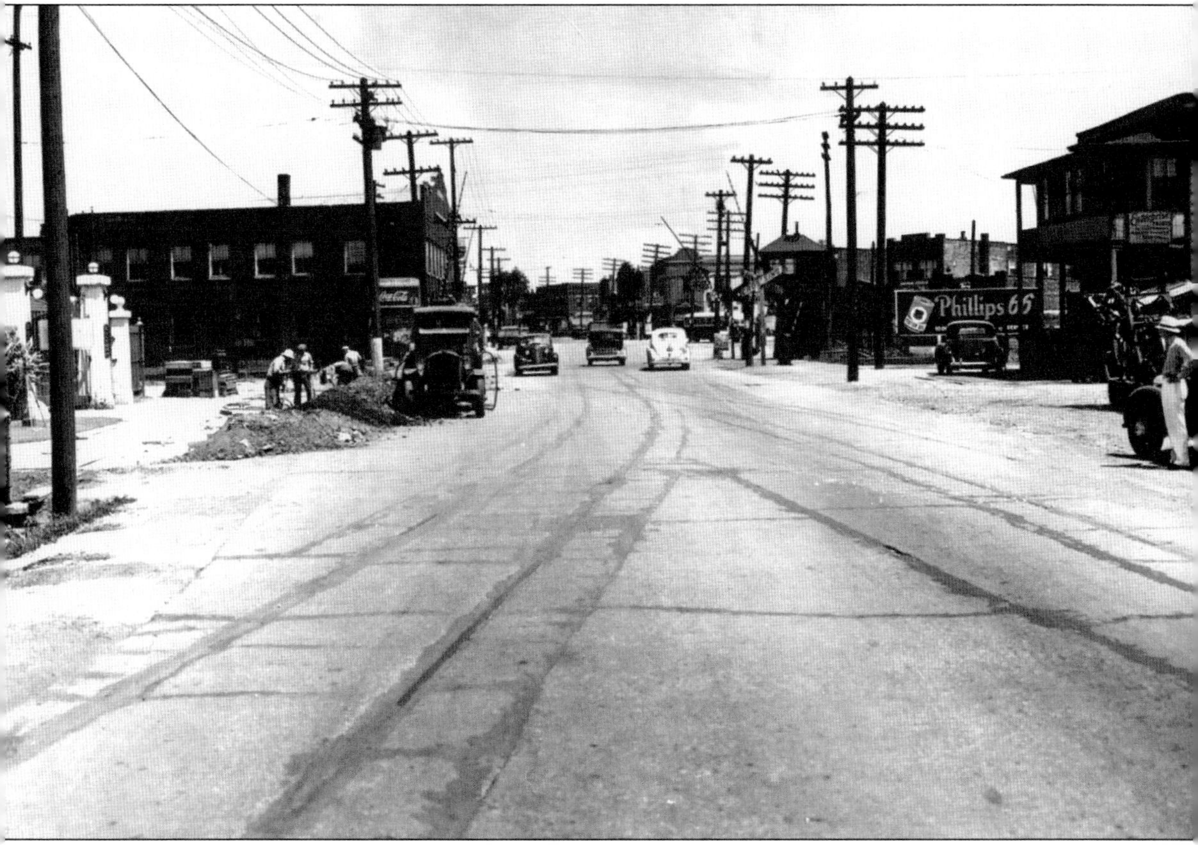


**GATEWAY TO ARGO.** Seen here is a street scene of Archer Avenue looking north from Bedford Park around 1939. The streetcar tracks are but scars on the pavement. To the near right is Wagner Coal and Building Supplies, and to the left is the entrance to the Corn Products Refining Company. The viaduct under the IHB tracks has not been constructed yet, but it is in the planning stages. The railroad gates were lowered by an attendant who stayed in the peaked tower to the right, who would exit the lookout and manipulate the gates by hand. (Courtesy of C. C. Wagner and Company.)

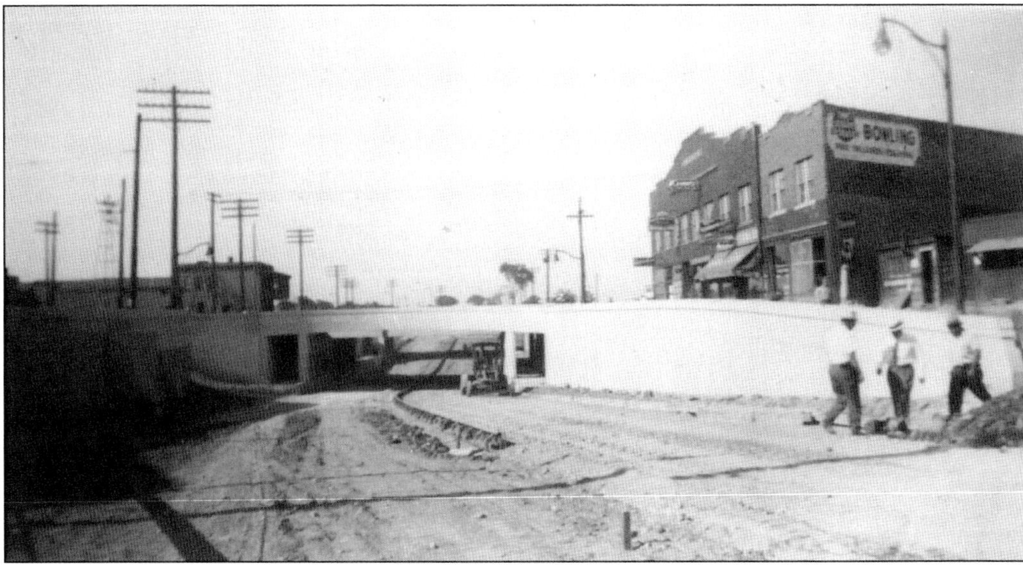


**VIADUCT CONSTRUCTION.** After years of traffic congestion at the IHB crossing south of Sixty-third Street on Archer Avenue, a grade separation was put out for bids. In 1939, the plans were made, and in 1940, the whole project was completed. Seen here is the southwest corner of Sixty-third Street and Archer Avenue looking south. (Courtesy of the Summit Public Library Historical Archives.)

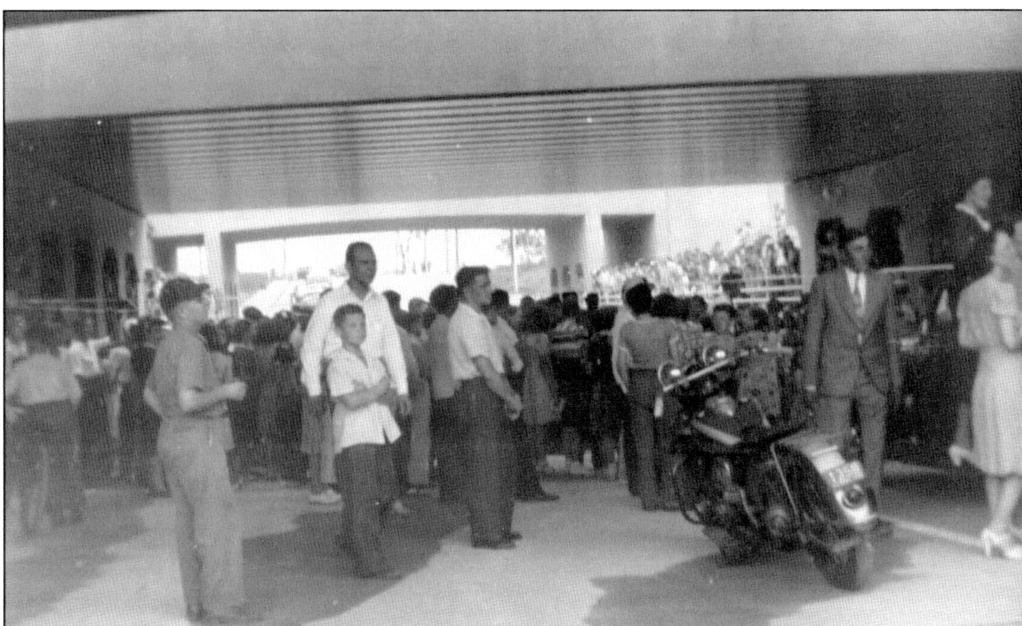

**VIADUCT COMPLETED.** The viaduct under the IHB tracks was completed officially on Labor Day 1940. This image shows a gathering under the new overpass structure. (Courtesy of Ted Ronczkowski.)

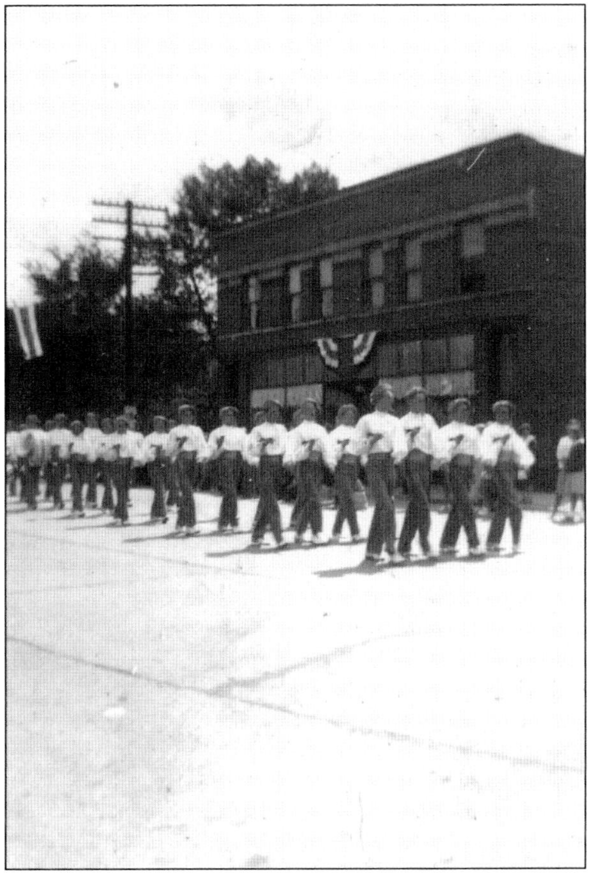

**Fiftieth Anniversary Parade.** In 1940, the Village of Summit celebrated its 50th anniversary. A parade and celebration was undertaken that served the purpose of the village's anniversary, the incorporation of Bedford Park which had officially occurred on June 18, 1940, and the completion of the IHB viaduct. This image is of the parade in Summit in front of Kabaker's.

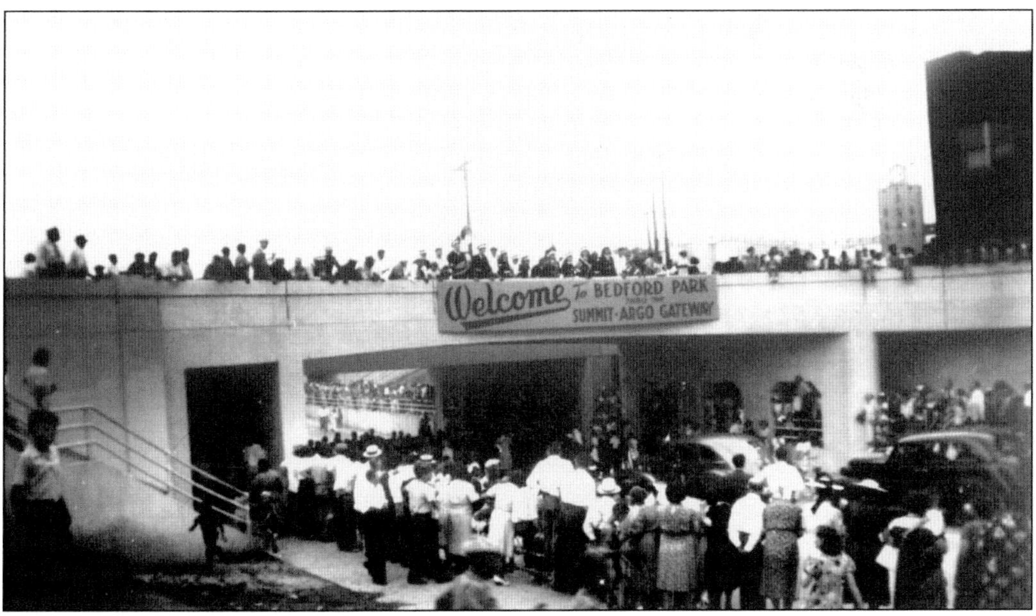


**Fiftieth Anniversary Parade, Argo.** The 1940 parade heads south on Archer Avenue into the newly formed Bedford Park.

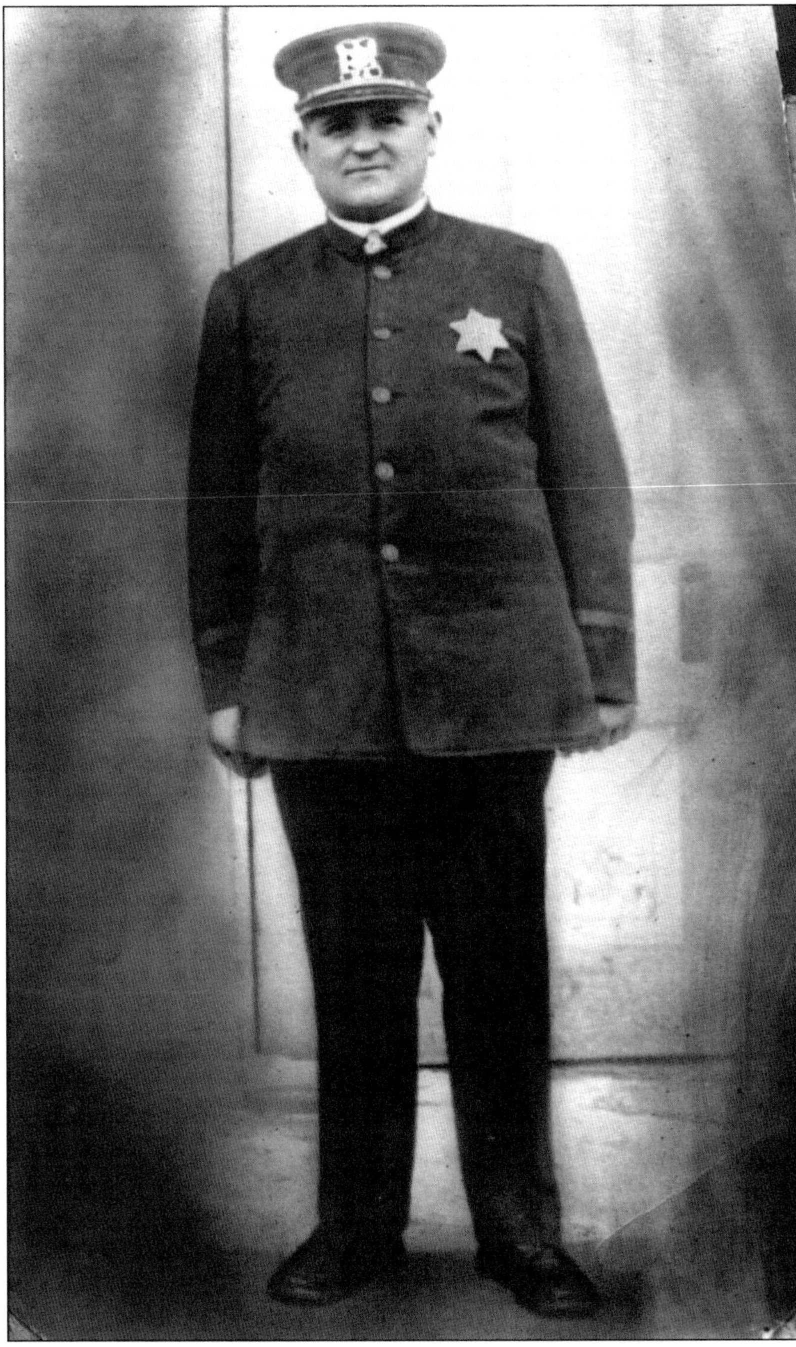

**STANLEY RONCZKOWSKI.** Stanley Ronczkowski was one of the first grocers in Argo. In 1926, he opened a gas and service station at 6200 South Archer Avenue. Later he was hired as a policeman for the village. In 1936, he responded to a fire call on Fifty-ninth Street. While attempting to control the scene, he injured his toe. The injury eventually required an amputation of the leg. Within three weeks, gangrene set in and he died from the infection. Ronczkowski is the first Summit police officer to die from a duty-related injury. His name appears on the police officers' memorial in Washington, D.C. (Courtesy of Ted Ronczkowski.)

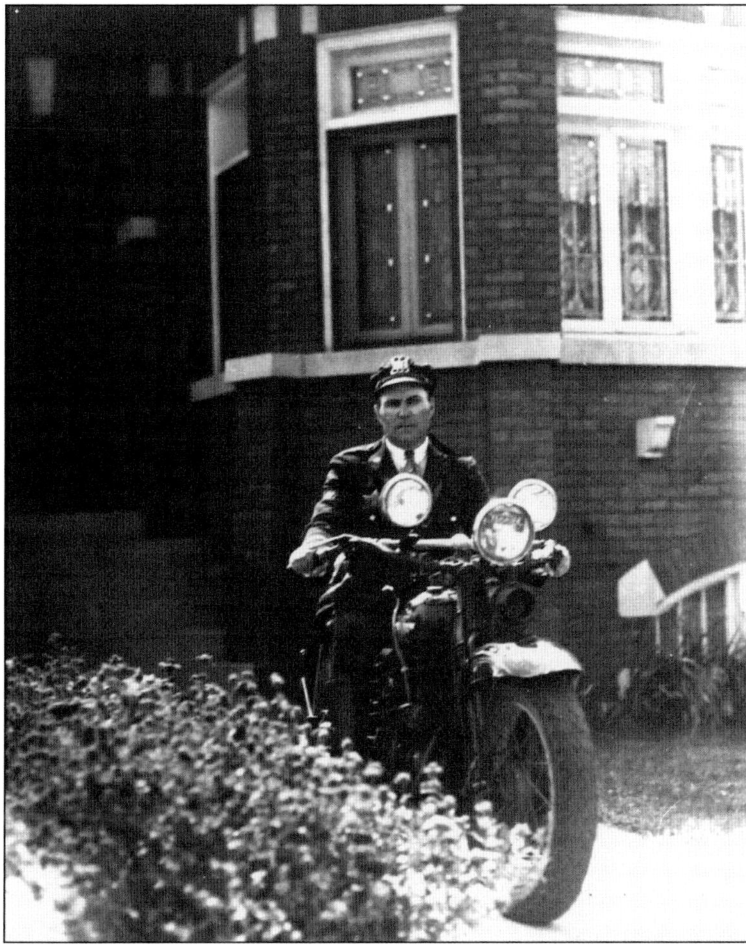

**Nick Henke.** Motorcycles were the mode of traffic enforcement going back before 1917, and although they were discontinued by the Cook County police by 1939, Summit kept them in service for years to come. Nick Henke, pictured here, was hired in 1926 and stayed on the force for many years. The first police car was bought by the village in 1926.

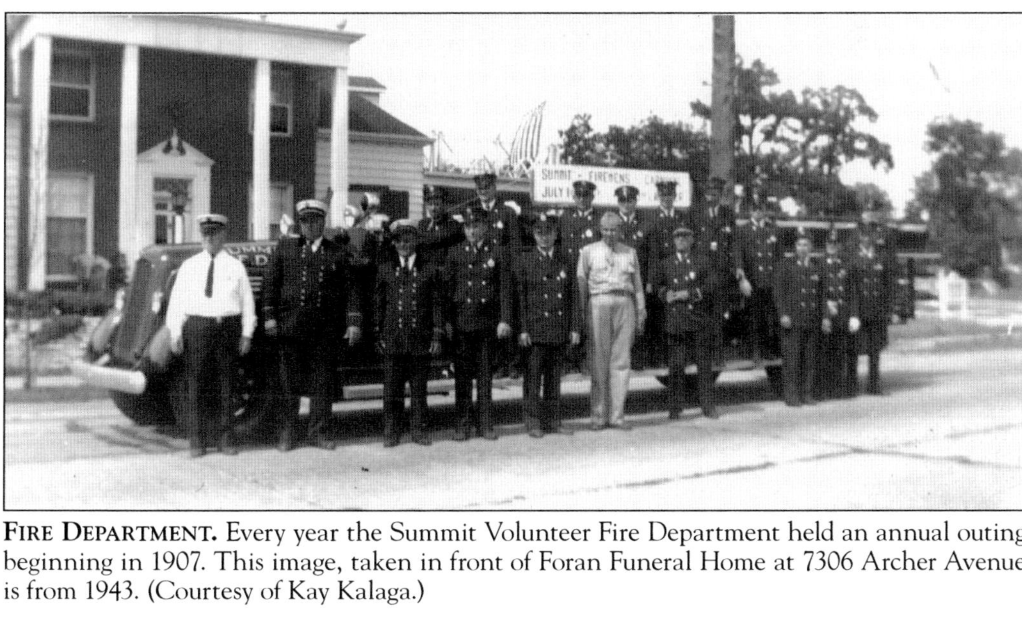


**Fire Department.** Every year the Summit Volunteer Fire Department held an annual outing, beginning in 1907. This image, taken in front of Foran Funeral Home at 7306 Archer Avenue, is from 1943. (Courtesy of Kay Kalaga.)

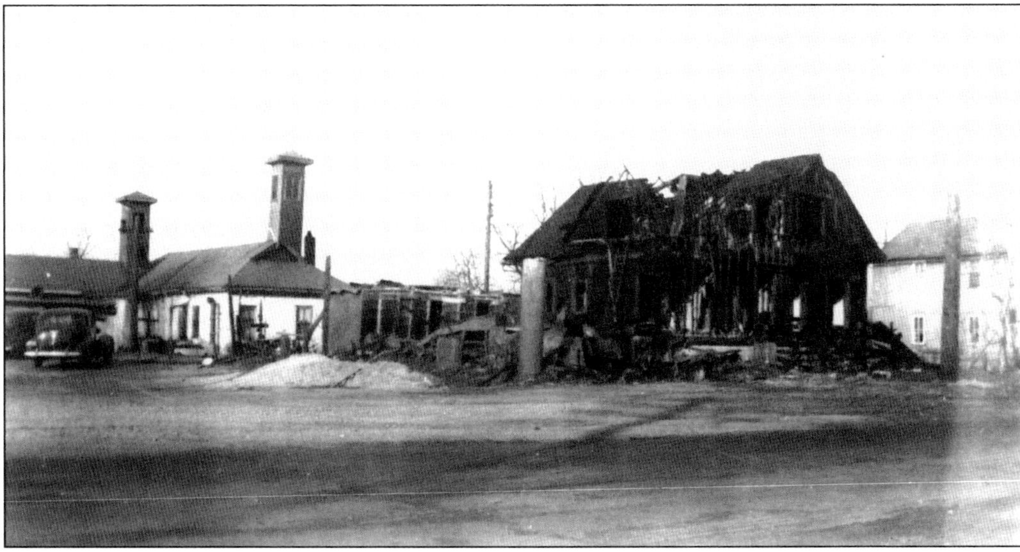

**Village Hall Burns.** The original village hall structure mysteriously burned on Christmas Day 1943. The Hellmuth house next door was also destroyed (right). Inside the garage were two fire engines. Village board meetings were already being held in the community center as the old hall was too small for large gatherings, but the loss of the fire equipment and official records was a hard blow on the village.

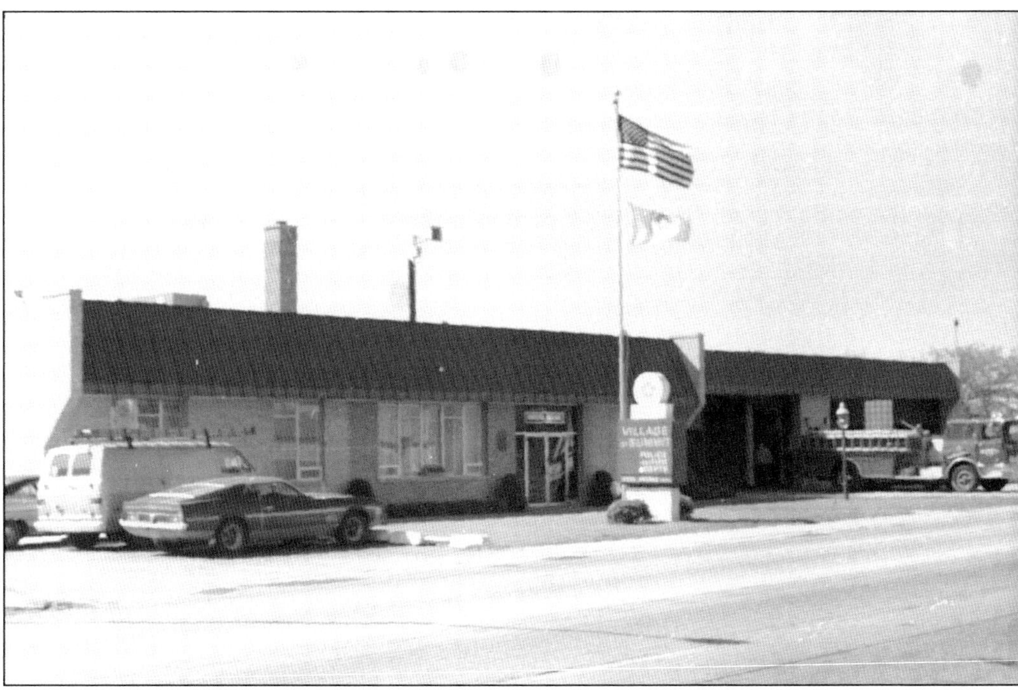

**Fire and Police Department.** By 1945, this building was constructed at 5810 Archer Avenue to house the fire and police departments. In the early 1950s, an addition was built to better suit the village's offices.

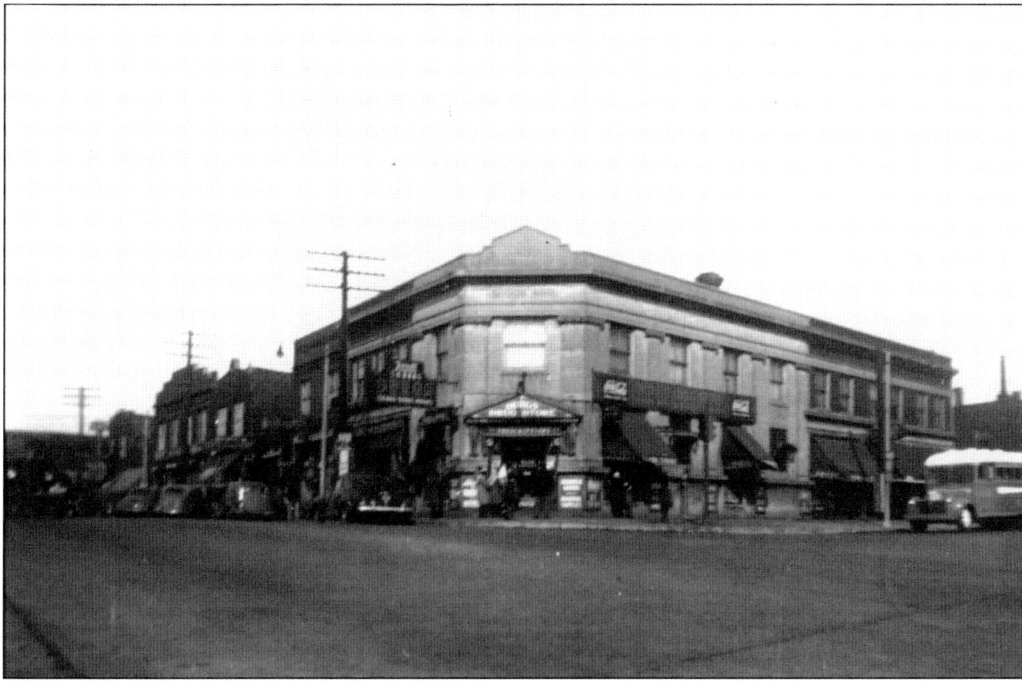

**BURG'S PHARMACY.** The savings bank building, better known as Burg's Pharmacy, is seen here at Sixty-third Street and Archer Avenue in the 1940s.

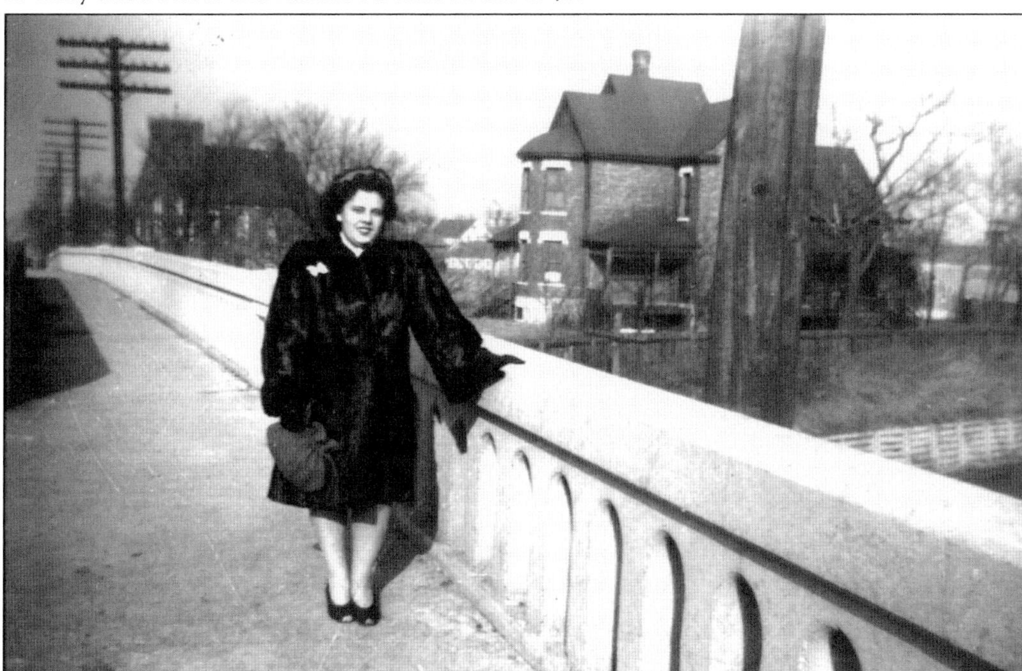

**ARGO BRIDGE.** The old Michigan Central Railroad bridge on Archer Avenue separates Argo from Summit. It is located south of Fifty-ninth Street. Seen here is an unidentified woman standing on the bridge with William T. Welbourn's house and Zion Lutheran Church in the background sometime in the 1940s.

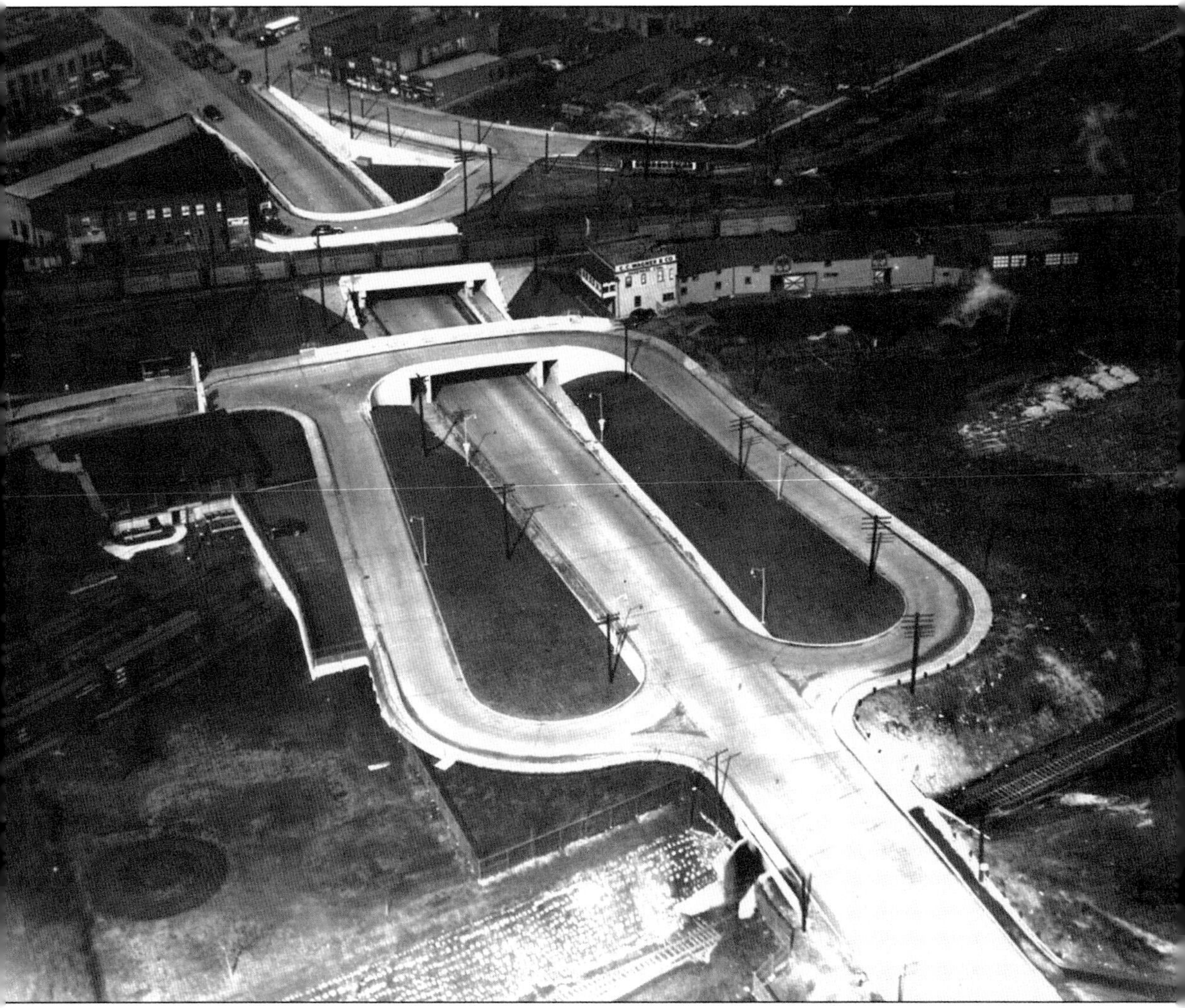

**Aerial View of Viaduct, 1940.** The completed IHB viaduct is seen here in the early 1940s. In view are Wagner Coal and Building Supplies (the lumber came in the 1950s) and the Horseshoe, the road that the Blue Bird buses turned around on. The buildings along both sides of Archer Avenue (called Archer Square) were occupied mainly with juke joints at this time. A Chicago Surface Line streetcar is seen leaving its terminus to Sixty-third Place. The new administrative office for the Corn Products Refining Company is seen on the west side of Archer, and south of that, the original Dolese and Shepard farmhouse, once Argo Hospital, has been torn down. (Courtesy of C. C. Wagner and Company.)

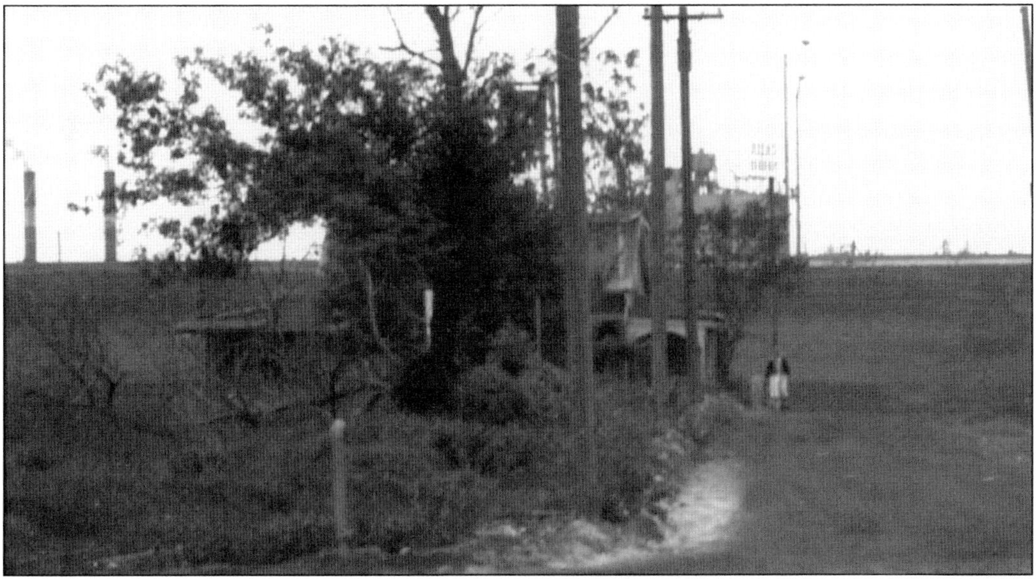

**HOME ON THE ILLINOIS AND MICHIGAN CANAL.** An unidentified woman is seen here in 1967 living along the canal towpath in the heart of old Summit, just southwest of the canal bridge.

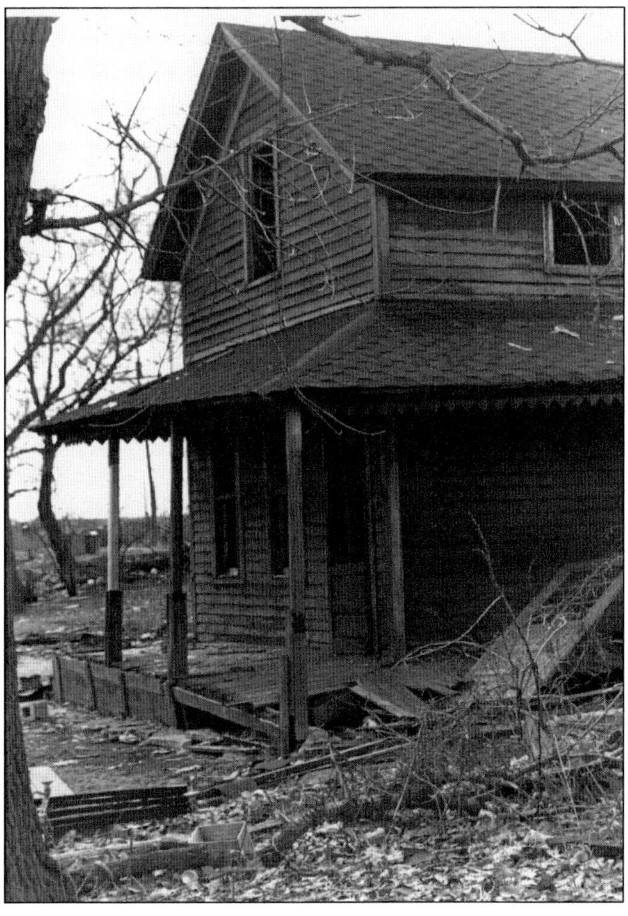

**ABANDONED HOME ON THE ILLINOIS AND MICHIGAN CANAL.** This 19th-century building, photographed by the author in 1975, eventually burned to the ground. It stood several hundred feet southwest of the original location of Ossian Guthrie's boulder cairn monument to Fr. Jacques Marquette and was across from the old Chicago and Alton Railroad depot.

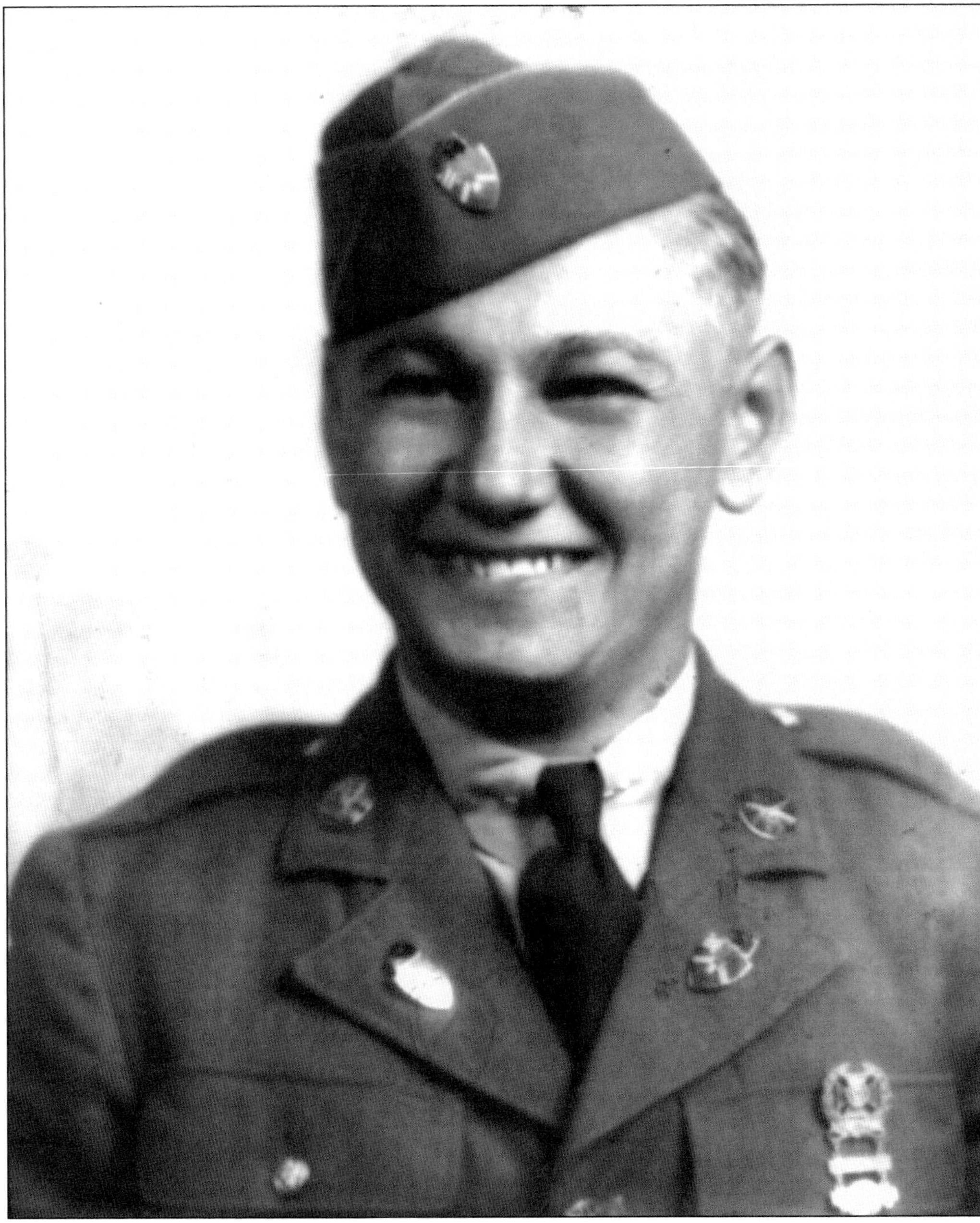

**PVT. EDWARD KOTT (1919–1942).** According to the *Des Plaines Valley News*, "This is the first man from Argo Summit to die in action during this war [World War II]." He volunteered for the U.S. Army in February 1941 and was attached to Company K of the 30th U.S. Infantry. He took part in Operation Torch on November 8, 1942. In his own words, "Perhaps there will come a time when this will all be over with. . . . If I don't come back you will always know that I went down for that which we hold precious, Our Liberty, Our Country—and don't just feel sorry for me. I am only one of millions. Some of us must die so the rest of us may live in peace." Although he lived on Sixty-third Street in Argo, he was buried in the Sunday American Cemetery, plot G, row 18, grave 99, in Carthage, Tunisia, North Africa—one of many.

# *Eight*

# Arrival at Maturity

After the prosperity experienced in the 1920s, population growth and industrial/commercial expansion along with urbanization held reign over the blue-collar village of Summit, and its population almost doubled by 1940 and increased another 30 percent by 1960 as truck farms and the last patches of prairie were being populated and improved to provide the structure for this growing workers' community. However, by the mid-1980s, many of the commercial establishments and industries declined for various reasons.

Since American cities grow or decline as a result of their roles in the national economy, even Chicago was already in decline when the population of Summit fell slightly. Contributing factors included the development of the West Side Redevelopment project, which forced many landlocked people from Argo to move on to other communities. Large industrial employers like the Corn Products Refining Company, Reynolds Metals of McCook, and the Electro-Motive Division of General Motors were declining, and even closing up shop. Summit was a community in decline—saved because of its strategic location on the much-used venerable transport routes through town—as an industrial/commercial town it had reached maturity and now had to face the challenges presented by that status. The changes in heavier reliance on the newer, improved transport facilities like Midway Airport in Clearing, the Stevenson Expressway, and the restrengthening of older railroad facilities through town and new growth in the expanding commercial and service industry expansions eventually brought the population up to its saturation point again with spikes in immigration to the area from Chicago and particularly Mexico.

The adaptations Summit had to go through wreaked havoc on the village's history as new progress and natural maturity required new ways of facing old problems. Hard decisions had to be made, and more often than not, the reinventing of Summit required the recycling of historic sites and architecture.

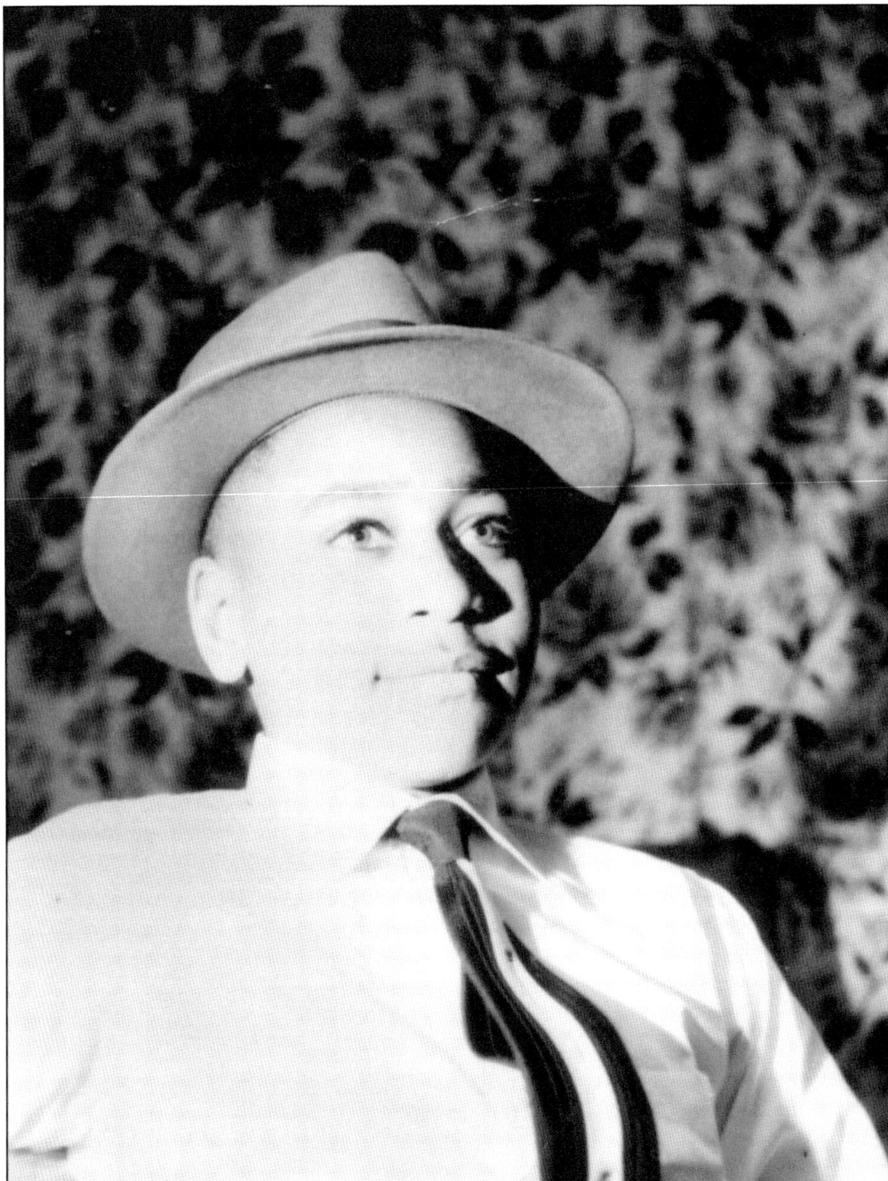

**Emmett Till.** Emmett "Bo-Bo" Till, credited for jump-starting the Civil Rights movement in America, may have been born in Chicago on July 25, 1941, but he was an Argo native. Till lived with his mother and grandparents on Sixty-fourth Street in Argo until he was 12 years old when he and his mother, Mamie, moved to Chicago to escape Argo's overcrowding. Till attended Argo Grade School (now Wharton Elementary) and spent his early days playing with his family and friends under the smokestacks of the Corn Products refinery. In August 1955, Till, his uncle, and his cousin Wheeler Parker Jr. were on vacation in Mississippi when he was kidnapped by two white men who accused him of flirting with one of their wives. He was later murdered. His body was found in the Tallahatchie River on August 31, 1955, beaten and disfigured. He was shipped back to Chicago where his mother ordered an open casket wake to show the world what had happened to her only son. Thousands of people viewed Till's remains between September 3 and 6, 1955. (Courtesy of Wheeler Parker Jr.)

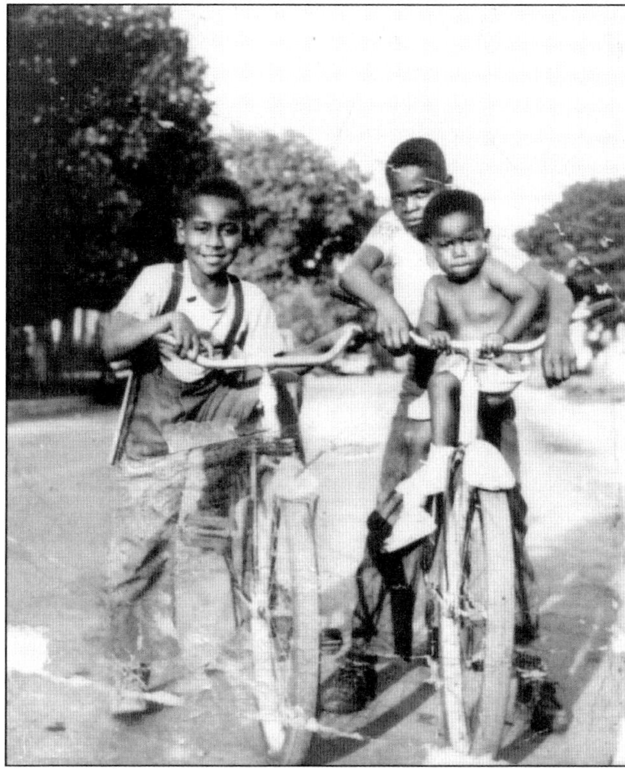

**Wheeler Parker Jr.** Emmett Till's cousin, who was in the room with him when he was kidnapped, still resides in Argo and is a successful businessman and retired pastor of the Argo Temple Church of God in Christ. Wheeler is seen here on the right with Joe B. Williams (toddler), with Till on the left. This photograph was taken in 1950 on the 7500 block of West Sixty-fourth Street. (Courtesy of Wheeler Parker Jr.)

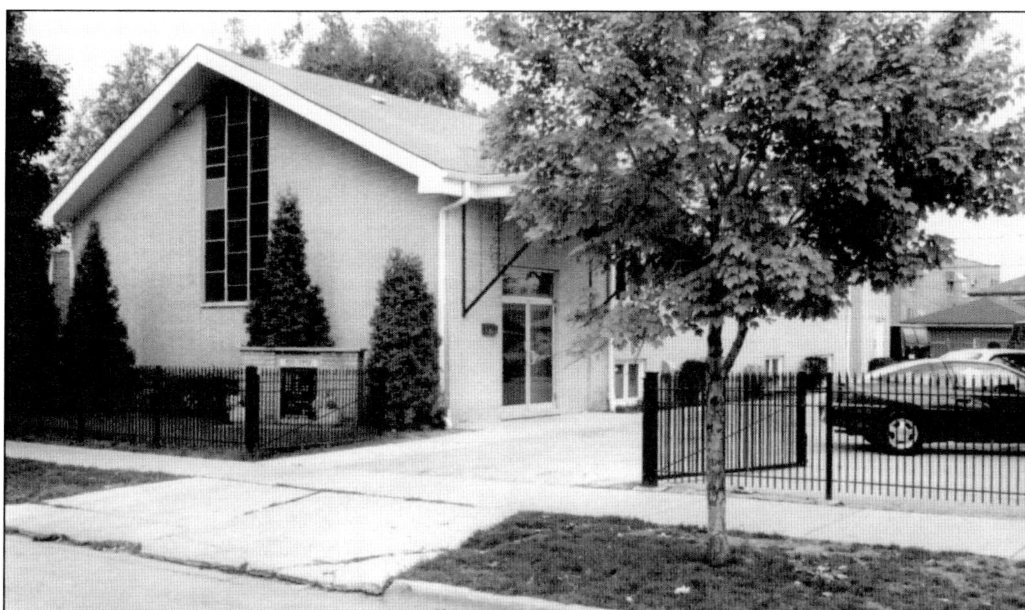

**Argo Temple Church of God in Christ.** Argo Temple Church of God in Christ was organized in 1926 at the home of Emmett Till's grandmother Alma Gaines Spearman. The first building was located at 7533 West Sixty-fourth Street (1933–1970). In 1971, a new church was dedicated at 7435 Sixty-fourth Street where it remains to this day. (Courtesy of Wheeler Parker Jr.)

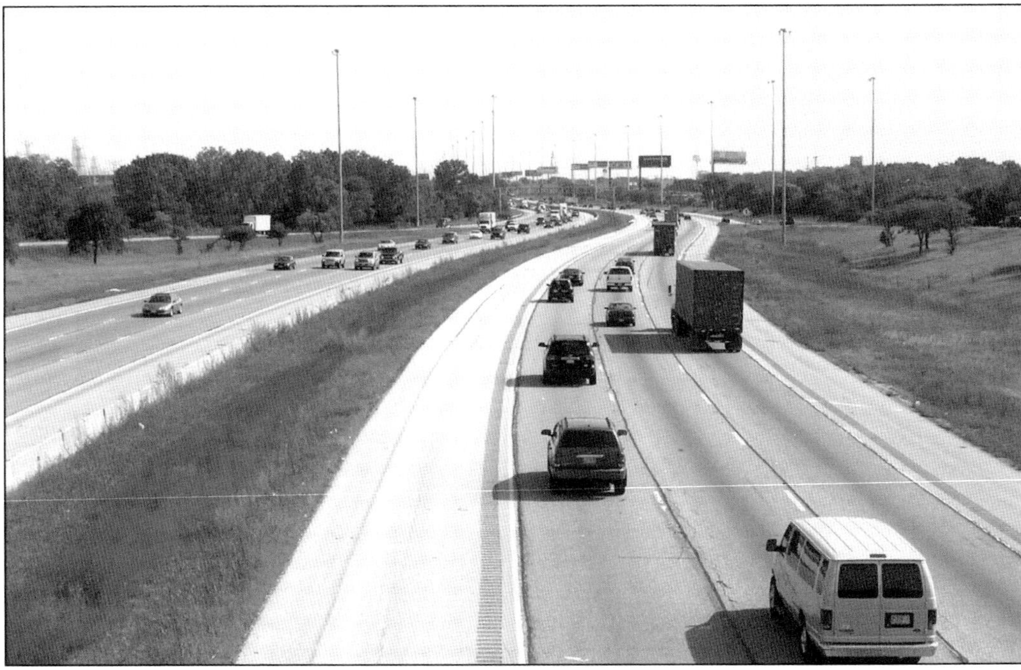

**STEVENSON EXPRESSWAY.** Built over the bed of the old Illinois and Michigan Canal from Chicago to Summit, the Stevenson Expressway, a major freight and transportation route, was built in 1964. Its construction required the further alteration of the natural transport route through the old Lake Chicago Outlet.

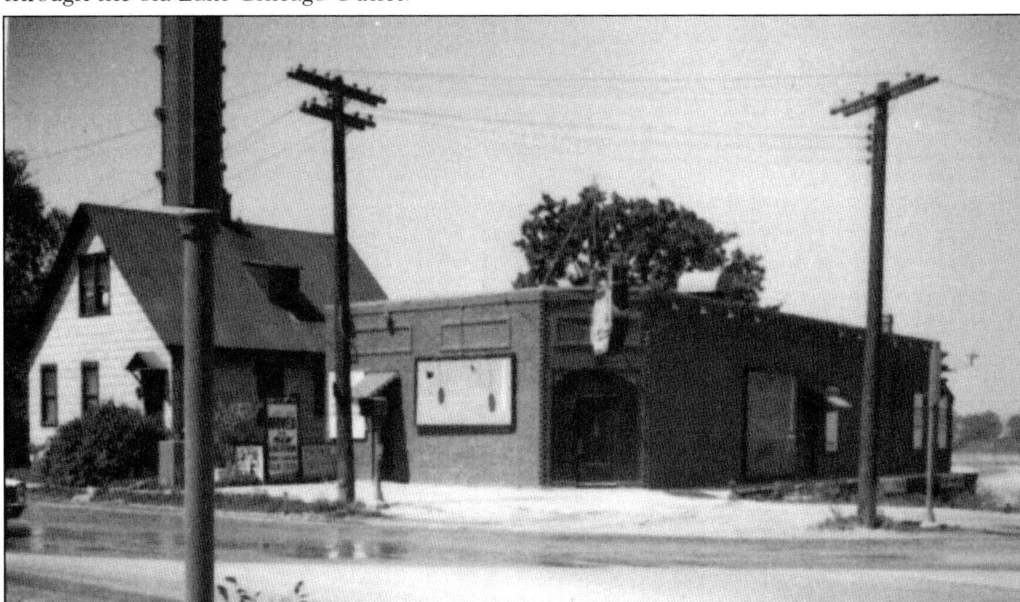

**CANDLELIGHT DINNER PLAYHOUSE.** Another icon of the community, the Candlelight Dinner Playhouse was the brainchild of William Pullinsi and Anthony D'Angelo, who pioneered the concept of dinner theater. Their first location was at this converted tavern at 5508 Archer Avenue in 1961. They constructed a new building at 5620 South Harlem Avenue and moved in 1964.

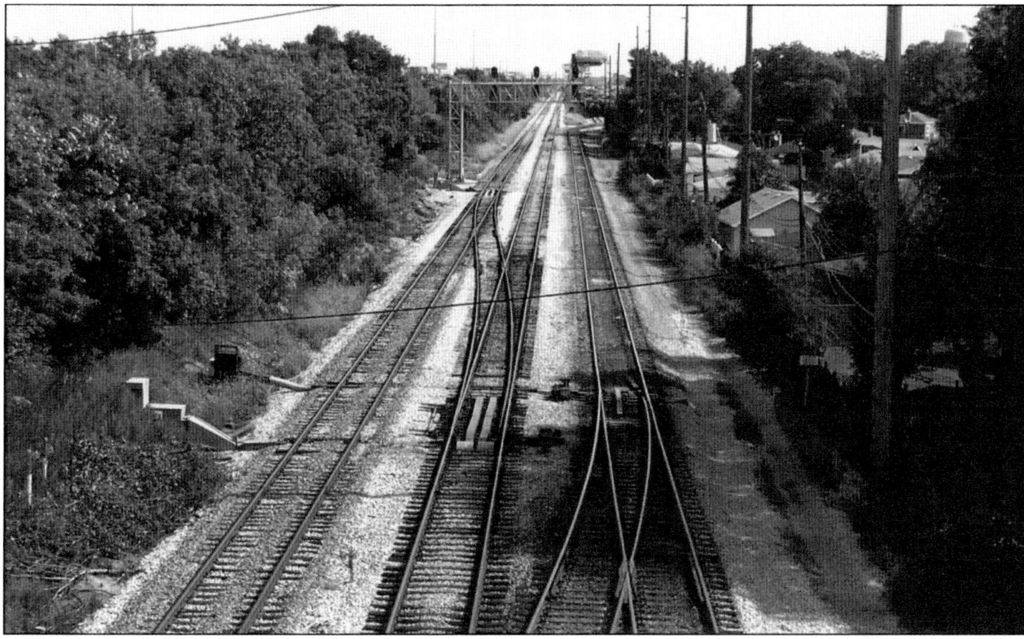

**The Illinois Central Railroad, 2008.** In a view looking east from Harlem Avenue into the old Lake Chicago basin, these old Chicago and Alton Railroad tracks once paralleled the Illinois and Michigan Canal (now under the expressway to the north). It is hard to believe, but Pres. Abraham Lincoln's body traveled over these tracks and met up with thousands of mourners at the Summit whistle stop in 1865 when his body was being carried to its last resting place in Springfield, Illinois.

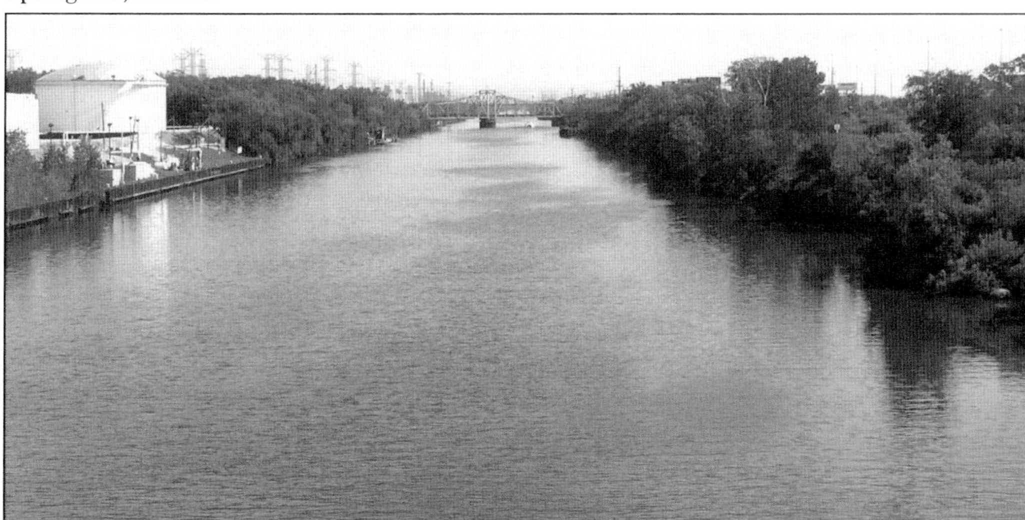

**The Sanitary and Ship Canal, 2008.** The 1900 answer to Chicago's sewerage and transport, this waterway, an engineering wonder of the world, reversed the flow of the Chicago River and provided for sewage disposal from the Chicago metropolitan area as well as a deep waterway to the Illinois River to conduct freight barges, another lifeline of the city of Chicago. The concept of this canal was issued from Ossian Guthrie, an engineer and master planner who conceived the idea of digging it in the 1880s.

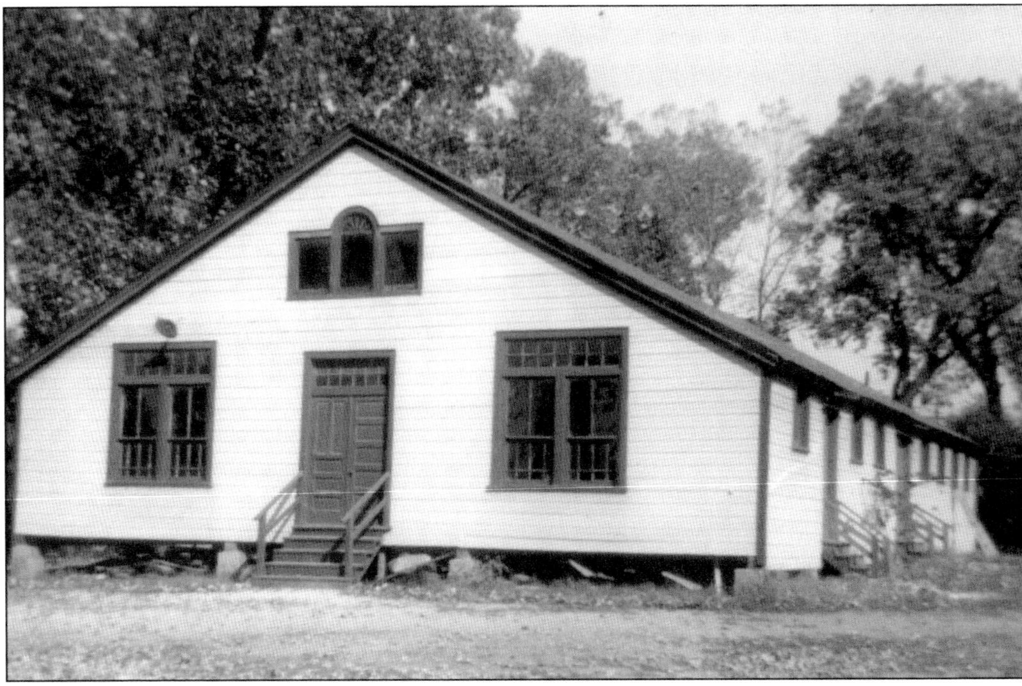

**Zopelis's Grove.** The old Zopelis's Grove Field House on Center Avenue was built by John Welbourn in 1893. The trees on the property were planted by W. W. Walker and Frank O'Heran. The property is now occupied by the Heritage Commons Condominiums. Being part of Anton Zopelis's tavern property on the Summit Corner, it was frequently rented for community events and private parties.

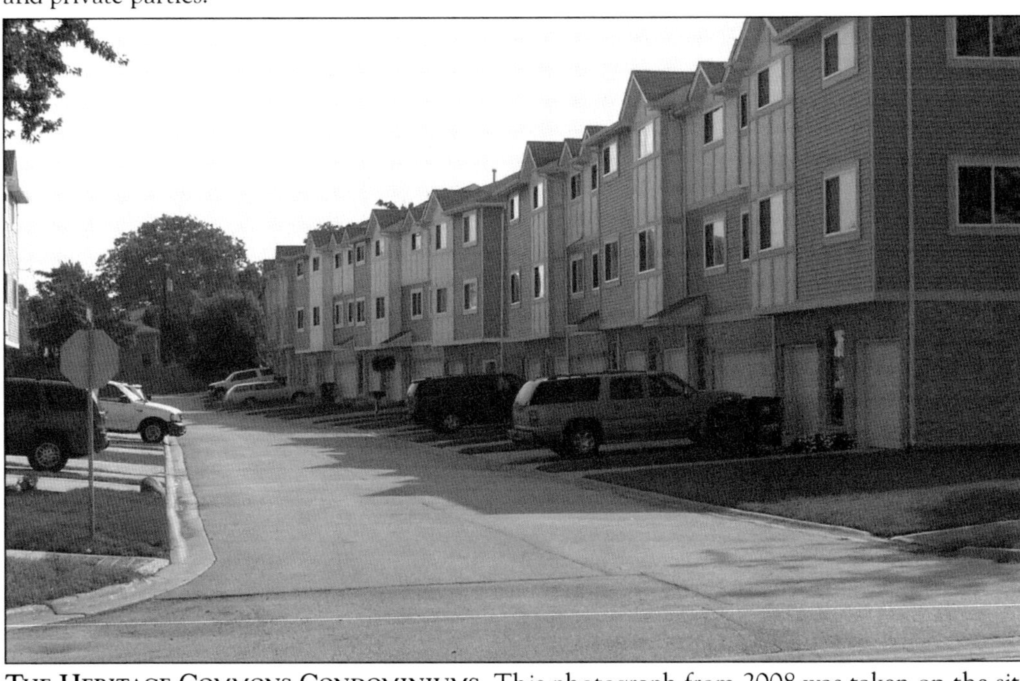

**The Heritage Commons Condominiums.** This photograph from 2008 was taken on the site of the oldest subdivision and first stagecoach stop in Summit.

# *Nine*

# A New Age

In today's progressive village of Summit, it takes a discerning eye to recognize the traces of its historical development that are still there. Most people are satisfied that it is easy to travel down the Stevenson Expressway or Archer Road or Avenue through town, unaware that these arteries of transport have been around for the length of time they have, in one form or other. The ages of foot, canoe, horse, wagon, stagecoach, canal boat, and trolley travel are largely over, while the railroad, freight barge, automobile, and truck have still survived as modes of transport basically over the same venerable routes that first carried people conveniently as their invention and times to flourish arrived. And time has wrought changes in population to the riverine areas; beach, swamps, and prairies of Summit were recognized for their suitability for commerce and agriculture. At first owned by primarily three men by the 1830s—John S. Worth, Dale Alexander, and Nehemiah King by 1835—the original Summit caught the interest of farmers and speculators. Pioneers like Russell Heacock, Peter Kern, Frederick Petersdorf, and "Long John" Wentworth were among others who settled. With the strategic importance of this region as a link between the waterways of east and west, which bottlenecked here, came the building of the Illinois and Michigan Canal and the settlement of the region by an influx of population with the removal of the American Indians and sale of prime lands.

Growth since the mid-19th century has steadily filled and refilled the land of the Summit by an extremely diverse ethnic mix that has arrived and utilized the benefits of living here. From about 300, the resident population of the 1880s grew to 547 by 1900 and soon became 4,019 by 1920, 7,043 by 1940, 10,374 by 1960, 10,110 by 1980, and 10,637 in 2000. The original subdivision was resubdivided; adjacent areas annexed; homes, industries, businesses, and residences grew; and transport routes were improved and added until progress necessitated the urbanization of the land to its present state. Although progress has continually reinvented Summit, its basic geologic legacy remains as do some traces of the architectural, residential, and historic past, giving way to a new age of progress.

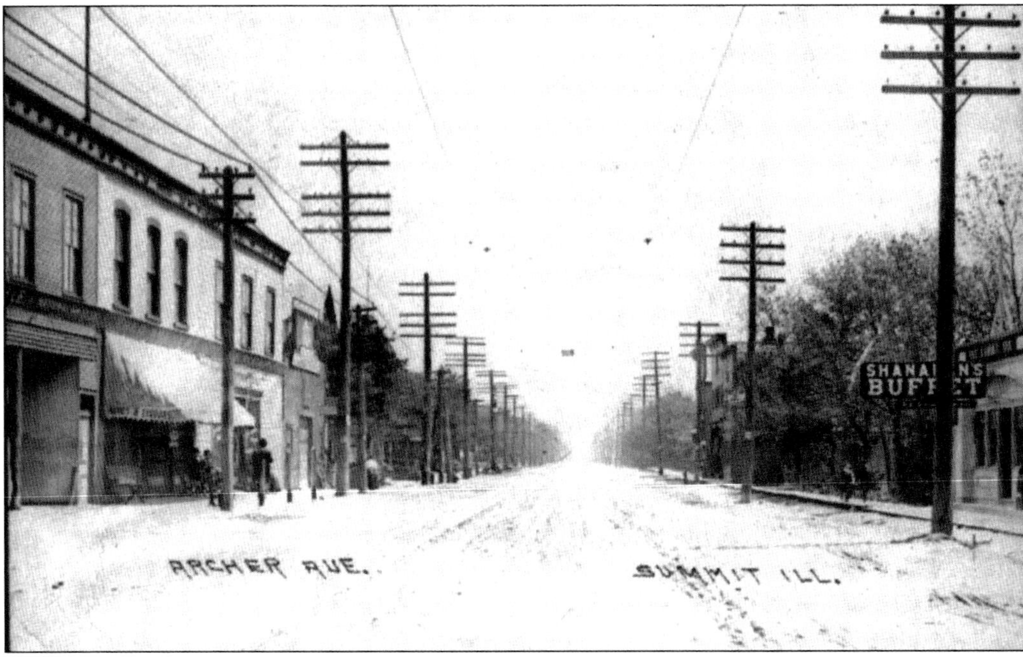


**ARCHER AVENUE LOOKING EAST, 1910.** Historic Archer Avenue was designated one of the first roads of Cook County in 1831. For many years it was the primary southwesterly road to Joliet from Chicago. It was improved for wagons in 1834 and represented the northern part of the old Chicago trail from Bloomington, over which the first wagons of grain bound for Chicago and eastern ports were hauled.

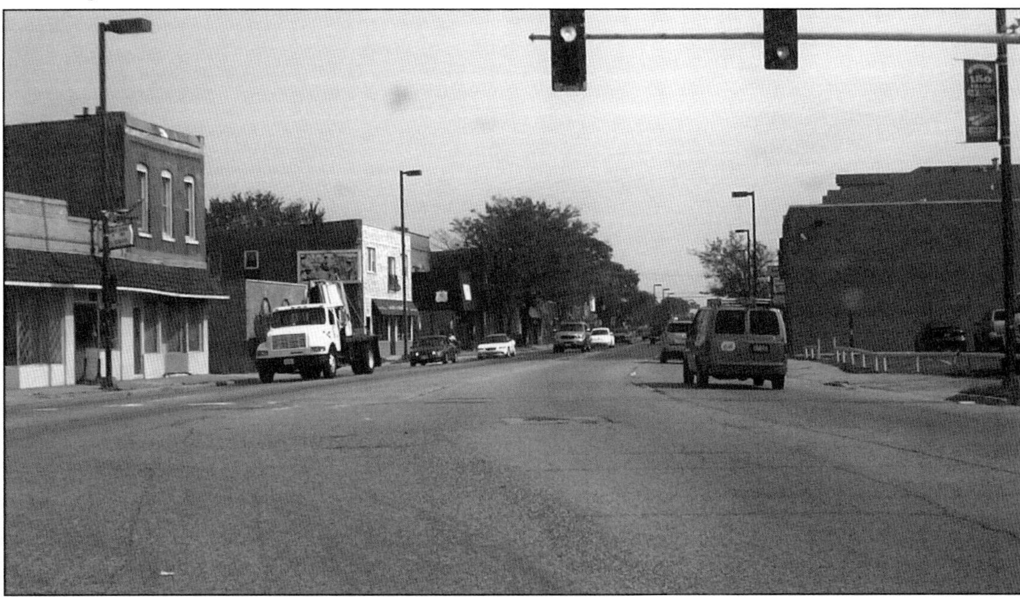

**ARCHER AVENUE, 2008.** This photograph is looking east to Chicago in 2008. Originally an American Indian and portage trail, Archer Avenue has been continually widened and improved since 1834. The present-day Archer Avenue is a main thoroughfare in and out of the city of Chicago and onto Interstate 55 and the Stevenson Expressway. It has been the site of homes, businesses, and industries since the 1830s.

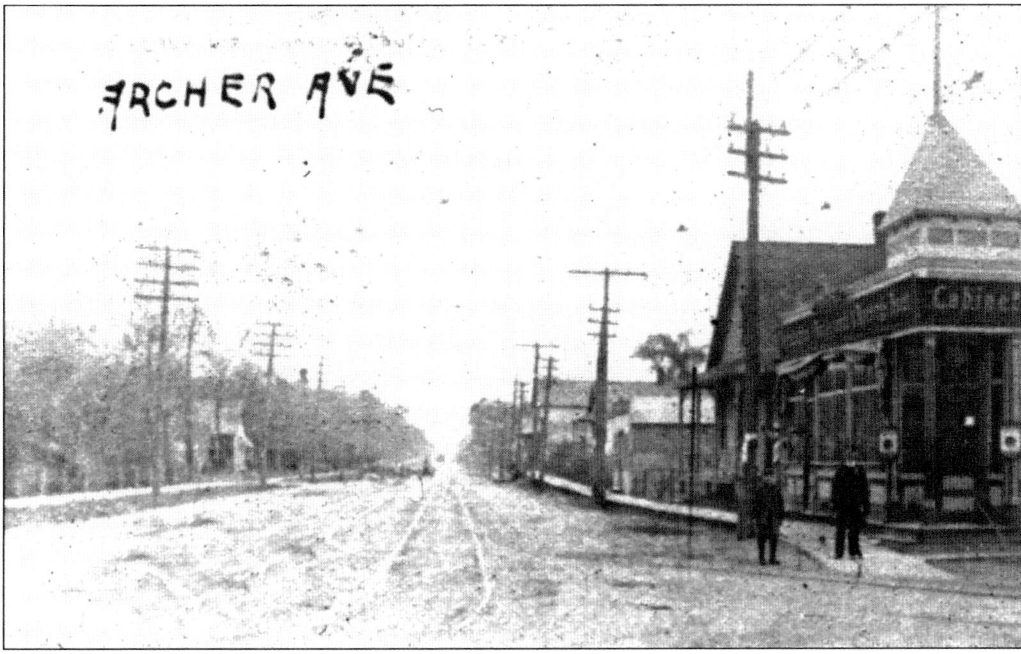


**ARCHER ROAD, C. 1910.** Looking south from the bend in the heart of old Summit, this postcard shows the DePaole Tavern and some of the early pioneer residences on the west side of Archer Avenue, an area populated by merchants, farmers, and boarders to Fifty-sixth Place. Part of the road was improved by Col. William Beatty Archer and the Illinois and Michigan Canal commissioners in 1836 to facilitate the building of the canal.

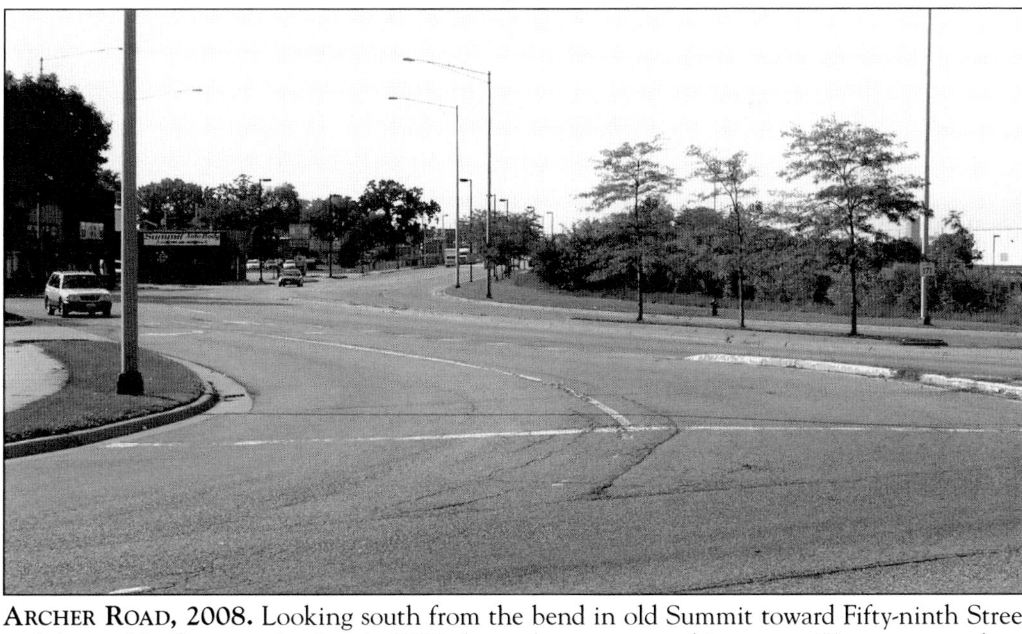

**ARCHER ROAD, 2008.** Looking south from the bend in old Summit toward Fifty-ninth Street and Argo, this photograph taken in 2008 shows the restructured Interstate 55 west access above the old site of Zopelis's Grove, now the Heritage Commons Condominiums. Notice the removal of the old settlement buildings that once lined the west side of the road. Kabaker's corner is now an automobile maintenance business.

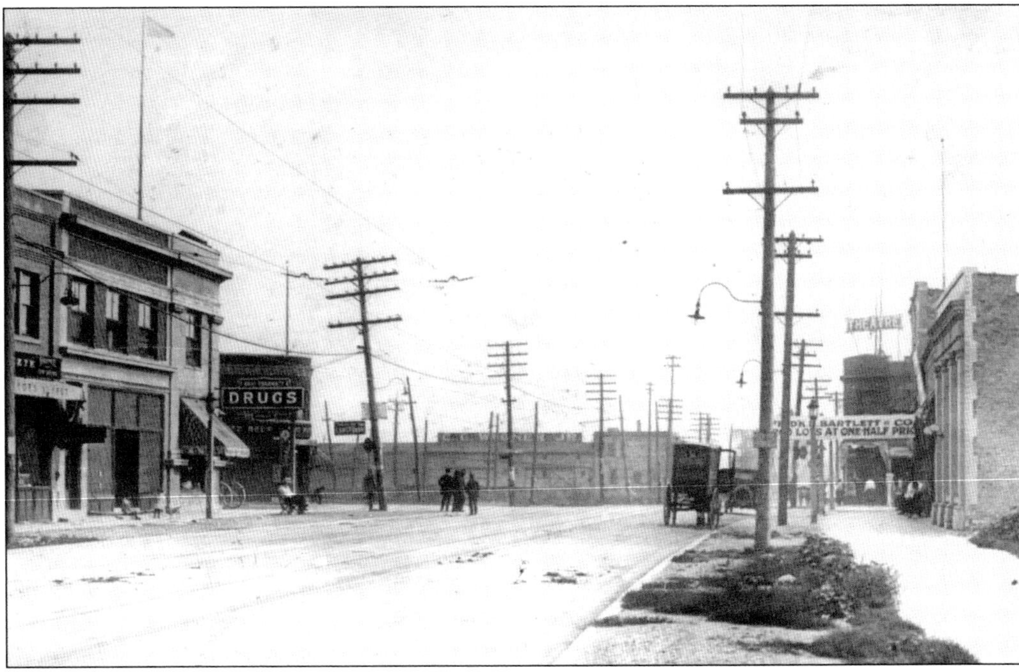


**ARCHER ROAD.** Looking south toward Sixty-third Street, this area has always been legally part of Summit. However, it is traditionally referred to as part of the Argo boomtown. This photograph was taken in 1915 and shows the 1908 Argo Commercial and Savings Bank building with a Drugs sign attached, as it was Burg's Pharmacy at this time.

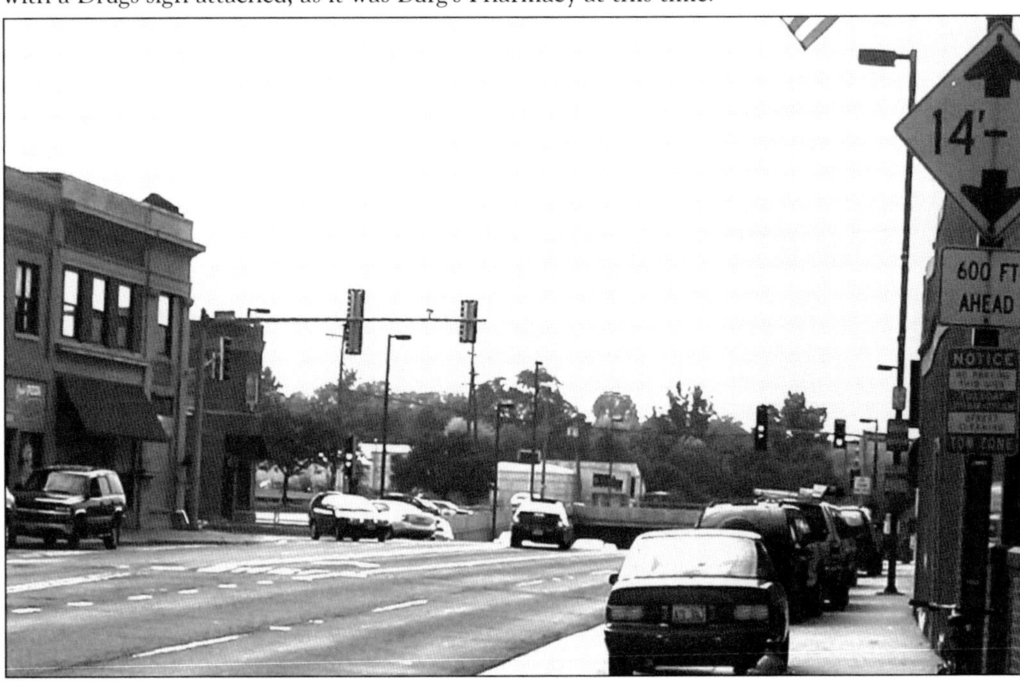


**SIXTY-THIRD STREET AND ARCHER ROAD.** Many of the old brick structures have been rehabilitated for use by current businesses. This photograph taken in 2008 shows how the intersection has changed since 1915

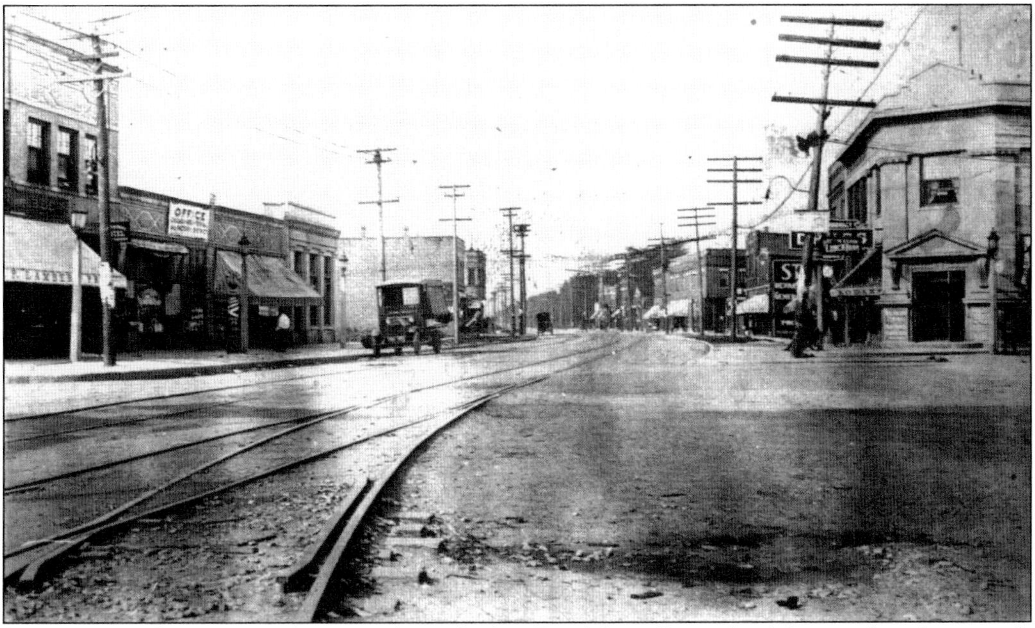


**SIXTY-THIRD STREET.** Looking north on Archer Road from Sixty-third Street, this photograph shows the Argo business district with a trolley from the Chicago and Joliet Electric Railway around 1913.

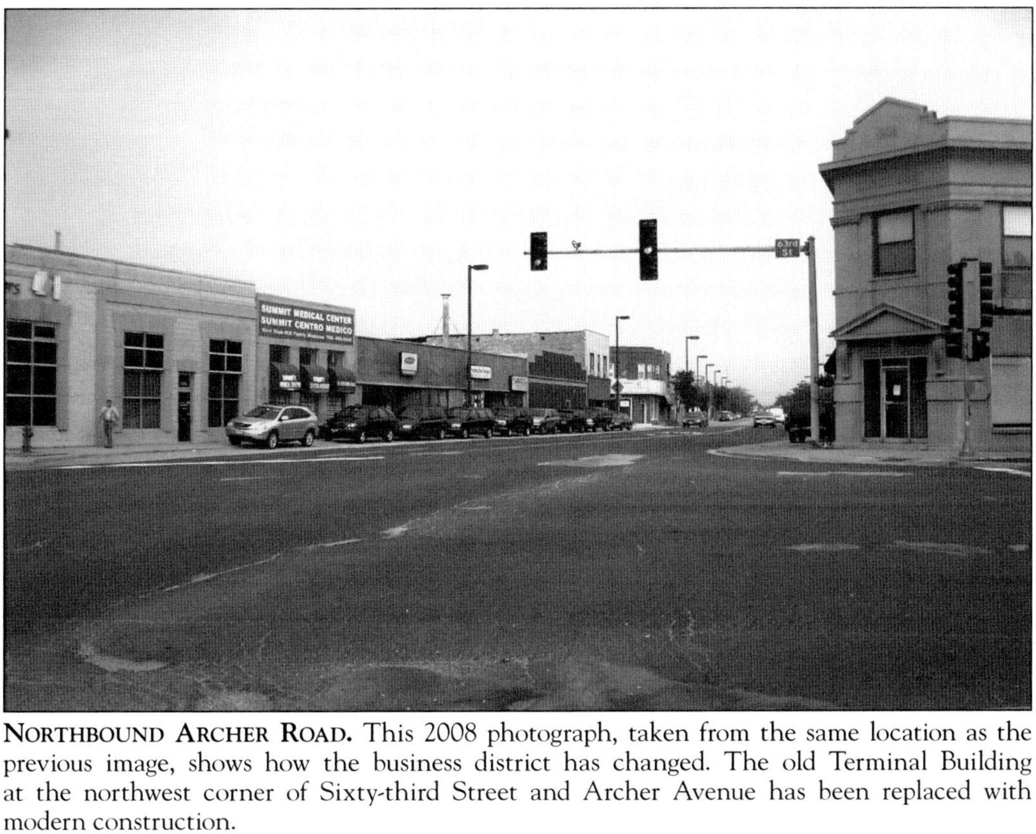


**NORTHBOUND ARCHER ROAD.** This 2008 photograph, taken from the same location as the previous image, shows how the business district has changed. The old Terminal Building at the northwest corner of Sixty-third Street and Archer Avenue has been replaced with modern construction.

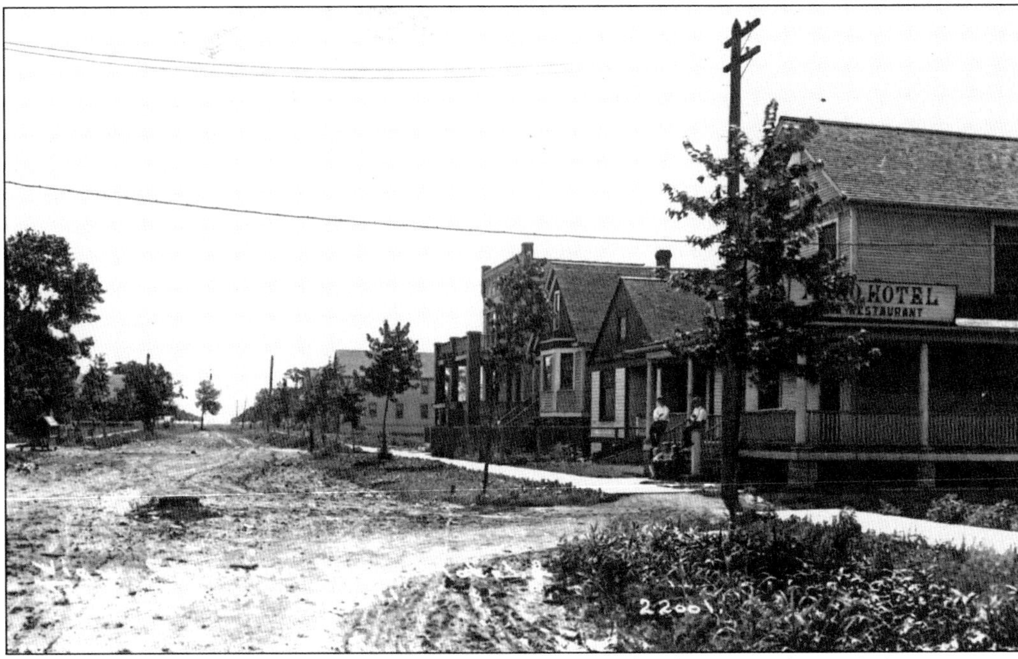


**SIXTY-SECOND PLACE LOOKING EAST.** The old Argo Hotel is shown on this real-photo postcard from around 1915. The third building down in brick is the office and home of Dr. Robert D. Barclay. At this time the Argo district was growing at a fast pace with the Corn Products Refining Company, Elgin Motor Car Company, and the Anderson Engine Company, whose workers lived and availed themselves to the local business district and trolley lines. (Courtesy of the Paul Rush collection.)

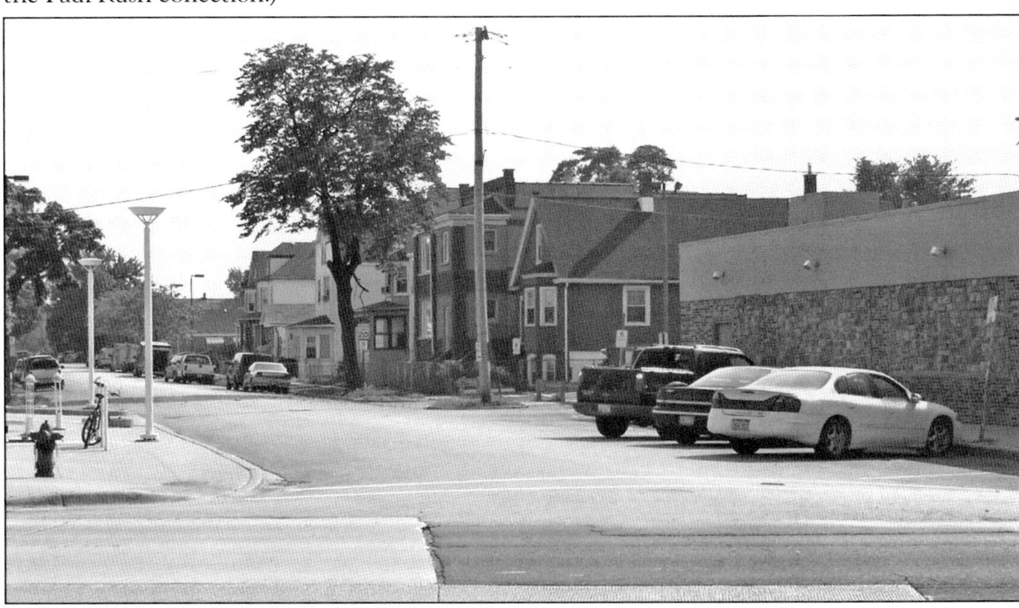

**EAST SIXTY-SECOND PLACE.** A 2008 photograph of the same area now shows a vacant parking lot between the brick and frame buildings at the site of the old Argo Hotel and the now residential refurbished Dr. Robert D. Barclay building. This area is now practically all residential with some older residences still standing but architecturally altered to appear more modern.

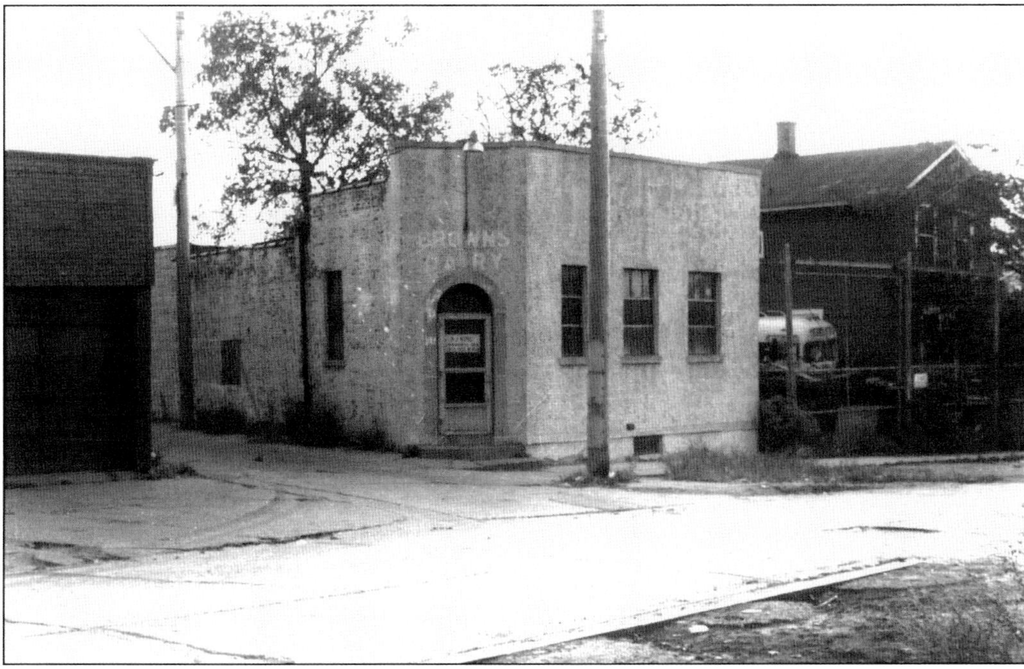

**Brown Dairy Building.** The Brown Dairy building is seen here as it appeared in 1976 after the business ceased operations at 7717 Sixty-second Place. The brick facade was added to the original wooden frame structure in 1926.

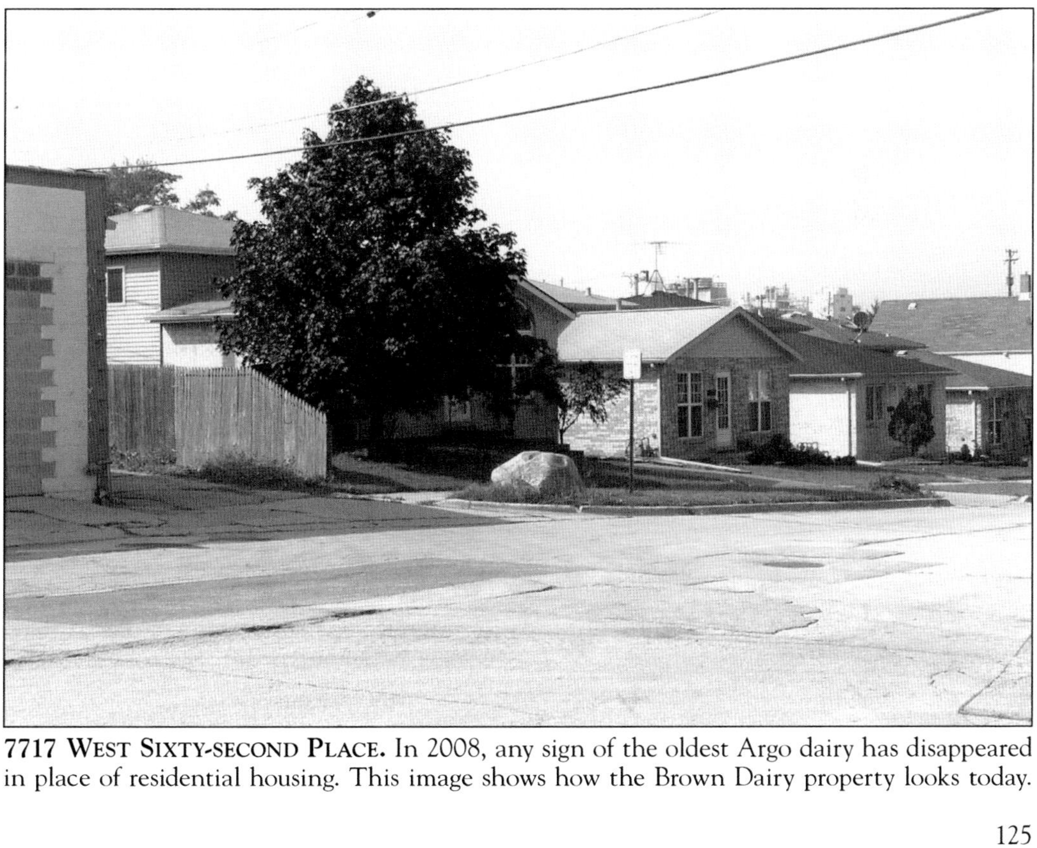

**7717 West Sixty-second Place.** In 2008, any sign of the oldest Argo dairy has disappeared in place of residential housing. This image shows how the Brown Dairy property looks today.

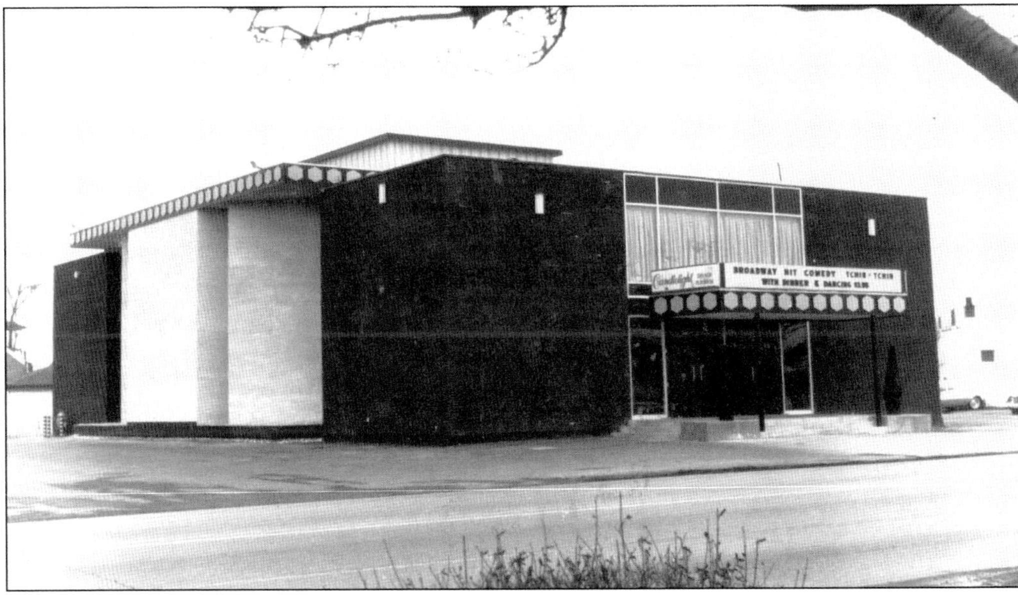

**Candlelight Dinner Playhouse.** The Candlelight Dinner Playhouse started out in a converted tavern owned by William Altier at 5508 South Archer Avenue. With the success of the business, this building was constructed at 5620 South Harlem Avenue in 1964. An addition called the Forum Theater was built in 1972. By 1998, the theater was sold and torn down to make way for a parking lot of Portillo's Hot Dogs, which occupies property just to the north of where the theater once stood.

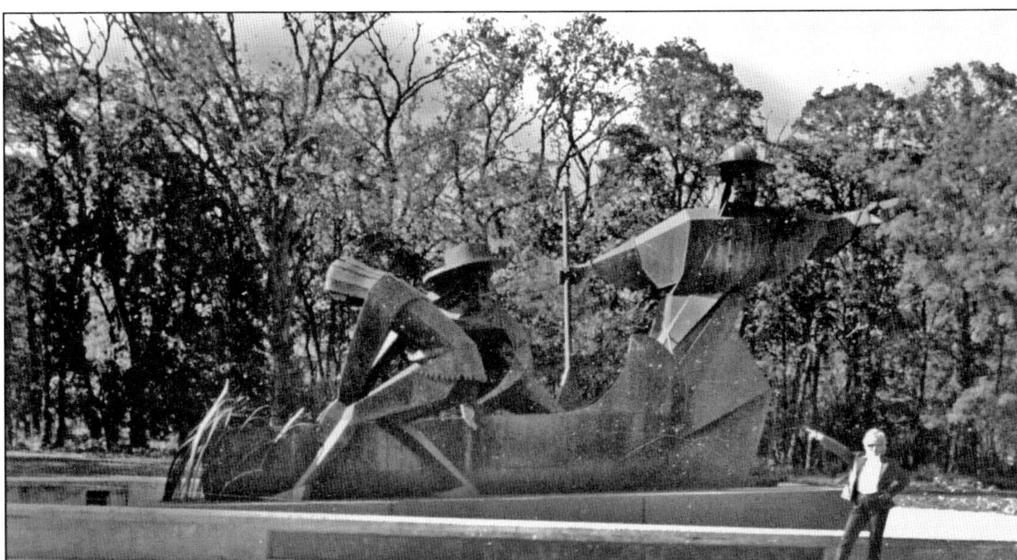

**The Waterway West Monument.** Seen here is where the European exploitation of the Lower Des Plaines Valley and Lake Chicago Outlet began. The 91-acre western terminus of the Chicago Portage Route has been a national historic site since 1952. This is the new monument of 1989, photographed in 2007. The viewer is reminded that the 1673 journey of discovery took place northeasterly from the Summit to Portage Creek and overland east to the Chicago River and the future site of Chicago.

# Bibliography

Alden, W. C. "Description of the Chicago District," Chicago Folio No. 81. In *Geologic Atlas of the United States*. Washington, D.C.: United States Geological Survey, 1902.

Andreas, Alfred T. *History of Cook County Illinois*. Chicago: Self-published, 1884.

Bannister, Henry M. "Geology of Cook County." In *Geological Survey of Illinois* Vol. III by A. H. Worthen, 239–256. Springfield: Geological Survey of Illinois, 1868.

Bretz, J. H. *Geology of the Chicago Region*. Part I. Bulletin No. 65. Urbana: Illinois State Geological Survey, 1939.

Conzen, Michael P., and Kay J. Carr, eds. *The Illinois & Michigan Canal National Heritage Corridor—A Guide to Its History and Sources*. DeKalb: Northern Illinois University Press, 1988.

Danckers, Ulrich, and Jane Meredith. *Early Chicago*. River Forest, IL: Early Chicago, Inc., 2000.

Grossman, James R., Ann Durkin Keating, and Janice L. Reiff, eds. *The Encyclopedia of Chicago*. Chicago: University of Chicago Press, 2004.

Hamilton, Raphael N. S. J. *Marquette's Explorations; The Narratives Reexamined*. Madison: University of Wisconsin Press, 1970.

Howe, Walter A., comp. *Documentary History of the Illinois and Michigan Canal, Legislation, Litigation and Titles*. Springfield: State of Illinois Department of Waterways, 1956.

Knight, Robert, and Lucius Zeuch. *The Location of the Chicago Portage Route of the 17th Century*. Chicago Historical Society's Collection XII. Chicago: 1928.

Markman, Charles W. *Chicago Before History*. Studies in Illinois Archaeology 7. Springfield: Illinois Historic Preservation Agency, 1991.

Peine, John D., and Debra Neurohr. *Illinois & Michigan Canal Corridor: Illinois*. Denver: U.S. Department of the Interior, National Park Service, 1981.

Putnam, James William. *The Illinois and Michigan Canal*. Chicago Historical Society's Collection X. Chicago: University of Chicago Press, 1918.

*Report of the Canal Commissioners of Illinois to Governor John R. Tanner*. Springfield, IL: Phillips Brothers, 1901.